Amos Norton Craft

Modern Spritualism

Amos Norton Craft

Modern Spritualism

ISBN/EAN: 9783741116797

Manufactured in Europe, USA, Canada, Australia, Japa

Cover: Foto ©ninafisch / pixelio.de

Manufactured and distributed by brebook publishing software (www.brebook.com)

Amos Norton Craft

Modern Spritualism

EPIDEMIC DELUSIONS:

CONTAINING AN

EXPOSÉ OF THE SUPERSTITIONS AND FRAUDS
WHICH UNDERLIE SOME ANCIENT AND
MODERN DELUSIONS,

INCLUDING

Especial Reference to Modern Spiritualism.

BY

REV. AMOS N. CRAFT, A. M.

———•◆•———

CINCINNATI:
WALDEN AND STOWE.
NEW YORK: PHILLIPS & HUNT.
1881.

Copyright
By AMOS N. CRAFT,
1881.

DEDICATION.

TO MY WIFE,

Mrs. Alice Steadman Craft,

WHOSE VALUABLE ASSISTANCE

IN MY

BUSY PASTORATE HAS AFFORDED ME LEISURE FOR
ITS COMPOSITION,

This Volume is Inscribed

BY

The Author.

PREFACE

THE author has not aimed to write glowing sentences, but to give a simple sketch of some historic and scientific facts which relate to his theme. He seeks to point out a field of thought which has been suggested to him by personal contact with one of the most subtle and hurtful members of the great family of delusions. His opinions concerning modern spiritualism have been gained and confirmed by seven public debates with apostles of that strange compound of skepticism, credulity, and sensuality. In addition to the authorities referred to in the following chapters, he acknowledges especial indebtedness to Ueberweg's "History of Philosophy," Taylor's "Primitive Culture," Mackay's "Memoirs of Extraordinary Popular Delusions," "Human Nature and the Nerves," by J. S. Grimes, Boismont's "Rational History of Hallucinations," and Salverte's "Philosophy of Magic."

A. N. C.

CONTENTS.

CHAPTER	PAGE
I. The Origin of Delusions,	7
II. Superstitions of Philosophers,	17
III. Superstitions of the Uncultured Concerning the Spirit World,	38
IV. Superstitions of the Uncultured—Animism,	45
V. Superstitions of the Uncultured—Continued,	51
VI. The Sleep of Reason,	62
VII. The Power of the Excited Imagination,	77
VIII. Deception by Natural Phenomena,	95
IX. Legerdemain,	102
X. Ordeals,	119
XI. Epidemic Alarms,	123
XII. The Crusades,	133
XIII. Money-making Delusions,	140
XIV. Alchemy,	150
XV. The Witch-mania,	173
XVI. Haunted Houses,	189
XVII. Animal Magnetism,	196
XVIII. Mormonism,	211
XIX. The Origin of Modern Spiritualism,	217
XX. Mediums Exposed,	226
XXI. Tricks Explained,	259
XXII. Some Occult Laws of Mental Action,	287
XXIII. Theories Founded on Fraudulent Phenomena,	303
XXIV. Spirit Agency the Last Hypothesis,	318
XXV. Delusions and the Evil Passions,	324
XXVI. The Bible and Modern Spiritualism,	338

Googl

EPIDEMIC DELUSIONS.

CHAPTER I.

THE ORIGIN OF DELUSIONS.

THE principal sources of delusions are superstition, fraud, and dissatisfaction with previous customs and beliefs, inspired by the passions restless under restraint, or the imagination impatient with the limited horizon of human knowledge. All of these causes have been at work in every age of the world. Our first parents doubted the word of Jehovah; but the doubt only led them to believe the delusive suggestions of the devil, and all their sons and daughters who have had similar doubts have been led into like beliefs.

The first delusion may be taken as a type of all which have come after it. The forbidden fruit was "good for food," and the animal appetites, impatient under restraint, have always played a conspicuous part in the history of delusions. It was that which made Mohammed's paradise so attractive to the voluptuous Arab; and, also, the method of Mohammedan propagandism satisfied his thirst for blood, and his desire for military glory. It was that which impelled a large majority of the devotees of modern spiritualism to turn away from the Bible, and seek in spirit circles, not proofs of immortality—for on that subject they were never in doubt—but confirmations of the "Harmonial philosophy," which made evil good, sin a means of progress, and the spirit world a place of unrestrained sensual delight.

Also, the serpent was "subtile" and the tree was "pleasant to look upon." Delusions are often maintained by specious arguments, which to the inexpert masses are unanswerable; but being ever willing to mistrust the voice of God, rather than to suspect that there may be something beyond their powers of comprehension, they often suffer themselves to be misled by high-sounding words and plausible theories, simply because they do not understand them. They also forget that many things which are pleasant to look upon may be only fictions of the fancy. Mental indolence holds them back from toiling through the seeming to the real. Pride and self-conceit have played a part. Men are prone to overestimate their intellectual powers, and to underestimate the vastness of the universe. They think it not unreasonable that they may be "as gods." The first delusion, not only in its genesis, but in its ending, is a type of subsequent delusions; for error is ever hurtful, particularly where it involves the moral powers. But its end is death. No one is guiltless for following a delusion of this latter class, for every man knows that he is going astray when he is violating his moral convictions.

Superstition arises from the imagination reaching

out in the gloomy fog of ignorance, awed by the mysterious unknown. As the word superstition suggests, the imagination stands over an awful and dark abyss, filling it with creatures and forms of its own creation. It may be proper for the imagination, for pastime, to venture forth into the unknown; or, perhaps, to find some possible hypothesis, but never in quest of certainties. But the recreant imagination has ever been going thither for certainties, creating more than half of the world's beliefs and philosophies. In our own day the "scientific imagination" has too great liberty. Darwin, Huxley, and Tyndall, are examples of a class of scientists who spend quite as much of their time in sending the "scientific imagination" into the unknown and unknowable as in patient experiment with the visible realities near at hand; and, consequently, their "scientific imaginations" have added largely to the list of scientific superstitions. If this tendency is so strong in men of learning, what must it be in the uncultured masses of mankind, who have never been trained in the methods of scientific thought? We should expect that their beliefs would be still more largely furnished by the imagination.

By descending the various grades of human culture, we meet protoplasm, psychic or odylic force, animal magnetism and clairvoyance, spiritualism, witchcraft, alchemy, charms, omens, and the innumerable objects of superstition among the most uncultured tribes. The superstition receives a certain dignity by culture, but it is superstition after all.

The only remedy for superstition is a frank confession of ignorance concerning those matters of which we have no knowledge.

The superstitious are the ready victims for the impostor; and impostors, like the superstitious, have never been wanting. Since the days of Cain, every generation and every community has had its criminals. The law of demand and supply has always brought together dupes and deceivers. The former class being less culpable, not being bad enough willfully to deceive others, and judging others by themselves, are slow to believe that the man of agile tongue could be guilty of fraud, and thus the wily impostor has an easy path before him. The impostor is all the more successful if he has a theory to present which is in accord with some popular superstition. Joseph Smith was aided by a popular belief that the American Indians are the descendants of the ten lost tribes of Israel, and that when they wandered away from the known world, they bore with them some divine inspirations. A current belief in the existence of some chemical preparation by which men might enjoy perpetual youth was necessary to enable impostors in mediæval Europe to convince even kings that they were receiving guests who had associated with ancient warriors. Likewise the modern beliefs concerning mesmerism, clairvoyance, and spiritualism have enabled impostors to spring up from the criminal classes which exist in every community, and reap an abundant harvest of fun, frolic, money and sin.

Sometimes the deceivers are deceived. They

misunderstand the effects which they produce, or knowing themselves to be guilty of fraud, they can not disbelieve the cunning lies of their fellow impostors. Sometimes the deceiver is deceived by his dupes. The juggler, pretending to be assisted by spirits, may be assured by persons in the audience whom he has driven to an hysterical frenzy, that they see spirits which, of course, are invisible to him: and, being ignorant of the freaks of the excited imagination, he is bewildered into a belief of his own lying theories. Though conscious that he is not a real medium himself, he thinks he has discovered one in his audience. He who from mercenary motives advocates an opinion which he disbelieves may after a while become convinced by his own arguments and desires, and become a zealous apostle at last.

When we consider the moral and intellectual condition of mankind, we are not surprised that so many delusions have arisen, but are rather led to wonder that divine truth when planted in such soil has taken root and flourished so well. Christianity, which opposes the evil appetites, humbles human pride, and holds no compromise with sin, would have been slain with its founder and first disciples, if it had not had the perpetual aid of supernatural power in the influences of the Holy Ghost. We marvel, not that the Gospel has not made greater progress, but that it has triumphed at all. Delusions are usually in harmony with the desires of the depraved human heart. When they arise they tend to become epidemic.

Human beings are bound together by the law of sympathy. By this law of the mind we are caused to experience, to a degree, the joys and sorrows of our friends. Their hope and their faith strengthen our own. It is a wise law, for without it a parent's example would be lost to the child, the persuasive eloquence of the man of God would be lost upon the erring; there could be no pity for the unfortunate, and each human being standing alone, uninfluenced and uninfluencing, the family, the Church, and the state could not exist. Without this law of sympathy and those mental states which it produces, there could be no permanency to the cause of truth, and no progress of civilization, for each generation would be uninfluenced by the experience and convictions of the generations which had lived before it, and the world would be continually learning over again the rudiments of knowledge. The child must receive his opinions from his parents and teachers, until he is sufficiently mature to think for himself. The man must be guided by established customs and beliefs, except in the few instances where he may have time and opportunity for original investigation.

The hurry of practical life gives to the masses but little opportunity for reflection upon any other themes but those which are suggested by their physical necessities. Hence, we nearly indorse the remark of of W. R. Alger: "A crowd always thinks with its sympathy, never with its reason." If the crowd thinks with its reason, its reasons come at second hand. Leaders arise and crowds follow after them, snatching a moment now and then from their daily toils to memorize the sentiments and arguments of their leaders. If the crowd is pure in heart, and the would-be leader does violence to their moral instincts and convictions, they "think with their sympathies," and turn from him; if they are evil, they "think with their sympathies," and follow after him. A wise Providence has thus provided that the busy, toil-driven multitude shall not be led into wicked delusions unless their hearts are evil. If they are compelled to think with their sympathies, and they prefer the good to the evil, as they can soon discover the spirit and moral tendency of an evil teacher, their sympathies will at once lead them back to the good old way trodden by their fathers. And when they thus think with their sympathies, they think wisely; for the moral atmosphere surrounding any new system of belief is a sure criterion of its truth or falsity. A leader can not command the multitude, unless he strikes some vibrating cord in the popular heart, and thus the successful leader is but an index of the hearts of his followers. The wonderful career of Mohammed, leaving out the sensualism of his teachings, exhibits to us the latent longing in the Arabian mind for some higher statement of truth concerning the divine nature; while the careers of communists and "social reformers" show us the latent discontent, with the moral restraints imposed by Christianity, existing in the lower stratum of society. In order that a delusion may become epidemic, there must be a pre-existing state of mind, favorable to the disease, in the class of persons which is to be affected by it; and then when a leader arises he gains adherents, and the error spreads like a contagion. Like a fire kindled in dry stubble, it rages on until the fuel is exhausted. Often persons of undecided moral convictions, and sometimes for a little while men who are really good, are led to embrace a pernicious delusion when it is exciting public attention and its victims are many. When soldiers are in line of battle, facing the foe, if one coward runs all the cowards are likely to follow him—causing a panic, into which brave men are drawn. Fear, hope, and belief, sometimes sweep through an entire army. Despondency and distrust sometimes go from city to city, and extend through all the rural districts, causing creditors to chase down debtors, and capitalists to withdraw their capital, leaving workingmen unemployed, involving a nation in financial disaster.

Where the moral convictions are not especially involved, delusions have a wider and swifter course, for the popular understanding is more obtuse than the popular heart. The delusions of alchemy, witchcraft, and animal magnetism swept over all Christendom, opposed only here and there by the learned, because wealth and long life, a belief in and a dread of the power of demons, and a belief in a mysterious natural force, acting between mind and mind, and between mind and matter, involved no contradiction of the moral sentiments. Mormonism and spiritualism requiring an acceptance of new revelations, and a decreased attachment to the old, together with certain licentious philosophies, were confined within narrower limits. In delusions which do not involve the moral sentiments, the busy and uneducated masses are easily swayed by plausible theorists, whose high-sounding words or cunning deceptions feed their desire for the marvelous. Even the most educated are thus weak in reference to those matters which lie outside of their especial lines of investigation.

Thus we see that in those fields of thought in which the popular mind is uneducated, there is a vacant dream-land, in which the fancy has full sway. It is an unoccupied territory, open to any who may come first, providing they commit no nuisance. Any horde of delusions may come and dwell there, until their depredations upon adjacent regions of knowledge and belief render it necessary to drive them away. The law of sympathy impels a man to adopt the opinion of his neighbors in the absence of any fixed opinion of his own; and thus the teaching of one man concerning a matter about which the public judgment is in suspense, may be adopted by the multitude. This law of sympathy extends yet deeper. The mind controls the body, and two minds may so sympathize as to control their bodies in a similar manner; in walking, or running and jumping, for pastime, or in strange physical contortions, when they are mutually controlled by the same superstitious idea. If it were the common belief that hysteria is produced by some terrible demon, and a score of hysterical women were in a room together, and one of them from some cause should have an hysteric fit, we should expect that the whole company would be attacked in like manner.

Delusions are liable to become epidemic, and physical manifestations of the dominant idea may become epidemic also. Italy once witnessed a congregation of four hundred thousand persons, all drawn together by the same frenzy of superstition; while at another time a procession of fifteen thousand, men, women and children, dressed in white robes, singing songs and beating themselves with whips, was seen passing through the streets. Sometimes the multitude under the guidance of some delusion jerks and jumps as if it had the Saint Vitus' dance; or, again, it weeps, shouts, bites, or imitates the voice and manners of the wolf. Sometimes it goes into convulsions around a sacred fountain or a magnetic tree; while, again, it is distributed into little groups, scattered through the villages and cities of a whole country, listening for raps, tipping tables, or gazing into the air to see spirits. Whatever the form of the delusion, one of its chief elements is always superstition.

Chapter II.

SUPERSTITIONS OF PHILOSOPHERS.

BULWER LYTTON remarks: "A philosopher has a system; he views things according to his theory; he is unavoidably partial; and, like Lucian's painter, he paints his one-eyed princes in profile." The one-eyed prince may be discovered in all systems of human thought. That theologies as well as philosophies are not exempt, is sufficiently shown by the successive creeds of the Christian Church. It is freely admitted that theologians are liable to seek to be "wise above what is written;" and sometimes pursue an extra-biblical theory, until it leads them into the cloud-world of fancy; but it is the boast of philosophers, particularly those of the skeptical school, that they are exempt from this common frailty. The theologian, having established the fact of divine revelation, should divest himself of all preconceived theories, and derive his opinions from the teachings of the Bible. The philosopher, having satisfied himself that the natural world is a revelation of truth, should hold all theories in abeyance, until he has studied and classified natural phenomena. But as this requires toil of body and mind, and as mankind are naturally prone to inaction until driven by their necessities, the monk and the naturalist find it more agreeable to retire to some quiet retreat to idly dream and theorize. Infidels and skeptical philosophers have been more prone to this than any other class.

No human being can be wholly skeptical. The imagination of the skeptic is imprisoned, and his hope is bound in fetters. Therefore, he who begins a skeptic and denies the established beliefs of his fellows, being left alone with an empty mind and heart, must soon begin to look about for some positive system of belief. Having scorned the foundation rock and being impelled to build, he must build on the sand. Having rejected the true materials, he must build a castle of the air. Thus the most daring skeptics become the wildest visionaries. As two men setting out to travel in opposite directions shall meet face to face when each has gone half-way around the world, so skepticism and superstition are two extremes which meet, though starting forth in opposite directions. The superstitious and the skeptical are sure to be found in each other's company at last. Who was more skeptical than Comte? Yet his skepticism ripened into a superstition, which Professor Huxley describes as Romanism, with Christianity left out. Who is more skeptical and who is more superstitious than Andrew Jackson Davis, denying the existence of a personal God, the freedom of the will, moral obligation, the evidences of Christianity, the sacredness of the marriage bond, and striking a blow at the established convictions of Christendom; yet describing minutely the spheres of the spirit world, the color of the eyes of the people of the planet Mars, and the freaks and

SUPERSTITIONS OF PHILOSOPHERS.   19

appearance of the "Diakkas," a race of elementary spirits in the lower circles of the invisible world, and receiving, without the semblance of proof, the wildest dreams of his fellow spiritualists? The following formula exhibits the common sophistry of superstition: *If it is not* ——— *what is it?* *We do not know. Therefore, it is* ———. The name of any favorite fetich or force is inserted in the blank spaces, according to the desire of the individual who consciously or unconsciously employs the formula. Professor Crookes, F. R. S., looking upon the jugglery of Mr. Home and Mrs. Fay, asks: "If it is not psychic force, what is it?" He answers, "I do not know;" and concludes: "Therefore, it is psychic force." A spiritualist looking upon the same phenomena reasons in the same manner; but arrives at a different conclusion: "If it is not a spirit, what is it? I do not know; therefore, it is a spirit." "I do not know," is a hard saying, even for philosophers. They prefer the utterance: "I do not know; therefore, I know." Epictetus remarked: "The first business of the philosopher is to part with self-conceit." We trace this common sophistry of superstition in the entire history of speculative philosophy.

Thales (640 B. C.), who has been called the father of natural philosophy, looked forth upon the mysterious phenomena of life in the world around him, and asked the question so often propounded by the thoughtful: "From what do they proceed?" Observing that germinating seeds in the earth are moist, he reasoned: If it is not water which causes the phenomena of life, what is it? We do not know. Therefore, it must be water. By this sophistry he convinced himself and many eminent disciples after him, that water is the source of all things. By the same process of thought he came to the conclusion that the magnet is a living creature, because it attracts iron. His error of substituting hypothesis for proof, may still be found among some of the most conspicuous scientists of our day. A logical possibility is often confounded with certainty, and the scientific teacher stands before us like a high-priest of nature, bewildering us into belief by announcements *ex cathedra*, and silencing opposition by the ever ready interrogatory: "If that is not it, what is it?"

Anaximander (611 B. C.), by the common sophistry of superstition, came to the conclusion that at the beginning of the universe matter in a rarefied state existed in infinite quantity; and, being subject to eternal motion, condensations and combinations occur, producing worlds and spiritual beings. The earth being in the center of the universe, and in the form of a cylinder, remains motionless. Living beings are generated from the substance of the earth, by heat and moisture. Anaximenes, who lived about this time, affirmed that the earth, being flat and round, like a plate, floats on the air which fills the universe, and which is the essence and cause of all things. Diogenes also entertained the same theory of the origin of the universe. "If it is not air, what is it?" would silence objections and make innumerable disciples.

Heraclitus gave his disciples an elaborate description of the manner in which substances and life were caused by fire; while the followers of Pythagoras, being fond of mathematics and music, affirmed that numbers are the substance of things, and that the human soul is a harmony.

Parmenides (of the fifth century B. C.) taught that plurality and change are illusions of the senses. This bold skepticism led him to the equally bold superstition implied in the belief that he and all his neighbors, together with serpents, beasts, and birds, and all animate objects, were not many objects, but one; that when he seemed to talk and walk he was silent and motionless; that he had never been born and would never die.

Zeno, of the same century, was yet bolder in his avowals of skepticism and consequent credulity, denying the existence of plurality, space, motion, and sound; bidding utter defiance to the testimony of the five senses. He shows wonderful shrewdness in the invention of sophisms by which to defend his positions, and exhibits to us to what depths of darkness and absurdity a giant intellect may plunge, when not guided along the pathways of thought by the lamp of divine truth.

Leucippus and Democritus, who are so much admired by some of our own scientists, and whom they have frequently imitated, in using the common sophistry of superstition, taught that the "full" and the "void" are the first principles of all things. The "full" consists of indivisible atoms distinguished from each other by their form and position.

Fire and the soul are composed of round atoms. Sensation is caused by material images, coming from objects to the soul, through the organs of sense. Organized beings arose from the moist earth. We inhale soul-atoms from the air, until the whole body is filled with them, and they become so distributed as to produce thought in the brain, anger in the heart, and desire in the liver.

The eloquent Gorgias, who was contemporary with Socrates, with persuasive rhetoric and wonderful arguments, affirmed that nothing exists; that if any thing does exist we can not know it; and, if we could know it, we could not communicate our knowledge to others. The students of nature were held in check from the wild extremes of superstition and skepticism by Socrates for a time; but we soon find Euclid of Megara affirming that only the one exists, and that the opposite of the good has no existence; implying the horrible notion that crime is a virtue misunderstood.

Plato assumed that ideas are eternal, and that individual objects are images of pre-existing ideas. His followers afterwards made the archetypal ideas of their master living beings, endowed with personality and life. Plato himself regarded his "ideas" as efficient causes, creating the objects of the visible world. He taught that God first created the soul of the world by creating two elements of opposite nature, the one divisible and changeable, and the other indivisible and unchangeable; and, after joining them by an intermediate substance, he scattered this invisible compound throughout space. This was the soul of the world, to which He afterwards gave an appropriate body. The embodied world-soul contained certain cubiform elements which formed themselves into the earth; elements of pyramid shape forming fire, icosahedral elements forming water, and octahedral elements forming air. The universe taken as a whole, according to Plato, is in the shape of a dodecahedron. The divine part of the human soul was made like the world-soul. Man possesses, however, three souls, one of them being an appetitive soul, such as is possessed by plants. Plato also taught that the soul transmigrates through the bodies of men and animals, for a period of ten thousand years. He affirmed that the celestial spheres are separated from each other at distances corresponding to the lengths of the strings of a musical instrument, and that the earth is wound around a solid bar, which extends from one end of the axis of the universe to the other.

Aristotle, who was Plato's greatest pupil, affirmed that the sphere to which the fixed stars are attached is in immediate contact with Deity, and that the moving planets are each moved by a spiritual being, or inferior god.

Pliny, the great Roman naturalist, believed that a round stone with a hole in it, if found in an eagle's nest, would prevent diseases and shipwreck, if carried about the body.

These philosophers whom we have named occasionally reasoned truly and profoundly; but we see that the wisest of them frequently mistook hypothesis for proof, and used their own ignorance as the sole proof of knowledge. As the spiritualist in the presence of a dark *séance*, or the excited visionary in a "haunted house" reasons: "If it is not a spirit, what is it? We do not know; therefore, it is a spirit:" so they reasoned concerning their particular hypothesis or dream, by which they sought to explain the inexplicable. "We do not know," has always been a difficult sentence for mortals to utter. It is even easier to say: "We do not know what it is; therefore, we do know what it is." Natural philosophy had but little place in the thoughts of mankind during the dark ages of Romish supremacy; but with the dawn of the Protestant Reformation the fetters were gradually removed from the reason, and the stirring controversies which it produced provoked independent thought, and awakened the sleeping intellect. We are considering the history of speculative philosophy in its relations to the phenomena of external nature. Until recent times, speculative philosophy and natural philosophy were one. It is a modern discovery, that the true method of determining the laws of nature and the facts of natural history is to go forth upon land and sea, to make actual observations and experiments, and not to shut one's self up with the midnight lamp, to enter the regions of abstract thought and fantasy, to determine what the external world contains.

Every investigator is entitled to build an hypothesis upon observed facts, and when his data have accumulated to a sufficient extent, he may announce his hypothesis as a scientific verity. But the facts must prove the hypothesis, and not the hypothesis the facts. Furthermore, the assumed facts must be verified as genuine, and it must be demonstrated that, among many possible hypotheses, only the one hypothesis can serve to explain them. If a given phenomenon may be produced by any one of many given causes, the whole matter must be left in suspense in the absence of further proof, and the assertion that it is produced by any particular cause would be an irrational procedure. A traveling "spirit medium" produces music in the dark, when his hands and limbs, and whole body are tied to a post, and the musical instruments are beyond his reach. Jugglers do this by adroitly unloosing themselves from their fastenings, or by the aid of confederates; therefore, the medium may produce the musical sounds in that way. If God so willed it, a spirit from the invisible world might produce them. Or it is among the infinitesimal possibilities that Professor Crookes's psychic force, under the control of the will of the medium, or some one in the flesh, might produce them. To affirm without further proof that they are produced by either of the two last named causes exhibits the sleep of reason, and shows that the thinker, for the time, has become irrational.

Supposing that these three hypotheses are equally uncertain in this particular case, we are bound to give preference to the former, being more in harmony with the common experience of mankind. This latter probability ripens into certainty when we seize the medium, turn up the lights, and find him unbound, with the musical instruments in his hands. But Professor Crookes's sleep of the reason, when he dreamed of psychic force, finds a parallel in the occasional dreams and dogmatic annunciations of most men who have tried to break through the narrow boundaries of human knowledge. Men are not willing to confess their ignorance. Nor are they willing to wait until they dig a tunnel through the impassable Alps of mystery; they throw aside the pick-ax and shovel, and explosive materials, and sit down and dream, and dogmatize as to what the mysterious transalpine realm of the invisible must be, and stigmatize as ignorant and non-progressive, and "theological," all who refuse to accept their dreams as eternal verities. Men who have devoted themselves to scientific speculation have subserved a worthy end; and, like the alchemists in search of the philosopher's stone, they have stumbled upon many valuable truths; but not infrequently their guiding star has been a will-o'-the-wisp, and they become impatient, because the world will not follow it into the dismal swamp of superstition or skepticism.

Lord Bacon (1561-1626) limited natural philosophy in its method to experiment and induction, and thus became the father of the natural sciences. He brought philosophy down to earth, and sent it forth to build laboratories for experiment and classification. But Bacon did not always follow his own method. His great intellect sometimes slumbered, and we find him employing the common sophistry of superstition. He dreams and dogmatizes when he affirms that man has two souls, the one spiritual and incognizable, the other physical. The latter is an object of scientific knowledge; it is a thin, warm, material substance. He also came near to fetichism, when he affirmed that all the elements of bodies have perceptions, which are manifest by attractions and repulsions. How did he know that the material elements, as gold and oxygen, which we suppose to be inanimate, have the power of perceiving? But using the sophism of the modern spiritist and the believer in witchcraft, and the fetich worshiper in South Africa, he says, unconsciously: "What causes attraction and repulsion among the material elements? If it is not perception, what is it? We do not know; therefore, it is perception."

Hobbes was a philosopher and a friend of Lord Bacon, and aspired to be even more severely critical than his honored associate. His criticism in many things went to the extreme of skepticism. He spurns religion from the realm of philosophy, and confines it to that which is natural and political. He affirms that bodies are composed of ultimate atoms, which are not, however, absolutely indivisible. Did he ever see one of them? Or by any demonstration prove its existence? Did he ever by experiment apply the edge of an infinitely sharp razor to a material atom, and with infinite force bear down upon it, to see that it is not absolutely indivisible? He resolves all real processes into motions. Thought is motion. The senses are affected by motions, which are transmitted inward to the brain, and from thence to the heart; a reaction sets in from the heart, producing a motion from the heart outward to the organ of sense producing sensation.

All very lucid and confirmed by "many infallible proofs!" If one body move another body, as by attraction, as in the case of the magnet, the body itself must be in motion, at least in its minute parts. He also affirms that matter is not incapable of sensation and thought. This philosopher, who repudiated all religion, and who affirmed that conscientiousness consists in obedience to the king or civil rulers, becomes as wildly superstitious as any worshiper along the banks of the Ganges. Does the latter call the river divine? The former assumes that matter may feel and think. Their sophistries are identical. "If thought and sensation are not motion, what are they? We do not know; therefore, they are motion." The worshiper of the Ganges may be uttering his queries concerning some other natural mystery, and his visible or invisible fetich may be of a different class, but he arrives at his conclusions by the same sophism as that employed by our celebrated skeptical philosopher.

Hobbes also precedes our modern scientists in assuming that bodies can not act upon each other when separated by a vacuum. He assumed that the motions of the minute parts of a given body are communicated to the surrounding ether, and thus carried to the body to be acted upon. But from his stand-point, what formula of reason could he construct which would warrant him in arriving at such

SUPERSTITIONS OF PHILOSOPHERS.

conclusions? Had he ever seen the component atoms of bodies in motion? Had he ever seen the ether trembling with its burden of vibrations which it was carrying from one body to another? If a convenient hypothesis in the absence of proof is worthy of a philosopher, how could he rule out of philosophy all religion, with its convenient hypotheses, which surely are as well supported?

There are modern scientists of a small select school to whom we direct the same earnest question. Descartes (1596–1665) resolved to rid himself of all traditional opinions and "build from the foundation." He would not trust the testimony of his senses, for they are sometimes deceived. He could not tell whether his waking or sleeping state was spent in dream-land. So he begins at the foundation and builds by saying: "I think, therefore I am." He would not assume his existence without proof. But wait awhile and see him relapse into "dogmatic slumber." We find him declaring that wherever space is, matter is; that matter is infinitely divisible; that the universe is a limited sphere; that plants and animals and all phenomena are caused by pressure and impulsion alone; that each thought produces a certain material change in the brain, and that the soul lives in the pineal gland. Had he explored all space? Had he divided a particle of matter into infinitesimal parts, or witnessed the operation? Did he or any accredited witnesses soar to the outer surface of the universe, and measure angles and take observations to find out that the universe is a limited sphere? By what process did he build on his "*Cogito, ergo sum,*" the certainty that plants and animals and all phenomena are produced by pressure and impulsion?

Spinoza (1632-1677) affirmed that there is only one substance, and that is God. This substance has two fundamental attributes, thought and extension, which include and constitute all individual existences. In the causes and effects of the visible world we see only one mode of extension operating on another mode of extension, and one mode of thought operating on another mode of thought. All individual objects are but manifestations of God, and the substance within them is God. All human volitions, including crimes, are determined by God. To Spinoza good and evil have no absolute existence. Pantheism is but a return to the animism of the uncultured races, which sees vitality and intelligence in every object in nature. The fetich worshiper worships a part, the pantheist the whole of the material universe.

Sir Isaac Newton (1642-1727) objected to the formation of hypotheses not demanded by observed phenomena; but occasionally we find him soaring afar on the wings of unrestrained fancy. He assumed, for example, that shining bodies emit material rays, whose vibrations affect the organs of sense. That the rays are material was pure hypothesis. That they vibrate was not and is not demonstrable from any observed phenomena. The fact that some other elements and forces sometimes move in waves is not proof that rays of light vibrate and thus affect the nerve of vision. In a temporary slumber of his great intellect, he said: "If that is not it, what is it? We do not know; therefore that must be it." By this process of thought he came to the conclusion that the sensation of sight is produced by material rays, vibrating while they pass into the eye. Would it not have been more in harmony with his character as a philosopher to say, I leave this problem unsolved? But this Christian believer gives less evidence of credulity, and adheres far more closely to the rigid laws of scientific evidence, than those who boasted of their skepticism, and whose adherence to religion was doubtful, or whose opposition to religion as requiring excessive credulity was avowed.

Bishop Berkeley, who was so skeptical as to deny the existence of matter as a substance, wrote a book on the wonderful cures wrought on the human body by tar water. The superstition, headed by this great man, spread rapidly. Tar water houses were built in London, and many and marvelous cures were wrought. The effect was attributed to tar water until the power of the excited imagination in causing and curing diseases of a certain class became better known.

Galvani and Volta were searching for the mysterious principle of life when they made their discoveries, and they lived and died having a faith similar to the old alchemists.

Leibnitz (1646–1716) was the founder of the German speculative philosophy of the eighteenth century. With him active force is the essence of substance. A monad or atom is so small as not to occupy space, and yet it has the power of action. God is the primitive monad, from which all other monads have sprung. Every soul or spirit is a self-conscious and God-conscious monad. Plants and minerals are sleeping monads, with unconscious ideas. That which appears to us as a body is in reality a collection of many separate monads, which we could see as separate, were it not for the confusion in our sensuous perceptions. Every substance has perceptions, and a tendency or desire for new perceptions, possessing something similar to feeling and appetite.

Voltaire declares with emphasis, that it is possible that matter may think. We are prepared to expect such credulity on the part of an avowed infidel; but we are a little surprised to find Kant (1729–1804), the author of the immortal "Critique of Pure Reason," relapsing into "dogmatic slumber," and teaching that most of the planets are inhabited; and going so far as to say that the inhabitants of the planets farthest from the sun are the most perfect. He teaches that time and space have no existence outside of thought, that things in themselves, or objects as they exist independently of the observing mind, have neither unity nor plurality; that unity, plurality, totality, reality, limitation, substantiality, causality, reciprocal action and existence, do not belong to things in themselves, but are forms of thought. We have great respect for Immanuel Kant, but we have still more respect for the common sense of mankind. Kant teaches also that matter is infinitely divisible; that a repulsive force belongs to every portion of matter; that the sum of matter in the material universe is never increased nor diminished—all of which assumptions, whether true or false, are so far beyond the reach of human observation or demonstration, that we would suppose that one so critical as to reject the idea that the essence of rocks and rivers and mountains exists in time and space, and embraces unity, plurality, reality, substantiality and existence, as is popularly believed, would be unwilling to announce them as scientific verities.

Hegel (1770–1831) affirmed that the world is phenomenon or semblance *per se*; that pure being is identical with nothing, or that being and non-being are one.

Lotze, born in Saxony, 1817, who stands as one of the chief leaders of German speculative thought at the present day, affirms that matter and force are illusions, yet is so unskeptical as to believe in the existence of an invisible, intangible, imponderable, hypothetical fluid, which exists, like an atmosphere behind the atmosphere, and pervades all space; and that the hypothetical vibrations of the ether undergo certain transformations constituting color. He also talks of spiritual monads, and says that the soul dwells in that portion of the brain which is without fibers. All this, of course, he is able to demonstrate by more convincing proofs than those upon which we rely for the existence of matter and force.

Trendelenburg (1802–1872) was also one of the principal leaders in German speculative thought.

Looking about him he found that all activity in the physical world is connected with motion, and concludes that motion is common to thought and being. He assumes that motion is eternal, and that time and space, and form, are its products. Ideal motion is self-conscious. The soul may be defined as a self-realizing final idea. Motion also is the organ of design. Many of these great names in a future age will be consigned to the oblivion in which the old alchemists are buried, and the philosophers of common sense will be their less conspicuous but more worthy successors.

Hartley (1705–1757) explained the origin of sensation by assuming that the white medullary substance of the brain and of the spinal marrow and nerves contains infinitesimal particles of matter which vibrate when excited by external objects.

Hume avowed a skeptical philosophy, by which he declared experience untrustworthy, and denied the existence of causation, and yet planted himself upon the reliability and uniformity of experience, when he sought to overthrow the Christian doctrine of miracles, and used arguments founded upon the very doctrine of causation which he had disowned.

John Stuart Mill (1806–1873), with an intellect of unusual power, whose processes of thought were like a mountain in labor, brought forth the notion that matter is nothing more than a permanent possibility of sensation; and that mind is succession of feelings, and a permanent possibility of feeling.

Skepticism becomes superstition when its denials are unsupported by evidence. To believe that a mere nothing, a vacuum, can think and feel, as is implied in the denial of the real existence of spirit, or that it can hurl forth before our eyes the phenomena of the material universe, as is implied in the denial of the real existence of matter, is as startling an exhibition of superstition as may be found among those savage tribes which give food and drink to trees and stones, and seek to entertain them with agreeable discourses.

The prevailing superstition among a class of living philosophers is embraced in the extreme statements of the doctrine of evolution. In "Fragments of Science" (page 453, Fifth Ed.), Professor Tyndall remarks: "Strip it naked, and you stand face to face with the notion, that not only the more ignoble forms of animalcular or animal life, not alone the nobler forms of the horse and the lion, not alone the exquisite and wonderful mechanism of the human body, but of the human mind also—sensibilities, intellect, will, and all their phenomena—were once latent in a fiery cloud." If one fiery cloud contained latent Huxleys, and Spencers and Tyndalls, surely other burning materials may contain them, and those peoples, to whom we shall hereafter refer, are profoundly philosophical in their views who give the fire a portion of their food before meals to keep it in good humour, and who avoid spitting in the flames or on burning coals, lest they may become enraged at the insult and burn the house.

It is not our purpose in this place to controvert the doctrine of evolution as taught by those evolutionists who refuse to admit that God is the evolver;

but to bring forward the idea as a kind of scholastic fetichism, which is unsupported save by the common sophistry of superstition. If Professor Huxley were to see his "protoplasm" transforming into some higher forms of animate existence, that would not be proof that the visible substance before him contained in itself the power of transmuting mechanical into vital forces. The substratum of the phenomenon would belong to the invisible realm, and would most rationally be referred, not to a visible, but to an invisible cause. If that which comes first is, on the sole ground of its priority, to be regarded as the cause of that which comes after it, the Roman historian was right who associated the fact that a soldier had sneezed, with the subsequent success of the army; and those other Romans were right, who believed that the eclipse-monster who was about to devour the sun, gave up his intended repast, because they had hurled firebrands at him.

Professor Huxley observes that the human body is a mechanism, and that mechanism precedes the mental faculties in the order of its development. He therefore concludes that which appears first must produce that which comes after it, and declares that animals "act mechanically, and their indifferent states of consciousness, their sensations, their thoughts, their volitions, are the products and consequences of the mechanical arrangements." He further affirms, that "molecular changes in the brain give rise to those emotions which in ourselves, we call volition." Has he subjected the assumed molecular changes in the brain to scientific examination? And, granting that the invisible molecules tremble and leap about while we are thinking, has he traced the steps by which the molecules produce emotions and thoughts? He ventures to assume that the motions of the molecules precede thought, and from that undemonstrable hypothesis concludes that, as that which appears first is the cause of that which comes after it, therefore thoughts are the products of molecular changes in the brain. His process of thought is: "If that is not it, what is it? I do not know; therefore, that is it."

Chapter III.

SUPERSTITIONS OF THE UNCULTURED CONCERNING THE SPIRIT WORLD.

THE mythologies of all primitive nations, and the innumerable pictures of the spirit world furnished from the lips and pens of sorcerors, wizards, spirit mediums, and false prophets, have taken their origin mainly in the belief, which is common in low stages of culture, that dreams are realities, and that the soul is actually absent from the body during sleep. Even Saint Augustine, who could give a system of theology to subsequent ages of the Christian Church, had not outgrown this primitive notion.* We find this idea among the New Zealanders, the Greenlanders, and the North American Indians. The Tagals of Luzon are unwilling to awaken a man who is sleeping, lest the absent soul may not come back. The Fijians believe that a living man's soul may go and trouble other people in their dreams. If they dream of seeing a neighbor in their sleep, they believe that the neighbor's soul has left the body and is actually present before them. Doctor Fian was tortured in the presence of King James, of England, because a dreaming woman had been with the culprit in a fleet of sieves at sea.

---

*Augustine, De Civ. Dei, xviii, 18.

As we shall see hereafter, a belief that dreams are realities was that which kept alive the witch mania of mediæval Europe, the poor witch confessing in the flames that she had ridden on a broomstick through the air simply because she dreamed that she had been doing so. Thus Hercules and Venus, gods and monsters, vampires, incubi, succubi, and salamanders, flying witches and wizards, ghosts and goblins, have found a place in the popular belief because dream-land has been mistaken for a land of realities. But the ever accumulating fables of the unseen have received accessions, from the mistaken notion that dreams which arise from the state of the entranced, and which are produced by the use of narcotics, are not dreams, but real visions of the unseen universe.

Mankind, guided by an unerring intuition, look forward to some kind of existence after death. As the magnetic needle points towards the north-pole, so there is that within us which points to a country beyond the grave; and like the magnetic needle, it can give us but little information concerning that unseen land other than that it exists, leaving the superstitious fancy free to people it with all kinds of shadowy creatures, engaging in all kinds of employments and being subject to all kinds of possible and impossible laws. "If that is not it, what is it?" is a sufficient answer to every objector, and a sufficient vindication of the faith of any spiritualist or visionary. Customs which arise from this firm yet indefinite idea of the future life are often savage, yet not without an appearance of plausibility.

Until recently in the Fiji islands, when a man died his wives and slaves were killed to accompany him into the spirit world. This custom has been quite wide-spread in some parts of Africa, Central America, Mexico, Bogota, and Peru. Widow burning in India took its origin in the same idea. In Dahomey the absent king in the spirit world is kept posted on all affairs occurring in his former realm by telling the news to slaves, who are then killed and sent into the spirit world to bear the message with them. Shall not their disembodied spirits meet and converse with their former master? Who can demonstrate that they may not?

It is the prevailing notion, not unmixed with truth, that spirits people the world and are constantly mingling in mundane scenes. North American Indians of the Algonquin districts bury their children by the way side, that their spirits may be near to enter into the bodies of women who pass and be born again into this earthly life. In Northwest America, among the Tracullis, the medicine-man puts his hands on the body of the dead or dying, and puts them over the head of some living friend, and then blows through his hands, believing that he has blown the soul of the dying man into the body of his friend, and that the next child born to him will be animated with the soul thus conveyed to him.

This idea has been wide-spread. We find it in Old Calabar, Guinea, Lapland, Tartary, Africa, ancient Mexico, and Brazil. In New Zealand the priest repeats a list of the names of ancestral spirits until the child sneezes, and the name repeated at that time is the name of the child, and of the spirit which has taken possession of it. The Congo negroes were accustomed to abstain from sweeping their houses a whole year after a death had occurred, lest the dust should be hurtful to the ghost. Roman Catholic Christendom is accustomed to pay religious homage to a multitude of saints, whose spirits are supposed to be pleased with their adorations; while throughout the great empire of China, lanterns are lighted to show the ancestral spirits the way back to the feasts of their mortal relatives, who provide vacant seats, baths, separate apartments and choicest delicacies of food for the ghosts who may choose to visit them. Louis XIV, after he was dead, was served with food, over which a priest said grace for forty days. We may still trace the survival of this custom, in Spain, Bulgaria, and Russia.

Very often, however, invisible spirits are objects of superstitious terror. In Australia the natives carry firebrands in the dark to protect themselves from evil spirits. The Indian tribes of Brazil, the natives of Southern India, have had a similar custom. The Hindoo sometimes lights a lamp in daylight to drive off the demons. The aborigines of Queensland and some North American Indian tribes beat the air with clubs to drive off the dead. The ancient Norsemen, of Iceland, carried fire around islands before they took possession of them, to expel the demons. In the Malay peninsula a fire is kindled near a mother in child-birth for the same purpose. When a baby was born in a Kalmuck tribe, the neighbors rushed about beating the air with clubs to drive off the spirits who might do harm to the mother and child. The Australians annually drive off in this way the ghosts of those who have died during the year. It is said that the Matamba widows, in Africa, have themselves ducked in water, to drown off the souls of their former husbands who clung to them, so that it may be safe to marry again. The Greenlanders were accustomed to remove the dead through a window and not out of the door of the house, while an old lady walked behind the corpse, waving a firebrand, crying: "There is nothing more to be had here." The Hottentots, Siamese, natives of Siberia, and others, have adopted various expedients to scare away the dead man's ghost, and to render it impossible for it to return. The Siamese carry the corpse through an opening in the wall, and carry it three times around the house at full speed, so that the ghost becoming confused may not find its way into the house again.

It is also a prevalent notion among all barbarous and semi-barbarous tribes, that by certain magical arts or invocations, departed human spirits and demons, and monsters can be brought down to earth, or up from the abyss below the world, to do the behests of mortals. Among the Fijians, "when any one faints or dies, their spirit, it is said, may sometimes be brought back by calling after it; and, occasionally, the ludicrous scene is witnessed of a stout man lying at full length and bawling out lustily for the return of his own soul." The Karens of Burmah suppose that when a man is sick his soul is temporarily absent from the body, and they will run about and try to catch it, and drop it down on the sick man's head, and thus hope to restore him. When a Chinaman is at the point of death, his soul is supposed to have already escaped from the body, and they seek to entice it back by holding up the sick man's coat on a pole, to which a white cock is fastened, while the Tauist priests utter certain incantations. When the pole turns in the hands of the holder, as it is likely to do by the movements of the air, or by the gradual relaxation of the muscles of the hand, they believe the spirit has returned to the coat.

The Chinese make a hole in the roof of a house in which a death has occurred, to let the dead man's soul escape. The superstitious in France, England, and Germany for the same purpose open a window of the room in which a man has just died. In Madagascar the sorcerer makes a hole in the burial-house to let a soul out, and placing his cap at the opening, he catches the spirit and carries it, and puts it on the head of a sick man, whose soul has departed, thus causing him to languish.

The methods employed to bring the spirits to earth are as various as the possibilities of the human fancy; yet, as the world is old, there has come to be in a general sense, "nothing new under the sun." Circles are formed and raps are heard among the Chinese. They also present fair examples of spirit writing. In all countries the excited imagination has done its work. Ignorance and superstition have been world wide.

It becomes monotonous and wearisome to multiply examples of the superstitious notions which mankind have entertained concerning spirits and the spirit world. The waking or sleeping dream of the visionary is dignified or disgusting, according to the degree of his moral and intellectual culture. And there is a surprising similarity in the conceptions of the future life among peoples of the same grade of culture. The modern spiritualist of low culture (and most of these dreamers are morally and intellectually degraded) describes the spirit world as a place of sensual delight, and filled with just such scenes and creatures as would be adapted to his own peculiar powers of appreciation. And as his tastes are similar to those of like intelligence in pagan countries, we find his dreams of the spirit world are but a repetition of similar dreams to be found among persons of his level in all countries and in all ages. Judge Edmonds, for example, who, having become a monomaniac, and thus sinking to the ordinary level of spiritualists and sorcerers, received convincing proof of immortality by drinking a bowl of buttermilk held in the dark by an unseen hand, finds himself indorsing the faith of the Chinaman who believes the spirits feed upon rice, and of the Australian savage who dares not rob a bee-hive without leaving a little honey for Buddai, the evil spirit, to eat.

CHAPTER IV.

SUPERSTITIONS OF THE UNCULTURED—ANIMISM.

IF Thales, Anaximander, Diogenes, Heraclitus, and Tyndall, and other ancient and modern philosophers, could find the origin of life and consciousness in the material elements; and if Lord Bacon could believe that the elements of material bodies have perceptions, manifest in attractions and repulsions; and Hobbes could teach that thought is motion, and with Voltaire could suppose that matter is not incapable of sensation and thought, and if Leibnitz could say that plants have unconscious ideas, we should not be surprised to find a similar method of reasoning among the uncultured. What the former are able to hold simply as a principle of philosophy, the latter with a bolder faith will carry out into all the details of practical life.

If matter is capable of thought and sensation, according to philosophers, the wild aborigines of Brazil act like philosophers when they bite the arrows which wound them and the stones over which they stumble. When we see rude Kukis of Southern Asia cutting into chips a tree which had killed a man by its fall, and a modern Chinese king ordering one of his ships to be flogged for misbehaving when out at sea, and when we read of Xerxes punishing the Hellespont, and at another time rewarding it with his golden goblet and sword, and Cyrus in a rage draining the Gyndes, we see an exhibition of a common impulse indulged by children and by people of low culture, and one that sometimes governs the conclusions of philosophers.

We even find courts of justice punishing inanimate objects as if they were responsible beings. According to Herodotus and Porphyry,* a court of justice was accustomed to assemble in the Prytaneum to try an ax or piece of wood which had been charged with causing the death of a man, without human agency, and if found guilty it was sentenced to exile, and solemnly carried beyond the borders of the country. An English law repealed during the reign of Queen Victoria provided that a cartwheel or tree which kills a man shall be sold and the proceeds given to the poor. Here we find a survival of the idea far into the higher stages of culture.

According to Alger, in his critical history of a future life, barbarians generally believe that every thing else, as well as man, has a soul or ghost.† The custom of burying objects dear to the deceased in the same grave with him, a practice common in all savage tribes, and the Chinese custom of burning objects which they design to give to the dead, point back to the idea that inanimate objects have souls. In some parts of Africa, when a negro cuts down a certain tree, he protects himself from the de-

---

*Herod., i, 189; vii, 34; Porphyry, de Abstinentia, ii, 30.
†Page 81.

mon inhabiting the tree by dropping palm oil on the ground, and he makes his escape by running while the tree spirit stops to eat the oil. Tree worship prevails to a great extent in Africa. The idea that plants have souls which may be propitiated by human sacrifices is found in Borneo, in ancient India, and elsewhere. The Talein of South-east Asia believes every tree has a demon, and offers prayers before cutting one down. The Ojibwas, of North America, belived that hatchets and kettles have souls, which must cross to the great city at the place of the setting sun. The Fijians had the same notion. It is this same idea which gave origin to the custom still observed by ignorant people in France, of throwing down on the floor or into the fire a spoonful of food, for luck and good health, before beginning a meal, and which causes the Bohemian to avoid insulting the fire by spitting into it, lest it should burn the house. To make the fire good-natured the Carinthian peasant occasionally feeds it with bits of lard.

The Tartars believe that the rags, bells, and bits of metal which the magician carries about his person contain spirits which aid him in his work. In certain parts of Norway, as late as the end of the eighteenth century, people preserved round stones, washed them every Thursday evening, smeared them with butter, and laid them on beds of straw, and occasionally steeped them in ale, that they might bless their homes.

The Tyrolese will not pick their teeth with grass for fear that some invisible devils in the straw may get into them by the process. For the same reason the Bulgarians fumigate flour if it has been ground at a mill owned by a Turk.

Some of the modern Parsees bury the hair and finger and toe nails when they cut them off, fearing lest retaining some of the spirit which once animated them they may do harm to their former owners. Some German peasants refuse to lend any article out of the house during the time between a child's birth and baptism, lest the absent articles may become possessed by some unfriendly spirit which shall cause the child harm when they are returned. Articles in the house are supposed to be possessed by the spirits of the inmates or by spirits on friendly relations with them. In some parts of Africa the natives object to having their portraits taken for fear that a portion of the soul of the subject may be lost by going into the picture. It is a notion somewhat akin to this which causes the young Hessian to carry a baby-girl's cap in his pocket to avoid being drafted in the army. The spirit of the fish, doubtless, returns to the sea; so the Cornishman must reason when he is careful to eat fishes from the tail towards the head in order that more fishes may come head first towards the shore.

Some North American Indians fear to kill a rattlesnake lest its spirit should revenge the deed if slain. The Tartars lead the favorite horse of the deceased to the grave and kill him, that his master may ride him in the land of shadows. We find this notion among the Esquimaux, Arabs, Mongols,

SUPERSTITIONS OF THE UNCULTURED. 49

Hindus, and many other peoples. The ancient Egyptians worshiped cats, jackals, hawks, bulls; and the mummies of some of these sacred animals are still in existence. The worshipers believed that these animals possessed powerful and immortal souls which could reward them after death, or that some god was incarnate within them. In Southern Europe we find the peasant ducking the image of the Virgin Mary in water to produce rain, believing, in a half-unconscious way, that the soul of the virgin dwells in the image, and may thus be punished for her neglect of the faithful. We go back to the golden age of ancient Roman culture, and we find the great Augustus actuated by a similar idea, whipping a statue of Neptune for producing an ill-timed storm at sea.

Thus we find the sublimest truths merging into error, and pushed into extremes by the unreasoning fancy, when misled by the wayward human heart, ever prone to be too proud to permit the lips to utter a confession of ignorance.

Some hypothesis must ever be assumed to account for the visible phenomena of the world, and the idea of invisible spirits working out each separate phenomenon is the ever present and easy hypothesis. The modern spiritualist hears a rap on the table, which the traveling medium or juggler affirms he does not produce; but being unwilling to leave the mystery unsolved he assumes that there must be a spirit at work in the table. The superstitious have crowded the universe with ghosts and goblins, which have crowded out of their thoughts the omnipresent God of love and law, surrounded by his visible and invisible sons and daughters. M. Figuier, a modern scientist of the evolutional school, has attempted to elevate the common superstition of the ages into the dignity of a science, affirming that the rudimentary spirits (corresponding to the Diakkas of Andrew Jackson Davis) which swarm in the universe, transmigrate through all grades of animate existence until they arrive at the ultimate degree of advancement and become pure spirits, which constitute the burning gases of the sun. "If that is not it, what is it? We do not know. Therefore, that must be it," is the one great sophism of superstition.

Chapter V.

SUPERSTITIONS OF THE UNCULTURED—Continued.

WHY do men sneeze? The uncultured races say we do not know; therefore, sneezing must be a spiritual manifestation, and they silence every skeptic by the unanswerable inquiry, "If that is not it, what is it?" When a Zulu sneezes he will say: "I am now blessed. The Idhlozi [ancestral spirit] is with me; it has come to me. Let me hasten and praise it, for it is that which causes me to sneeze." If he sneezes when he is sick he believes that he shall get well. The Zulu sorcerers demonstrate the presence of the spirit in them by sneezing. This superstition is quite prevalent among many African tribes. Also, in Polynesia and in many parts of Europe and Asia. We read of the lucky sneeze of Telemachus in Homer's "Odyssey;" and Xenophon mentions that when a soldier sneezed a shout of adoration to a god arose from the army. Aristotle states that the idea that a sneeze is a manifestation of spirit presence was extant in his day. Pliny mentions that Tiberius Cæsar required his subjects to cry "*salve*" when they heard a person sneeze.

This superstition is still prevalent among the Hindus and Thugs of India. When a Jew sneezed his brethren would exclaim, "Good life." The Mohammedan exclaims "Praise God" when he sneezes, and receives the congratulations of his friends. In France, in the seventeenth century, when a man of nobility sneezed, the bystanders were required to pull off their hats and bow to him. A similar custom was prevalent in England and Germany in mediæval times. Some peoples have believed that the sneezing is produced by an evil spirit, and would accompany the act of sneezing with gestures and exclamations to drive him away.

What causes people to gape and yawn? If it is not a demon what is it? The Hindu, reasoning in the same manner as the modern spiritualist, says, "We do not know; therefore, we do know it must be a demon;" and when he gapes he snaps his thumb and finger and repeats the name of a god. To neglect this would be as great a sin as to murder a Brahmin. The same notion is extant among the Persians and Mohammedans. When the modern Mohammedan yawns he puts the back of his left hand to his mouth, and says: "I seek refuge with Allah from Satan, the accursed." He believes that the devil is preparing to leap into a gaping mouth. Influenced by a similar idea the inhabitants of Tyrol cross themselves when they yawn. We find the same idea existing in Iceland. It has been a wide-spread superstition, and we would be likely to meet with it in all uncultured races which regard all things mysterious as being produced by spirits and monsters of the invisible world.

Josephus relates* that he witnessed a Jew, named Eleazar, curing those who were possessed of devils,

* Antiq. Jud. viii, 2, 5.

by drawing the invisible demons out through the nostrils of their victims, by means of a ring containing the root of a certain plant. We also meet the sublime and the ludicrous in the custom of the Messalian heretics, who were accustomed to spit and blow their noses to expel the devils which they may have breathed in from the air.

What can be more mysterious to the uncultured than a volcano? The savages of Kamtchatka believe that spirits go into volcanoes to cook their food, the fires having been kindled by them for that purpose. And they reason after the manner of Professor Crookes, F. R. S., and others, concerning the so called psychic force, exhibited in the *séances* of Anna Eva Fay. "If that is not it, what is it? We do not know; therefore, that must be it." By the same sophism it was established among the ancient Greeks and Romans that a volcano is the chimney of a spiritual blacksmith's shop, where a spirit named Vulcan worked at his trade perpetually. Certain New Zealanders cast their dead into the crater of volcanoes, believing it to be an opening into the spirit world. Christendom at one time believed volcanoes to be the entrances to hell. The people of Kamtchatka know that the mountain spirits heat up their house and throw firebrands out of the chimney, when a volcano bursts forth.

By the same false method of reasoning the Japanese and some Chinese prove that water-spouts are produced by long-tailed dragons ascending from the sea into the clouds. The same notion is to be found among the Mohammedans, and particularly among savage tribes. Sand pillars, caused by the whirlwinds of the desert, are regarded by native Mohammedans and others, as being caused by the flight of a demon.

New Zealanders, the Karens of Burmah, the Zulus, the natives of Dahomey and others, regard the rainbow as a living creature. Surely the rainbow to the uncultured must be a profound mystery, and by the method of argument we have already indicated, they would be justified in regarding it as a spirit manifestation. The Chiquitos, Caribs, Peruvians, Hurons, Cumanians, Ojibwas, the South Sea Islanders, the Africans, the common people of India, the Chinese, Siamese, looking at an eclipse, say: "If a monster spirit is not devouring the sun or moon, or if they are not sick and dying, what is it? We do not know; therefore, that must be it." Hence these peoples are terrified by an eclipse; and by sacrifices, prayers or threats, and the beating of drums, or shooting guns and arrows, seek to induce the devourer to give up his intended repast.

Popes have issued bulls against comets, and an eclipse has struck supernatural dread into the hearts of Christian peoples. The ancient Romans threw firebrands into the air, beat upon pans and blew trumpets during an eclipse. Similar customs were in vogue among the Irish, Welsh, and Turks; while at such times the Germans would throw aside their beer and hasten to the church to repent of their sins. Some of our Anglo-Saxon fathers believed that when the air was full of smoke and the sun was red, he was thus red because he looked on hell.

What causes an earthquake? "If it is not
... what is it? We do not know; therefore,
it must be . . . ." In the Indian Archipelago it
is believed that an earthquake is caused by the
world-supporting hog rubbing his itching sides
against a tree. Some North American Indians say
at such times that the world-supporting tortoise is
moving; the Chibchas, that the tired god is shifting
the heavy earth to his other shoulder; the people of
Kamtchatka, that the earthquake god's dog is shaking off snow or fleas; the Hindoos and the Mohammedans, that the world-bearing elephant and the
world-bearing bull are stretching themselves, or
shifting their burden. The Japanese think that
earthquakes are produced by great whales from the
sea creeping under the land. "If that is not it,
what is it?" This question a skeptical Japanese
can not answer, and must silently assent to the
popular faith.

Some workmen at Plymouth, England, found in
a quarry some mammoth bones and teeth, such as
are familiar to every geologist. They were identified as the bones of one Gog-Magog, a giant, celebrated in early British mythology. At a similar
discovery elsewhere, the workmen held an inquest
over the mysterious remains, and concluded that
they had belonged to one of the fallen angels, who
had, I suppose, been fatally bruised by his tumble
from the battlements of heaven. It was once the
notion that the fibrous asbestos was wool from salamanders, the spirit monsters which dwell in the fire.

Traces of ancient tillage on the wild Highlands of Scotland were believed to be elf-furrows, The native Mexicans, looking on the aqueduct of Tezcuco, being unable to account for such ancient art existing among ordinary men, believe that it was built by Montezuma. "If he did not build it, who did build it? We do not know; therefore, it was built by Montezuma," is their method of reasoning. By the same process of thought, great buildings of uncertain date and origin in Russia, are ascribed to Peter the Great; in Persia, to Autar; in Spain, to Boabdil or Charles V. Ancient Europeans attributed prehistoric monuments of human art to the handiwork of the devil. Recent Indian tribes accounted for the works of the ancient mound-builders of Ohio by affirming that the great Manitou built them, as a pledge that game should be plenty in the invisible hunting grounds of the spirit world.

Mythology took its origin and grounded itself in the popular faith by the use of this common sophism of the ignorant, which we are discussing in this chapter. A whim or dream is stubbornly asserted to be true, in the absence of proof to the contrary—the dreamer forgetting that no proposition not self-evident should be assumed to be true in the absence of reasonable proofs. He who affirms must establish his cause. His opponents must not be called upon to affirm a negative. We can not demonstrate that the man in the moon does not have his ears in his heels. If any man is of that opinion, we must leave him undisturbed in his faith.

The soil in certain countries has a peculiar red

color, and often fungus growths on old walls and stones, and on the ground, give a red color to the surfaces on which they grow, and for these singular appearances the common sophistry of superstition yields various solutions. The Cornishman beholding the red film on stones believes that they contain blood marks of murder committed near the place; while the red stains on the stones at Saint Denis Church in Cornwall were supposed to be produced by the blood of the saint when his head was cut off, at a time and place far distant. German peasants still go out in search of the blood of John the Baptist, and the New Forest peasant sees in the red marl he digs the blood of the ancient Danes. It was a similar fancy which enabled the ancient Greeks to see the blood of Adonis in the swollen river which was tinged with the red soil which lay towards its source. The mysterious rising of the Nile was sometimes caused by the tears of the gods, and sometimes created by the benevolent impulses of superhuman spirits.

What causes bodily disease? It often comes on insidiously and invisibly, without any natural cause which the human understanding can trace. The Australian believes that a dead man's ghost will, when offended, creep into his body and stealthily consume his liver. The Mintira, of the Malay peninsula, tell us that the spirit "Kalumbahan" brings on small-pox, while the spirit "Jrari," by an invisible process sucks a fresh wound, and hence it is that the blood will flow. One tribe in that country strew thorns in the path leading to a place infected with the small-pox to prevent the small-pox demon from going forth to commit his ravages elsewhere. The Dyaks, of Borneo, believe that invisible spirits with invisible spears inflict invisible wounds, and thus cause disease. In the Indian archipelago men seek to appease the disease spirits with feasts and dances, and to tempt them away by putting offerings into little boats, which they send out to sea. The spirit thus tempted away from the bowels of the sick man may not find his way back. A belief in disease demons may be found in the Georgian and Society Islands, in the West Indies, among various tribes in Africa, in Siberia, and elsewhere over the world. In ancient times the idea was prevalent among the most cultured nations.

Idiocy, insanity, hysteria, epilepsy, Saint Vitus's dance, and similar diseases, have ceased to be regarded as freaks of the denizens of the spirit world only in countries where the revelations of modern science have taught better. A Chinaman, when suffering with dizziness or any disease of a mysterious nature, still believes that he is being beset by invisible spirits, and may solemnly affirm that he has been captured by a wife he possessed in some former state of existence. In Burmah, when a man has the ague a spirit is shaking him for some misdeed. In classic times we find that Homer and Pythagoras believed that the diseases and pains of mankind were caused by evil spirits. The word epilepsy, taken from the Greek, implies seizure by some supermundane power. Socrates said that those who denied demoniacal possession were themselves demoniacs. Among the Greeks and Romans the insane were "full of ghosts." The same notion was current among the Jews. Justin, Tertullian, Chrysostom, Cyril, and Cyprian, believed that diseases and insanity were caused by demoniacal possession. When Charles VI, of France, was possessed of a certain demon, a priest chained twelve men together, and tried to coax the demon to enter them and leave the king, but the aristocratic imp would not enter into common blood. In 1861, in Morzine, near Lake Geneva, there were a hundred and ten raving demoniacs, some of them insane, and some possessed by an excited fancy, who proved to be too much for the incantations of the Romish priest of the place. Among the Zulus of Africa, a sick man being attacked by a departed human spirit of mischievous tendencies, is cured by taking some of his blood and burying it in an ant-hill.

What causes water to boil? To the savage some troubled ghost resides in the pot. Whence come our dreams? The majority of mankind have regarded them as visitations from the invisible world. The word nightmare means night-spirit or elf, showing the sober belief of those who coined the word for us. Why do some men become so lean? Some invisible vampire is growing fat by sucking their blood. The Greenlander asks, Why do seals and wild fowls start and stare without visible cause? It is because they, too, are gazing into the spirit world. According to Homer the dogs can see spirits. The Jew and Mohammedan know when the dogs howl at night they see the death angel. In

Australia when the wind whistles the savages know to a certainty that the bush demon is whistling, and that people must take care or he will reach down his long arm and seize them. The Dakotah Indian asks 'What are these mysterious foot-prints in the rocks?" and after settling the matter in his mind will show you the prodigious strides of the thunder-bird, as demonstrated by his foot-prints, twenty-five miles apart.

Why does water slowly disappear when exposed to the heat of the sun? The people of Madagascar and many other countries believe that invisible spirits are drinking it to slake their thirst. They reason after the method adopted by Prof. Wallace, F. R. S., and Prof. Crookes, F. R. S., in their investigations of psychic force, and by Baron Reichenbach in his investigations of odylic force, and by Mesmer in his studies of animal magnetism, and by Hon. Robert Dale Owen and others in their investigations of the phenomena exhibited by spirit mediums: "If it is not ———, what is it? We do not know. Therefore, it must be ———." They say to the objector, "affirm your negative." They tell us that if we can not point out any other cause for their phenomena, we must admit their hypothesis. The spiritualist, for example, appealing to some *seance*, and using our inability to explain the manifestations as proof that they are produced by the spirits of the dead, makes use of the following foolish sophism:

Major premise: Every thing we can not explain is produced by the spirits of departed human beings.

Minor premise: We can not explain the phenomena exhibited in this particular *seance.*

Conclusion: Therefore, the phenomena of this particular *seance* are produced by the spirits of departed human beings.

How does the hair grow on the top of one's head? We can not explain it; therefore, it must be caused by spirits of departed human beings, for by the principle assumed above, they produce every thing we can not explain. We thus have a departed relative or ancestor with his invisible workshop at the root of each hair on our heads, in each mysterious nerve and fiber of our bodies, in each cell and pore of the vegetable kingdom. There are in this mysterious universe many things which we can not explain.

The above sophism is that which is employed by the fetich worshipers in South Africa, by the witch-maniacs of the mediæval ages, by mesmerists and visionaries everywhere. We find a lingering survival of it among men of scientific repute. It will be a long time yet before even educated men in all their reasonings will cease to utter the foolish paradox, concerning some mysterious phenomenon: "We do not know what it is; therefore, we know what it is."

Chapter VI.

THE SLEEP OF REASON.

THE mother of Constantine the Great, it is alleged, discovered the true cross in the holy city of Jerusalem, since which time fragments have been preserved in nearly every city of Europe. These fragments were looked upon with religious awe, and are to be found in many cathedrals at the present day. The United States comes in for a share. In a cathedral in Buffalo, New York, is an inscription: "Parts of the original Cross in and about this altar." These fragments if all gathered together would build a cathedral. Tears of the Virgin Mary and St. Peter were preserved in bottles; the blood-drops of Jesus and martyrs, and the milk of the Holy Virgin, have been exhibited to the ignorant worshipers by the Romish priesthood. The hair and toe-nails of sacred personages were brought down through the ages, and sold to fill the coffers of the Church. A bushel of St. Peter's toe-nails have been sold, and some of them still exist as objects of reverence to the faithful Romanist.

There is still exhibited in Rome the stairs by which Jesus ascended into the presence of Pontius Pilate; while at Port Royal, in Paris, is exhibited a thorn from the Savior's crown. The thigh bone of the Virgin Mary is in Halle, while the thigh bone of Charlemagne cures lameness at Aix-la-Chapelle. In China, the boots which have been worn by an upright judge attain a great value, and when he resigns his position, they are drawn off and preserved with great care. As an illustration of how baseless and illogical a popular belief may be, we find among the Buddhists a belief that the god Gautama experienced five hundred and fifty births, during which he took the form of a frog, a fish, a crow, an ape, etc.; and the bones and feathers and hair of these bodies of the god have been preserved in Buddhist temples, to confirm the faith of the worshipers.

Beginning with the sixth century, the bones of the martyrs were broken into fragments and sold to Churches. Skulls and other bones of favorite saints were multiplied to a wonderful degree. It is marvelous how many skulls some favorite saint possessed. These bones possessed wonderful power. The bones of St. Lawrence, it is said, moved in the grave to make way for those of another saint. These relics, it was believed, healed the sick, converted heretics, bestowed spiritual benefits, served for charms to ward off evil, when carried to battle would ward off the weapons of the foe, and when attached to towers served as lightning rods to ward off the thunderbolt. They were inserted in royal crowns, to give prosperity to kings, and worn in rings as protection against poison and disease. They were laid with the Bible on the altar, to give double solemnity to judicial oaths. Constantine had a nail from the "true cross," made into a bit for his horse. Gregory of Tours relates, in his "Glory of Martyrdom," that a nail from the cross thrown into the Adriatic Sea by Queen Radegunda, made it safe for navigation. Napoleon the First, at Milan (A. D. 1805), wore the iron crown of Lombardy, which was made, it was alleged, of a nail from the true cross, and which no monarch since Charles V had dared to wear. Napoleon put on, exclaiming: "God hath given it me; let him take heed who touches it."

On marble tablets in the church of Saint Prassede, in Rome, is a list of the treasures of that church: A tooth of Saint Peter, another of Saint Paul, a part of the chemise of Mary, a part of Christ's girdle, and some of the earth on which he prayed, a piece of Moses' rod, a part of the reed and sponge used by the soldiers in offering drink to our Savior during the crucifixion, three spines from the crown of thorns, a part of the towel used by our Savior in wiping his disciples' feet, and a part of his swaddling clothes and seamless robe. This seamless robe was once on exhibition at Treves, where the worshipers repeated this prayer: "Holy coat, pray for us." In 1854, the official "Gazette of Vienna," announced that the tooth of Saint Peter, which Pius IX gave to the emperor of Austria, would be exposed to the gaze of the public four days. The great toe of the Trinity was on exhibition before the Reformation of the sixteenth century.

In the days of Saint Augustine, the dung-heap upon which Job sat was still visible. In Saint Peter's, in Rome, are the thirty pieces of money for which Judas betrayed his Lord. They were made by Terah, Abraham's father, and passed into the hands of Joseph's brethren, Moses, Solomon, Nebuchadnezzar, and the Magi, who offered them to the infant Savior, after which Mary cast them into the treasury of the temple, from which the priests took them and gave them to Judas.* The sovereigns of England are crowned while sitting upon the stone which Jacob used for his pillow at Bethel. In the Cathedral of Genoa is the holy grail or the cup put into the mouth of Benjamin's sack, and out of which our Savior partook of the last supper.

D'Aubigné relates that the Church of All Saints, at Wittenburg, contained fragments of Noah's ark, some soot from the furnace which contained the three Hebrew children, together with ninteen thousand other relics. The breath of St. Joseph was exhibited at Schaffhausen, while at Würtemberg was shown a feather from the wing of the archangel Michael.† In 1870 A. D., the newly discovered bones of a virgin martyr of the third century were brought from Italy and deposited in a cathedral in Cincinnati, Ohio. The Roman Catholic cathedral in Buffalo, New York, contains a slab from the Roman catacombs, on which is the inscription in Latin, "Peregrinus, buried the twelfth day before the calends of March, who lived . . . months;" but the infant is represented in wax as a man with gaping wounds. A phial of his blood is deposited at the feet of the image. The inscriptions on the

---

* Withrow, Catacombs of Rome, p. 141.
† Hist. Ref. i, ch. 3.

walls assert that the building contains "a large piece of the true cross on which trickled the sacred blood of Christ," and "particles of the bones of Saints Peter and Paul, and of many other holy martyrs."* All this surely indicates the sleep of reason on the part of the deluded worshipers.

In England relics of notorious criminals and their victims have sometimes been in great demand. In the year 1828, when Maria Martin was murdered by Corder, people came from Ireland and Scotland to take away pieces of the barn where the murderer secreted his victim. A lock of her hair was sold for two guineas. The rope by which the famous Dr. Dodd was hanged was sold at a great price. The executioner at Newgate at one time derived no small income from the sale of relics and by permitting people to stroke themselves with the dead hands of criminals to cure diseases and prevent misfortunes.

The blind freaks of superstition are so various that we can indicate but few of them. In New Zealand the hoot of an owl is regarded as an evil omen, while the flight of a hawk over one's head is indicative of good fortune. The Kalmuck is happy when a white falcon flies on the right, but is gloomy if it flies by on the left, reminding us of the present popular superstition in Christian countries concerning seeing the new moon over the left and right shoulder. In Central Africa the sorcerer cuts a fowl into two equal parts from head to tail. If any blemishes appear in the backbone, a mother and grandmother

---

* Withrow, Catacombs, page 143.

have been guilty of treachery. A blemish near the tail of the fowl fixes guilt upon the wife, while any unusual appearance on the wings convicts the children of treachery to the suspicious father. Augustus Cæsar expected a double empire because the liver of a certain animal was malformed.*

In the Edda or sacred books of the ancient Scandinavians, we find the sober statement that "a dog's hair will heal a dog's bite." The familiar adage, so often upon our own lips, "you got out of bed wrong foot foremost," carries us back to the time when it was the current notion in Germany that to get out of bed, using the left foot first, would cause the day to be full of trouble.

Henry, the confessor to Emperor Frederick III, was also an alchemist, and as we look into his crucibles we find the following substances: Salt, copperas, aquafortis, egg shells, mercury, lead, and dung. These substances he believed could be so combined as to form gold. Still more absurd were the recipes for compounding mummies and other objects into a salve or liquid by the application of which the alchemists sought to attain perpetual youth.

Pliny, the great Roman naturalist, informs us by what method pains in the human stomach may be transmitted into the body of a puppy or duck, which, when the magical ceremony is performed, will probably die in agony while the human sufferer will experience relief

In England and our own country many people believe that if warts are touched with a pebble, and

―――――――
*Pliny xi, 73.

the pebble put in a bag and laid by the roadside, the one who finds and opens the bag will have the warts, which will disappear from the hands of their former possessors. We also meet very frequently the notion that a horseshoe put over the door will ward off evil and bring good luck to the inmates of the house.

In Brandenburg people determine whether there shall be a death in the family by the position of the spleen in the pigs they kill. The shah of Persia will wait for days outside the walls of the capital until the position of the stars permits him to enter. We have before us a book published in Harrisburg, Pennsylvania, in 1856, by John George Hohman. The author affirms that the book was partly derived from a work published by a gypsy, and partly from materials collected by himself from all parts of the world. It is a fair sample of books of this class, and contains a good compilation of the superstitious whims of the most uncultured class of modern Christendom. The author and those he represents are firm believers in the Bible, to which they have added their absurd beliefs. We extract the following:

"*A Good Remedy for Hysterics, to be Used Three Times.*—Put the joint of the thumb which sits in the palm of the hand on the bare skin which covers the small bone which stands out above the pit of the heart, and speak the following at the same time:

'Matrix, Patrix, lay thyself right and safe,
Or thou or I shall on the third day fill the grave."

It is evident the patient will make a mighty effort to have no more fits.

"REMEDY FOR WORMS:

Mary, God's mother, traversed the land,
Holding three worms close in her hand;
One was white, another was black, the other was red.

"This must be repeated three times, at the same time stroking the patient with the hand, and at the end of each application strike the back of the patient, to wit: at the first application once, at the second application twice, and at the third application three times: and then set the worms a certain time [to expire], but not less than three minutes."

"*Remedy Against Slander.*—Take off your shirt and turn it wrong side out, and then run your thumbs along your body close under the ribs, starting at the pit of the heart, down to the thighs."

"*Remedy for Colic.*—I warn ye, ye colic fiends! There is one sitting in judgment, who speaketh: Just or unjust? Therefore, beware, ye colic fiends."

"*Remedy for Fever.*—Good morning, dear Thursday! Take away from [*name*] the seventy-sevenfold fevers! O thou dear Lord Jesus Christ, take them away from him. . . . This must be used on Thursday for the first time, on Friday for the second time, and on Saturday for the third time, and each time thrice. The prayer of faith has also to be said each time, and not a word dare be spoken to any one until the sun has risen. Neither dare the sick person speak to any one till after sunrise; nor eat pork, nor drink milk, nor cross a running water nine days."

Here we find a survival of some old heathen incantations, blended with Christian beliefs. Thursday was Thor's day, and dear Thor was the god first invoked. Friday and Saturday were days sacred to two other pagan deities which our forefathers worshiped, and from whose names the names of these two days of the week have been derived. But the sun-god, worshiped on Sunday, was the great deity on whose power the suppliant most relied. Hence not a word was to be spoken until the sun had risen. In the words "thrice" and "nine," we see the Christian idea of the Trinity. In the prohibition against pork we find a Jewish and Catholic notion; while the running water is animated by the water demons of pagan times, which may enter into the body of the patient. This recipe for curing a fever suggests to us the ages of superstition through which it has come to us, and the multitude of human beings which have used it in its ever varying forms.

"*To Make a Dog Stay with You.*—Draw some of your blood, and let the dog eat it along with his food, and he will stay with you. Or, scrape the four corners of your table while you are eating, and continue eating with the same knife after having scraped the corners of the table. Let the dog eat those scrapings, and he will stay with you."

"*Remedy Against Injuries.*—Whoever carries the right eye of a wolf fastened inside of his right sleeve, remains free from all injuries."

"*How to Obtain Things Which are Desired.*—If you call upon another to ask for a favor, take care to carry a little of the five finger grass with you, and you shall certainly obtain what you desired."

"*To Destroy Warts.*—Roast chicken feet, and rub the warts with them, and then bury them under the eaves."

"*To Banish the Whooping-cough.*—Cut three small bunches of hair from the crown of the head of a chick that has never seen its father; sew this hair up in an unbleached rag, and hung it around the neck of the child having the whooping-cough. The thread with which the rag is sewed must also be unbleached."

"*How to Banish the Fever.*—Write the following words upon a paper, and wrap it up in knot grass, and then tie it upon the navel of the person who has the fever:
"Potmat Sinent,
Potmat Sinent,
Potmat Sineut."

Our author also presents the two following recipes, taken from the writings of Albertus Magnus, the great alchemist, who was the friend of Thomas Aquinas:

"*How to Prevent Hair from Growing.*—If you burn a large frog to ashes, and mix the ashes with water, you will obtain an ointment that will, if put on any place covered with hair, destroy the hair and prevent it from growing again."

"*How to Make Enemies, Friends.*—If you find the stones which a vulture has in his knees, and which you may find by looking sharp, and put them in the victuals of the two persons who hate each other, it causes them to make up and be good friends."

"*How to Make Cattle Come Home.*—Pull out three small bunches of hair, one between the horns, one from the middle of the back, and one near the tail, and make your cattle eat it in their feed."

"*How to Gain a Law Suit.*—Take some of the largest kind of sage, write the names of the twelve apostles on the leaves, and put them in your shoes before entering the court house."

It was believed that the Scotch witches ruined their neighbors' fortunes by making a hash of the flesh of unbaptized babes and dogs and sheep, and placing a dish full of it in the house of their victims, repeating the following incantation:

> "We put this untill this hame;
> In our Lord the Devil's name;
> The first hands that handle thee,
> Burned and scalded may they be!
> We will destroy houses and hald,
> With the sheep and nolt [cattle] into the fauld;
> And little shall come to the fore [remain],
> Of all the rest of the little store."

The German witches gained the help of the devil by repeating the following:

> "Lalle, Baches, Magotte, Baphia, Dajam,
> Vagoth Heneche, Ammi Nagaz, Adomator
> Raphael Immanuel Christus, Tetragrammaton
> Agra Jod Loi. Konig! Konig!"

To show the intellectual apathy of the more ignorant classes we take the following specimen quoted by Mackay from a popular dream and omen book:

"*Twenty-ninth of February.*—This day, as it only occurs once in four years, is peculiarly auspicious to those who desire to have a glance at futurity, especially to young maidens burning with anxiety to know the appearance and complexion of their future lords. The charm to be adopted is the following: Stick twenty-seven of the smallest pins that are made, three by three, into a tallow candle. Light it up at the wrong end, and then place it in a candlestick made out of clay, which must be drawn from a virgin's grave. Place this on the chimney-place, in the left-hand corner, exactly as the clock strikes twelve, and go to bed immediately. When the candle is burnt out, take the pins and put them into your left shoe; and before nine nights have elapsed your fate will be revealed to you."

Some of the inhabitants of Stamfordham, England, walk to a gibbet on Elsdon Moor, ten or twelve miles distant, to obtain a splinter for a tooth-pick, and thus cure the toothache. At Tavistock, in Devonshire, some people cure the toothache by biting a tooth taken from a skull in the churchyard. A churchyard tooth they also carry in the pocket as a charm against the toothache. In the Netherlands the aching tooth is rubbed by a bone from the churchyard, while in some parts of Ireland water drunken from a skull possesses the same magical effect. Superstitious people in Sussex prevent the toothache by putting the stocking and boot on the right foot first, and by putting the right leg into the trousers before the left. In Wiltshire a fore-leg and a hind-leg of a mole put into a bag and worn about the neck is a charm through which the toothache is completely subdued. In Rosendale the parings of the finger and toe nails put under the bark of a live ash tree is fatal to the toothache. A similar notion exists in Gloucestershire. Shakespeare, in "Much Ado About Nothing," exhibits a popular belief when he represents that the toothache is caused by a worm in the tooth. Hence, we read of various charms employed to induce the worm to leave his lurking-place. In some parts of North Germany people who have the toothache complain to a pear-tree for relief, going three times around it, saying:

"Pear-tree, I complain to thee,
Three worms sting me;
The one is gray, the second is blue, the third is red,
I would wish they were all three dead."

We find a similar superstition in New Zealand, China, and elsewhere. Thus we see that superstition sometimes amounts to an utter sleep of the reason.

When bits of wood alleged to be taken from the original cross, or milk and tears of the Virgin Mary, are exhibited in Roman Catholic cathedrals, the poor dupe gazes, wonders, believes, and worships, but does not reason. He demands no evidence upon which to ground his faith. He may possess passion and emotion and a vigorous pulse, but he has sunken down to intellectual apathy and inaction. In his relation to a wide realm of research and knowledge he is as if he were not a rational being.

We see the same sad spectacle of intellectual slumber in the modern spiritual *séance*. Some clever jugglers, after placing the observer at a safe distance, or delegating one of their number to hold his hands so that he can not investigate the phenomena too closely, hold up before him in the dim gas-light a paste-board mask, and he goes into ecstasies over the idea that he is looking through the open doors of the invisible world. Perhaps it is a "Katie King" séance, and he clasps in his arms a living body in human form, a spirit materialized. Some other investigator grasps the hand of the spirit and daubs it with ink, and when the lights are turned up the ink is found on the hand of the medium. He is bewildered till the theory is announced by one of the jugglers that as the spirit had extracted materials from the body of the medium with which to materialize itself, it is but natural that when the material was returned to the body of the medium that the ink should be deposited with it, and hence appear on the hand of the medium, though originally placed on the hand of the materialized spirit. The dupe is once more in an ecstasy of faith, and now there is no method by which any materialized spirit can be demonstrated to be a fraud. If the medium is untied, some tricky spirits have untied her. If he grasps the spirit, and turns up the light and discovers that he has hold of the medium, the spirit has suddenly vanished, returning its bodily substance to the body of the medium, and hence he grasps now the medium, whereas he was holding to the spirit a moment before.

Upon this irrational faith, as we shall see further on, modern spiritualism is based, and will be, until, like the witch mania, it shall be laughed out of Christendom. In can not be argued down from its present pitch of absurdity, for no argument can make it more absurd. The dupe has become irrational. It was impossible to answer the statements of the once celebrated Judge Edmonds, who, when he asked the spirits in the *séance:* "If they had cows up there?" and on being answered in the affirmative, affirms that they finally quelled his rising and rebellious doubts, by bringing him a drink of buttermilk. The dark *séance* was typical of this temporary sleep of his intellect.

Chapter VII.

THE POWER OF THE EXCITED IMAGINATION.

BOISMONT in his valuable treatise on the "Rational History of Hallucinations* relates, that a cook on a certain ship having died, the mate shortly afterwards believed that he saw the cook walking on the water. The captain was called, and he likewise affirmed that he saw the same mysterious object, which he soon recognized as the cook. The vision grew before him, until he recognized the gait and dress of the deceased. Further investigation, however, revealed the fact that the object was only a fragment of a mast from some wrecked ship, floating before them on the sea. The author relates many similar facts, from which we select the following: At Saint Patrick's Hole, in Ireland, the inhabitants imagined the sounds produced by the wind to be human voices, issuing from purgatory: A lady sewing suddenly saw four hands and four needles instead of one: A certain man afflicted with monomania, spent much of his time licking the wall, declaring that it tasted like an orange.

Hallucinations occur when the subjects are in a bad state of health, and among the ignorant they may become epidemic. This is evident from the

---
* Pages 106–180.

first case given above. A conspicuous example is furnished in the dancing mania of the middle ages. Perhaps, some genuine cases of Saint Vitus's dance may have given origin to the epidemic; but it spread until whole multitudes would jump up and down until they fell exhausted. They often thought they saw spirits or the Virgin Mary. Sometimes they supposed they were wading through streams of blood, and that was the reason they jumped so high. Other authors mention the biting mania in certain nunneries. One nun fancied that the devil possessed her, and compelled her to bite her associates. Others caught the infection, and the epidemic spread until it was threatened by the authorities that the next nun who began to bite should be branded with a red hot-iron, when the epidemic ceased.

According to Boismont, an hysteric epidemic broke out among the nuns of Saint Elizabeth, at Louviers, in which hallucinations of sight and hearing were common among them. Mediomania, which broke out with the Fox girls and Andrew Jackson Davis, has presented many similar examples. Hallucinations often accompany hysteria, usually at the beginning of the affection. Sometimes persons converse with imaginary beings, and Boismont mentions one particularly who saw her own face in an imaginary looking-glass. Sometimes hallucinations precede insanity, but often the insanity is but partial. The author also relates that one young man saw and conversed with his mother and sister, who were living but absent; and another beheld most beautiful landscapes. He also affirms that in mania one-third of the subjects have hallucinations, and that any of the five senses may be involved, and relates the following examples: A storekeeper saw oyster shells on the floor, but when he attempted to pick them up, he found none there. A soldier, who was of threatening mien, entered his store, but when he attempted to seize the intruder and thrust him out, he only grasped at empty space. One lady believed she experienced electric shocks every time she touched her feet to the ground. Upham, in his "Mental Philosophy," mentions a grocery-man, who, while in apparent health, could not tell his imaginary from his real customers.

The mediomaniac is subject to like hallucinations. She sits up till the small hours of the night, trying to see spirits, or to hear some sound to indicate their presence. Her mind has been intensely fixed upon the one awful theme, day and night. Perhaps her mind and body are worn down with intense thought. She has a pale, sallow countenance. Her sunken eyes have a wild, weird look. It may be also a dear friend, torn from her by death, whom she seeks in the spirit world. At last, in a waking dream, imaginary spirits crowd around her. She is satisfied, and thenceforward proclaims her faith, and gains a following in her neighborhood. Soon the field is ready, and the physical-test medium, with his lectures and his clever jugglery, gathers a rich harvest from the half-bewildered and gaping crowd.

The clairvoyant sees nothing outside of his own

fancy. Twenty thousand dollars were a long time deposited in the Bank of England for any clairvoyant who would see and describe the bank-note concealed in the vaults. Clairvoyant doctors, with or without the aid of spirits, for a dollar, will see through clothing, and flesh and bone, and discover a tubercle in the lungs of the applicant. We offered a thousand dollars, in a hall in Buffalo, New York, in a debate with J. G. Fish, in presence of clairvoyant doctors and mediums, to be given to any man who would see through a common cotton sheet, behind which we would station a black man and a white man, pledging ourself that if, without any chance to cheat, a medium would tell which was that white man and which was black, he should have the money. The offer was not accepted. We have repeated the offer many times in public debates elsewhere, with the same result. The whole matter of mediumship begins and ends in fancy, or fraud and ignorance.

That the early experimenters in animal magnetism unwittingly depended upon the excited imaginations of their subjects for success, may readily be discovered from their mode of operation:—

"In the center of the saloon was placed an oval vessel, about four feet in its longest diameter, and one foot deep. In this were laid a number of wine bottles, filled with magnetized water, well corked up, and disposed in radii, with their necks outwards. Water was then poured into the vessel so as just to cover the bottles, and filings of iron were thrown in occasionally to heighten the magnetic effect. The vessel was then covered with an iron cover, pierced through with many holes, and was called the *baquet*. From each hole issued a long movable rod of iron, which the patients were to apply to such parts of their bodies as were afflicted. Around this *baquet* the patients were directed to sit, holding each other by the hand, and pressing their knees together as closely as possible, to facilitate the passage of the magnetic fluid from one to the other. Then came in the assistant magnetizers, generally strong, handsome young men, to pour into the patient from their finger tips fresh streams of the wondrous fluid. They embraced the patient between the knees, rubbed them gently down the spine and the course of the nerves, using gentle pressure upon the breasts of the ladies, and staring them out of countenance to magnetize them by the eye! All this time the most rigorous silence was maintained, with the exception of a few wild notes on the harmonica or the piano-forte, or the melodious voice of a hidden opera singer swelling softly at long intervals. Gradually the cheeks of the ladies began to glow, their imaginations became inflamed; and off they went, one after the other, in convulsive fits. Some of them sobbed and tore their hair, others laughed till the tears ran from their eyes, while others shrieked and screamed and yelled till they became insensible altogether.

"This was the crisis of the delirium. In the midst of it the chief actor made his appearance, waving his wand, like Prospero, to work new wonders. Dressed in a long robe of lilac-colored silk, richly embroidered with gold flowers, bearing in his hand a white magnetic rod, and with a look of dignity that would have sat well on an Eastern caliph, he marched with solemn strides into the room. He awed the still sensible by his eye, and the violence of their symptoms diminished. He stroked the insensible with his hands upon the eyebrows and down the spine; traced figures upon their breast and abdomen with his long white wand, and they were restored to consciousness. They became calm, acknowledged his power, and said they felt streams of cold or burning vapor passing through their frames, according as he waved his wand or his fingers before them."*

The excitement of the poor dupes of ignorance and superstition sometimes amounted to temporary insanity. "Early in the eighteenth century the attention of Europe was directed to a very remarkable instance of fanaticism, which has been claimed by the animal magnetists as a proof of their science. The *Convulsionaries of St. Medard*, as they were called, assembled in great numbers around the tomb of their favorite saint, the Jansenist priest Paris, and taught one another how to fall into convulsions. They believed that St. Paris would cure all their infirmities; and the number of hysterical women and weak-minded persons of all descriptions that flocked to the tomb from far and near was so great as daily to block up all the avenues leading to it. Working themselves up to a pitch of excitement, they went off, one after the other, into fits, while

---
*Mackay's Memoirs of Popular Delusions, vol. i, 278.

some of them, still in apparent possession of all their faculties, voluntarily exposed themselves to sufferings which on ordinary occasions would have been sufficient to deprive them of life. The scenes that occurred were a scandal to civilization and to religion—a strange mixture of obscenity, absurdity, and superstition. While some were praying on bended knees at the shrine of St. Paris, others were shrieking and making the most hideous noises. The women especially exerted themselves. On one side of the chapel there might be seen a score of them, all in convulsions; while at another as many more, excited to a sort of frenzy, yielded themselves up to gross indecencies. Some of them took an insane delight in being beaten and trampled upon."*

Mr. Carpenter, F. R. S., LL. D., who has devoted much time to the study of electricity in its relation to the human system, in discussing some of the phases of modern spiritism, cites the following facts, which are published in the *Popular Science Monthly*, of November, 1872: In a factory a young girl had a fit, caused by a mouse put down inside her dress. Some others of the female operatives went into hysterics by sympathy with the one first affected. The notion arose that the fits were caused by the cotton, after which scores of women, day after day, went into fits. An intelligent doctor persuaded the women that he possessed a wonderful remedy. The drug was harmless, although possessing no especial value. The women took it, and the fits ceased. In the hospital at Bristol, England, one

---

*Mackay's Memoirs of Popular Delusions, vol. i, p. 273.

of the girls, in a ward filled with girls, had a hysteric fit. Others were wrought on by fear and sympathy, and were affected in like manner, until the fits became epidemic. The attending physician cured them instantaneously by threatening to duck them in water. In a nunnery one of the nuns being influenced by a morbid imagination, began to mew like a cat. The other nuns conceiving the notion that their sister was being wrought upon by some mysterious cause, began to be similarly affected, and soon all the nuns were mewing.

In a nunnery in Germany one nun was seized with a mania for biting her sisters who came into her presence. Soon her sisters began to bite each other. It was thought that the devil had taken possession of them. The matter began to be talked over in other nunneries. The idea that the devil had been let loose to plague the sisterhood in this way aroused the superstitious fears of all nuns who heard of it, exciting the imaginations of the most susceptible until they began to bite. When once the epidemic started in a nunnery nearly all of the sisters were affected by it. Thus nearly all the nunneries of Germany in a short time contained biting nuns. The priests reasoned, "If this is not the work of the demons what is it? We do not know; therefore it is the work of demons." They tried to exorcise the evil spirits, but only spread the contagion by alarming the superstitious fears of the sisterhood. The physicians at last brought the biting mania to a sudden termination by threatening to duck or whip all nuns who should be found bit-

THE EXCITED IMAGINATION.

ing, and by telling them it was their own excited fancy which impelled them to the act.

The St. Vitus's dance is a disease familiar to us now. But a few generations ago, in Europe, the victim of this disease was supposed to be affected by a spirit. One genuine subject would excite the imaginations of many others until a whole multitude of frenzied people would be dancing around him. They would often dance for twenty-four hours at a time, until they fell exhausted upon the ground. Some died from their frantic exertions. St. Vitus was the patron saint of these dancers, and hence the name of the modern disease.

Of the power of an excited imagination in furnishing some of the alleged phenomena of modern spiritism, Dr. Carpenter gives the following example which came under his own observation: He went to a *seance* where the spirits had been lifting tables. The table was lifted while the sitters placed their hands in a circle on the top of it. After a time the members of the circle imagined the table was rising upward, for they felt it pressing up against their hands. Dr. Carpenter, however, kept his eye on the legs of the table, which he saw resting solidly on the floor. They were pressing their hands down on the table, and by a freak of the excited imagination they thought the table was pressing upward against their hands. Professor Faraday also made a careful investigation of the table-tipping phenomenon of spirit mediums, and declared that the medium himself moved the table when he thought the table was moving by an invisible cause. He contrived a way to measure the amount of pressure exerted by the medium's hands, and found that the medium in every case tipped the table, though protesting that he was unconscious of it.

Sir John Herschel relates in his volume of lectures that he often saw geometrical figures before his eyes when he was in the dark and with his eyes shut; and sometimes, also, when in perfect health, he saw in this manner faces of living people and landscapes.* He says that for many people it is easy to see pictures in the fire. In this way he accounts for the wide-spread notion that some people can see spirits, and gives many facts to support his conclusion.

It is well known that soldiers on picket often fire at imaginary foes. Sir Joshua Reynolds sometimes saw men as moving trees when he came from his studio.† Mrs. Howe, captured by the Indians, saw the half-decayed bodies of her children on the limbs of trees as she wandered in the forests. Dr. Johnson heard the voice of his mother calling him when she was many miles distant. Napoleon, before his Russian campaign, being in a state of great nervous excitement, would start suddenly and say, "Who calls me?" but no ears but his own could hear the voice. Sir Walter Scott, when in the West Indies, saw specters which, on closer examination, proved to be trees and other inanimate objects. Mr. Upham also relates the case of a lady who attended a concert, and heard the music no less dis-

---

*Popular Science Monthly, Vol. I, page 734.
†Upham's Mental Philosophy, chapter xiv.

tinctly for weeks afterwards, till she died. Nicolai, a bookseller in Berlin, saw specters, sublime and ridiculous, which would speak to him. Some were faces of the living and some were faces of the dead. Sometimes he was visited by birds and dogs. Bloodletting cured him. Here, again, we cite the case, related by Mr. Upham, of a shopkeeper who, in apparent health, could not tell for a time his real customers from those which were pictured by his imagination, until he attempted to touch them.

We thus see what the excited imagination may do, and we are prepared to find some singular statements from the medio-maniacs who have just now had their day. The conditions imposed for developing mediums are such as would naturally tend to throw the imagination of the medium into an abnormal state. The seeing mediums, according to the erratic and (among spiritualists) once famous P. B. Randolph, are to develop their powers by tying a bandage tightly around the head and over the eyes, and then lying down on the bed persistently try to see. The bandage upon the eyes will cause the dupe to "see stars" and other fiery forms which the excited fancy may shape into spirit forms. The poor devotee is already on the verge of insanity, and if he continues this developing process a few months he will behold the specters after which he has been seeking. The medio-maniac has cultivated her mania so as to produce the particular hallucination demanded by her faith.

Doctor Livingstone tells us that the South African, who believes in a god who has crooked legs, sees him with crooked legs in dreams and mediumistic visions.* The entranced Romanist sees in his visions the saints and the devil and the Virgin mother, just as the old artists had painted them in the frescoes of the cathedrals. The modern medium sees the spirit Indians, dressed in buffalo robes, wearing feathers in their hair, and carrying bows and arrows. The excited fancy is unable to free itself from the pictures which had frequently been seen in the books.

In Guinea, those who think they are possessed by a spirit, exhibit the fact by frantic gestures, convulsions, foaming at the mouth, gnashing of the teeth.† The Patagonian wizard beats upon a drum until the spirit takes possession of him, when in a state of nervous convulsion he answers questions with an unnatural voice. The "devil dancers" of Ceylon, and the Bodo priests of India, work themselves up into a frenzy by dancing and music, before giving forth their inspirations. The Fijian priest in solemn silence gazes at a whale's tooth, until he begins to twitch and jerk in every limb, increasing the frenzy until he breaks down with sobs. The sweat streams from his face, which becomes pale. In this state he gives the answer with which he thinks his god has inspired him. The same practice is found in the Sandwich Islands. The diviner there works up the frenzy to a desperate pitch, rolling on the ground, with eyes rolling, features distorted, foaming at the mouth, and

---
* South Africa, page 124.
† Taylor's Primitive Cult. vol. ii, page 130.

giving forth his answers in shrieks, which are so inarticulate that an attending priest must interpret them to the people.

Among the Manganga, of Central Africa, the medicine man utters incantations as he rolls himself about on the ground. Sometimes he communicates a charm to a stick, which will pull so that the holder has to hold with all his might to keep it from flying out of his hand. Sometimes the one holding the stick being frenzied and convulsed will roll about on the ground, being dragged, as he thinks, by the magical stick given him by the medicine man. This presents the same freak of the excited imagination as that detected by Professor Faraday in the table tipping séance described above. Occasionally these savage and civilized visionaries in their trances and convulsions experience hallucinations of sight and sound, sufficient to keep alive their faith. Often the practitioner brings on his convulsions to awe and convinces his dupes, who have no desire to see across the uncertain boundaries of this visible world.

The excited imagination can hear as well as see. The "raps" are generally produced by intentional fraud, but sometimes they are hallucinations of the diseased imagination. The "knocks" of the vampires in mediæval times and the "raps" of the spirits in recent times, were often produced inside of the skulls of self-made dupes. The sorcerer in Greenland prepares himself, by long fasting and silent gazing, and by self-imposed fits, and is often able to see images of men and animals rising up in the air before him. Among some North American Indian tribes the soothsayer prepares himself by fasting and by sweating baths, for the bodily convulsions and mental excitement necessary to receive inspiration from the spirits.* The Zulu fasts and wanders, and tortures himself until he faints, and lies in a state of semi-consciousness, during which he thinks he receives visions and inspirations from the spirits and gods. The Hindoo uses fasting for a similar purpose. The Pythia, of Delphi, fasted for inspiration.

The narcotic witch-ointment often brought visions of their own sabbath to the mediæval witches. Narcotic drugs have been used by the natives in the West Indies, Darien, Brazil, and Peru; among various North American Indian tribes, and, indeed, in all ages and in all parts of the world, to produce inspirations and visions, which were believed to be supernatural. The Mundrucus of North Brazil give narcotic drinks to their magicians, who see visions of men that have been guilty of crime. They detect criminals in this way. Pliny says, that in his day, thalassægle, a narcotic drug, was used to produce visions. Hesychius mentions that a certain drug was used to evoke Hecate from the invisible realm. Hashish is used by the Persian dervishes to bring on hallucinations of the senses, which they take for divine or spiritual manifestations. In this state small objects seem large, a human voice sounds like thunder, and miracles are constantly revealed to the senses. Indians will

---

* Taylor's Primitive Culture, vol. ii, page 413.

THE EXCITED IMAGINATION. 91

sometimes confine themselves in a small hut, and burn tobacco until the air is so filled with the smoke, that the victim becomes nearly unconscious, in which state he sees visions which he regards as supernatural. Whether the hallucinations of the imagination are produced by a sudden excitement, caused by narcotic drugs, or by long and wasting efforts to look into the unseen world, or by violent mental and physical exertion, resulting in hysterical convulsions, the poor dupe probably will ever afterward believe that his experience was supermundane.

Mr. Valentine Greatraks was a famous visionary, who flourished in Ireland, in the county of Cork, near the middle of the seventeenth century. While quite young he fell into a melancholy, involving partial insanity. His monomania took a benevolent turn, and he felt himself commissioned by the Almighty to cure the king's evil. He very solemnly communicated his convictions to his wife, but she, with a wife's faithfulness, pronounced him a fool. He soon found a credulous patient in one W. Maher, of Salter's Bridge, who was affected with the king's evil in the eyes, neck, and throat. Greatraks laid his hands on him, stroked him, and prayed over him. In a short time, by the aid of other remedies the patient was perceptibly improved. Encouraged by his apparent success, he began to receive additional commissions from on high to cure other diseases, which he proclaimed to all who met him.

His fame spread rapidly, and soon the sick came

to him in multitudes. He wrote to the Hon. Robert Boyle, that* "Such great multitudes resorted to him from divers places, that he had no time to follow his own business, or enjoy the company of his family and friends. He was obliged to set aside three days in the week, from six in the morning till six at night, during which time only he laid hands upon all that came. Still the crowds which thronged around him were so great, that the neighboring towns were not able to accommodate them. He thereupon left his house in the country, and went to Youghal, where the resort of sick people, not only from all parts of Ireland, but from England, continued so great, that the magistrates were afraid they would infect 'the place by their diseases. Several of these poor credulous people no sooner saw him than they fell into fits, and he restored them by waving his hand in their faces, and praying over them. Nay, he affirmed that the touch of his glove had driven pains away, and, on one occasion, cast out from a woman several devils, or evil spirits, who tormented her day and night. 'Every one of these devils,' says Greatraks, 'was like to choke her when it came up into her throat.'"

It was very evident that the woman he refers to had the choking sensation common in hysteria. He doubtless did produce immediate cures upon some cases afflicted with melancholy and with nervous disorders. Almost any disorder of the body with which the nervous system sympathizes may be relieved by instilling into the mind of the sufferer

* Mackay's Memoirs of Pop. Delus., vol. i, page 269.

THE EXCITED IMAGINATION. 93

the firm and invigorating faith that he is cured or rapidly recovering. A firm belief that he is slowly dying of some occult disease, in most cases, produces in the patient melancholy, lack of proper exercise resulting in a sluggish circulation of the blood, and consequent loss of appetite for food and the weakness of the whole physical system. Hereditary diseases under these favoring circumstances develop themselves, and erelong the victim of mistaken fancy dies. On the other hand, if a patient of this kind, before his depression has gone too far, is swept in by the tide of a popular frenzy like that described above, his absolute faith in the healer's power, after he has been touched by the magic hand, creates joy, hope, enthusiasm in the pursuits of life once more, a vigorous step, a bounding pulse, vigorous appetite, and consequent nerve and muscle and vitality sufficient to throw off or keep in abeyance a real disease. Hence, ancient visionaries and modern healing mediums have been able to point with triumph to the cures they have wrought.

In Van der Mye's account of the siege of Breda, which occurred A. D. 1625, it is related that the Prince of Orange sent the physicians two or three small vials containing a decoction of chamomile, wormwood, and camphor, with orders that they should tell their patients that it was a medicine of wonderful value, and very rare, being procured only in the far East, with great difficulty and danger, and that it was so strong that two or three drops would impart a great virtue to a gallon of water. The army was being crippled by the ravages of the scurvy, and was much dispirited. The soldiers had faith in the judgment and benevolence of the Prince of Orange, and took his wonderful medicine with gratitude and cheerfulness, and the disease rapidly disappeared. The soldiers as they recovered gathered around their benefactor to praise his wonderful remedy, and to express their heart-felt gratitude. When a soldier's hope is gone and his will gives way, he soon succumbs to the hardship of his lot. When he is in this condition the vital forces run low and the body is prepared for disease.

Chapter VIII.

DECEPTION BY NATURAL PHENOMENA.

THE mosque of Jethro, in the town of Hallch, on the Euphrates, for many generations was renowned for its trembling minaret. The priest would put his hand on the summit of the minaret and invoke the name of Allah, at which time it would begin to tremble so violently that those who were assembled near the priest to witness the miracle were afraid of being thrown down upon the ground below. A slight trembling would easily be exaggerated into a violent trembling by the excited spectators. But making all due allowance for possible exaggerations in accounts given of the miracle, we can not doubt that the priests were able to shake the minaret to a degree perceptible to the spectators. The occurrence after a time, however, ceased to be regarded as miraculous, as it was fully accounted for by certain accidental peculiarities in the architecture of the edifice. Such a phenomenon has been known to occur at other places, under circumstances which would remove it from the realm of the supernatural even in the minds of the most superstitious. A minaret of brick, near Damietta, could be moved at pleasure by the hand of a man pushing near its summit. In the church of Narcissus, at Rheims, the ringing of the bell would cause one of the great stone pillars to vibrate violently for some minutes after the bell ceased ringing. By referring to Dana's "Manual of Geology" we learn that great rocks are sometimes so delicately poised that the hand of a man is strong enough to cause them to rock to and fro. The priests of the temple of Jethro, taking advantage of the ignorance of the people, used a purely natural but unusual phenomenon to gain a reputation for possessing supernatural power.

The river Ida flows at certain seasons of the year in red colored torrents. The ignorant multitudes in ancient Greece were made to believe that at certain seasons of the year the river was mixed with the blood of Adonis, and they looked upon the phenomenon as supernatural. Modern travelers have discovered that during the rainy season, the red soil of Mount Libanus is washed into the river channel in great quantities, thus accounting for the red color of the waters. The once marvelous river of milk in ancient Phrygia has been found to be only an optical illusion, appearing when the spectators beheld it from a certain angle of vision.

The ancient Greeks thought the ship which Ulysses brought back to his country was changed into a rock by Neptune. The rock near the island of Corfu bears resemblance to a ship in full sail, so as to deceive the eye of the sailor beholding it at a distance. To the ancients the appearance was a reality. Near Eddystone rock is another resemblance of the kind, which has often deceived the eyes of French and German sailors. Niobe transformed into a stone is a rock which at a distance bears resemblance to a woman stifled with sobs; but when we approach it the illusion vanishes, and we see only a rock detached from Mount Siplus.

Rocks sometimes assume remarkably fantastic shapes, which may easily be imagined to resemble impressions made by human feet, or those of gods and heroes. The foot-prints of Jonah are still pointed out near Nazareth, while the mark made by Elijah's foot is shown on Mount Carmel. In a grotto near Medina the Mohammedan still sees in a stone the head of Mohammed, and the print of his camel's foot in a certain rock in Palestine. Near Tryas, in Scythia, we may yet find the foot-prints, two cubits long, of the great Hercules, while the foot-marks of his cattle are to be found near Agrigentum. In Savoy are the foot-prints of the devil's mule. Mohammed's foot-prints are also seen and venerated near Cairo, while north of Kano, in Soudan, is the rock which contains the foot-prints of the camel on which Mohammed rode to heaven. These natural excavations in the rocks are sufficiently similar to the objects which they are supposed to represent, to satisfy the ignorant and superstitious of their genuineness. "If that is not it, what is it?" is all the proof they require.

The use of hot-houses being unknown to the common people, the priests of Bacchus, on Mount Larysium, gained the reputation of possessing supernatural power by producing grapes before the season had sufficiently advanced for grapes to mature by the heat of the sun. Likewise, men who introduced the use of iron into Cyprus were supposed to be magicians whose very glance was to be guarded against. Anciently the effects of opiates were not attributed to the drugs, but to some supernatural power accompanying their use. Porphyry relates that when the priests of the heathen temples would give revelations to their applicants they used opiates for incense. At Didyma the priestess, before prophesying, prepared herself by inhaling the odor of a vapor exhaled by a sacred fountain. The priest of Claros was accustomed to prepare himself for his visions by drinking the water of the grotto of Apollo, which we are informed was of such a nature as to shorten his life. Priestesses at Delphi, when preparing for their convulsions and prophesies, breathed the exhalations of a certain cavern, the odor of which, according to Pindar and Plutarch, came to the room where the people waited for the response. The Delphic oracle became dumb when the exhalations of the cavern ceased. The Mexican priests uttered their oracles when intoxicated by the fumes of tobacco burnt on the altar.

Among nearly all primitive tribes the first discovered rudiments of medicine and of science in general have been in the hands of priests and magicians, and have served to establish their claims to superhuman power. We read that a daughter of Hegemon, a Grecian poet, predicted an eclipse, and thus convinced the Thessalians that the moon obeyed her incantations. In ancient Egypt all scientific knowledge was veiled from the people by

mysterious hieroglyphics, while among the Greeks
and Romans the magicians constituted a secret oath-
bound society, dealing out the penalty of death
upon any of their number who should impart their
superior knowledge to the people.

The uncultured, being ever ready to attribute
any thing, which is inexplicable to them, to some
supernatural cause, fall an easy prey to those intentional or unintentional deceivers who can control
those phenomena which they are unable to comprehend. When Mr. Carver was traveling in South
America, he opened a book at random, and told the
number of leaves from that place to the beginning
of the volume, by reading the figures at the top of
the page, and the Indians being unable to account
for the feat upon any other hypothesis, believed him
to be in league with invisible spirits.

In 1815 A. D., in Padua, red microscopic insects
appeared in the wheat of that country, causing general alarm. The priests, as ignorant and as superstitious as the people, declared that by some miracle
the wheat contained blood, and ordered fasts and
masses that the unwelcome miracle might cease.

But the most unfortunate freak of superstition
in mistaking the natural for the supernatural is exhibited in the manufacture of witch ointment and
poisonous compounds, the effects of which were
attributed to the magical power of the witch or
wizard from whom they were obtained. At a
time when the belief in witchcraft was giving way
in Europe, and the knowledge of science had somewhat advanced among the people, the witch oint-

ment was seized and analyzed by chemists, and was found to contain opium and henbane and other powerful drugs.* The ointment was prepared clandestinely, and sold usually to some superstitious and wicked persons who wished to form a temporary league with the devil to get revenge upon their enemies. The witch anointed herself until, in her delirium, she fancied herself away to the witches' sabbath, holding carnival with the devil; and when she awoke she would protest that, as usual, she had been bodily absent, engaged in her terrible vocation.

Witches often caused the deaths of their victims by what they believed to be the supernatural power of poisonous compounds. The parliament of France, in 1682 A. D., at last conceived the true idea of the character of witches and their work, excepting those who were the victims of trance and an excited imagination, when it resolved that they should not be punished "except as deceivers, blasphemers, and poisoners."

It is established by good authority that applicants to the Grecian oracles drank from a secret well or of some narcotic preparations, and they mistook their own dreams for revelations. Belladonna, applied to the eyes, would have been enough to make Pentheus say: "Behold two suns and two cities of Thebes." In ancient ceremonies the initiate was often elaborately anointed, and thus put under the influence of narcotics which he thought to be supernatural. We know that Pausanias (Book

---

*On this subject see Porta's Natural Magic and Forman's Tracts on Fascination.

IX, chapter xxxix), when initiated was caused by the priests to drink the waters of oblivion and then from the well of reflection, after which there followed his hallucinations, which he supposed realities. When he came to himself the priest caused him to write his own vision, proving that what he saw was visible to none but himself.

A magistrate of Florence was the first to detect the natural origin of the witch's supposed journey in the air to the rendezvous of her associates. He went to the room of a witch, had her anoint herself with ointment, and tied her to a bedpost. She fell asleep, he sitting by her side. When she awoke she declared she had been to the convocation of witches, and told who had met her there. It was fortunate for those she professed to have seen in her dream that this magistrate had obtained some hint of the power of drugs to excite the imagination, for otherwise they would have been burnt for witchcraft.

Chapter IX.

LEGERDEMAIN.

HUMAN nature is the same in all ages. The same impulse which moves the child to play "April fool" manifests itself in people of larger growth and has been exhibited in every age of the world's history. In every community some mischievous trickster has personated a ghost in a churchyard or in some haunted house to enjoy the grim fun of terrifying others more superstitious than himself. Sometimes the trickster can turn his skill to his advantage in gaining reputation and money, and whenever the state of society is such as to warrant the experiment adventurers are never wanting to take advantage of the unreasoning credulity of the ignorant.

While we are now writing, one Slade, of whom we shall speak hereafter, having been exposed by the reporters of the New York press, and having been seized in the very act of fraud by Professor Lankester, of London, and after having been arrested by the English courts for vagrancy, but getting out of jail on bail, is mystifying the mystic philosophers of Germany (some of whom are so skeptical that they can not accept the miracles of Jesus of Nazareth), so that they are writing learned articles in their scientific journals concerning his exhibitions.

Heathen priests could not have failed to possess this same impulse of erring human nature. We would expect to find it sometimes controlling the actions of Roman Catholic priests who were not always devout, and who were ever surrounded by an ignorant and superstitious people, hungry for some new marvel. Lucian has described the initiatory ceremonies of the Thaumaturgists. It was dark, and then there were flashes of light, specters, hisses of serpents, howls of beasts; the earth trembled, and the shivering candidate seemed to be raised mountain high and then to sink down into an abyss. Statues became alive and would weep and speak. Monsters, harpies, gorgons, hundred-headed serpents, and ghosts stood before him. There were thunder, lightning, and torrents of fire. Dry bodies fermented and turned into waves of foaming blood. Gods were seen with boiling water, melted metal, and burning firebrands applied to their naked bodies, while ferocious monsters crouched before them.

The cave of Trophonius, the seat of one of the most famous oracles of Greece, had a mouth too small for a man to enter it, but which was supernaturally enlarged (by machinery, doubtless) as the candidate approached. The movable floor of the temple of Ceres, in Greece, was, doubtless, terrible to the awe-struck worshipers; but it was moved by machinery, the remains of which have been discovered by modern travelers. The priests of Baal, in Elijah's day, doubtless cut their bodies in appearance just as the modern juggler does who seems to thrust a dagger through his wrist, while he exhibits the flowing blood to the beholders. The dagger exhibited for inspection is a genuine weapon, but is deftly exchanged by the operator for another dagger which has two parts joined by a semi-circular wire fitting to the wrist, which is covered with blood taken from some animal and provided for the occasion.

In the labyrinths of Egypt were doors so constructed in many places that they could not be opened without producing a sound, which would resemble thunder. Artificial lightning, such as is produced in our modern theaters, was probably known to Darius, son of Hystaspes, for when he mounted the throne the lightnings were around him. It has been shown that speaking tubes were used to produce responses in certain ancient temples, the priest thus personating the god, being conveniently concealed from the people. Memnon's musical statue, according to Juvenal, made its music by means of a peculiar mechanism concealed within it. A cavity evidently designed to conceal a living man, has been discovered in one of these ancient sonorous statues.

Eunus, the Syrian, and Barcocheba, who headed the revolt of the Jews, vomited flames from their mouths, while speaking to the people. It was done by means of a walnut shell filled with some burning materials, and the shell, being perforated, the flames could be forced out by the breath, without burning the mouth of the operator. The priestesses of Diana, in Cappadocia, and those in the temple of Mount Soractes, walked with naked feet on burning coals. Varro asserts that they were able to perform this feat by anointing their feet with a liniment, which made them hard and horny.* Explosions of chemical substances, and phenomena produced by petroleum and phosphorus, and electricity, were employed in the secret arts of the ancient sorcerer.† It is believed that Proteus, Cratisthenes, and Xenophon, the celebrated Theurgists, enveloped themselves with a circle of flames to conceal some other operations, by which they caused hidden reflectors (reflectors were then in use) to throw images into the air and smoke. According to Salverte, the Grecian magicians used wire gauze to protect themselves while walking through the fire.

The temple of Bacchus, in Andros, had a fountain which flowed wine seven days, and then flowed water during the rest of the year; showing, that the cunning priests of that temple were acquainted with some of the laws of hydrostatics. The superstitious beholders would be ready enough to accept the supernatural as an explanation of the phenomenon. The first production of iron instruments was regarded as a spirit phenomenon, and men, reasoning after the manner of our modern spiritualists, attributed it to Vulcan. We need not wonder that in those ancient times the people were so deceived, when we remember that scientific knowledge was often confined to magicians and oath-bound societies, who used their superior knowledge for purposes of deception and pecuniary gain. Sinan, a chief of the

---

* See Beckman's History of Inventions, vol. iii, page 277.
† Salverte's Phil. of Magic, vol. ii, page 157.

Ishmaelites, of Syria, concealed one of his pupils in a cavity, leaving the head exposed to view, the neck being surrounded by a disc of bronze, having the appearance of a basin of blood, in which seemed to be the head of a man who had been just beheaded, which talked of the invisible world. The trick gained the impostor the implicit obedience of the nation. The specter of a god at Temersa, two thousand years ago, came forth just like the materialized spirit, "Katie King" (which Robert Dale Owen, the veteran spiritualist of America, declared to be the greatest and most convincing test he had ever seen, and which he afterward acknowledged to be a fraud), and a virgin was annually sacrificed to the materialized god, until one Euthymus seized the specter, which was black and terrible, and clothed in the skin of a wolf, and discovered a priest in disguise, who afterwards drowned himself to escape the fury of the people.

There is nothing new to be discovered in the methods of fraud, mankind having studied this black art so long. Just as the modern medium will talk in indefinite terms, so that her words can neither be proved true nor false, so the ancient sibyl wrote her oracles on leaves, and scattered them on the wind, so that no certain meaning could be attached to her words.

In Upper Egypt a tree seemed to utter words in the voice of a woman, and in like manner the river Nessus spoke to Pythagoras. The priestess of Mars, in Gaul, also had the art of ventriloquism, as we learn from an inscription found in the vicinity of the ancient temple of that god. Salverte relates that in the beginning of the eighteenth century a man was burned alive as a wizard, for being a ventriloquist. The Chinese prophets and magicians use this art to keep the people in fear of their power. Chinese priests to-day often exhibit their supermundane power, by pretending to swallow knives and vomit flames. Ventriloquism is employed by the Esquimaux in their sorcery.

We find among the ancients a crude telescope, a tube with a glass in one end, used by magicians to cause distant objects to seem near. That which is a natural result seemed to them to be magical. The mediæval belief in alchemy, the pursuit of which became a mania in Europe, was sustained by fraud:

"With regard to the innumerable tricks by which impostors persuaded the world that they had succeeded in making gold, and of which so many stories were current about this period, a very satisfactory report was read by M. Geoffroy, the elder, at the sitting of the Royal Academy of Sciences at Paris, on the 15th of April, 1722. As it relates principally to the alchemic cheats of the sixteenth and seventeenth centuries, the following abridgment of it may not be out of place in this portion of our history. The instances of successful transmutation were so numerous and apparently so well authenticated, that nothing short of so able an exposure as that of M. Geoffroy could disabuse the public mind. The trick to which they oftenest had recourse was to use a double-bottomed crucible, the under surface being of iron or copper, and the upper one of wax, painted to resemble the same metal. Between the two they placed as much gold or silver dust as was necessary for their purpose. They then put in their lead, quicksilver, or other ingredients, and placed their pot upon the fire. Of course, when the experiment was concluded, they never failed to find a lump of gold at the bottom. The same result was produced in many other ways. Some of them used a hollow wand, filled with gold or silver dust, and stopped at the ends with wax or butter. With this they stirred the boiling metal in their crucibles, taking care to accompany the operation with many ceremonies to divert attention from the real purpose of the maneuver. They also drilled holes in lumps of lead, into which they poured molten gold, and carefully closed the aperture with the original metal. Sometimes they washed a piece of gold with quicksilver. When in this state they found no difficulty in palming it off upon the uninitiated as an inferior metal, and very easily transmuted it into fine sonorous gold again, with the aid of a little aquafortis.

"Others imposed by means of nails, half iron and half gold or silver. They pretended that they really transmuted the precious half from iron, by dipping it in a strong alcohol. M. Geoffroy produced several of these nails to the Academy of Sciences, and showed how nicely the two parts were soldered together. The golden or silver half was painted black to resemble iron, and the color immediately disappeared when the nail was dipped into aquafortis. A nail of this description was for a long time in the cabinet of the grand duke of Tuscany. Such also, said M. Geoffroy, was the knife presented by a monk to Queen Elizabeth of England, the blade of which was half gold and half steel. Nothing at one time was more common than to see coins, half gold and half silver, which had been operated upon by alchemists, for the same purposes of trickery. In fact, says M. Geoffroy, in concluding his long report, there is every reason to believe that all the famous histories which have been handed down to us about the transmutation of metals into gold or silver, by means of the powder of projection or philosophical elixirs, are founded upon some successful deception of the kind above narrated. These pretended philosophers invariably disappeared after the first or second experiment, or their powders or elixirs have failed to produce their effect, either because attention being excited they have found no opportunity to renew the trick without being discovered, or because they have not had sufficient gold-dust for more than one trial.

"The disinterestedness of these would-be philosophers looked, at first sight, extremely imposing. Instances were not rare in which they generously abandoned all the profits of their transmutations— even the honor of the discovery. But this apparent disinterestedness was one of the most cunning of their maneuvers. It served to keep up the popular expectation; it seemed to show the possibility of discovering the philosopher's stone, and provided the means of future advantages, which they were never slow to lay hold of—such as entrances into royal households, maintenance at the public expense, and gifts from ambitious potentates, too greedy after the gold they so easily promised."*

It makes the heart ache as we write this chapter, in which we must record the efforts which men have made and are yet making to deceive their fellows. No country has been exempt. Whether we go with the devotee to behold the foot-prints of Buddha on the peak of Adam, in Ceylon, or the foot-print of Guadama at a place in the Burmese empire, we see in the carving of the rock the handiwork of the deceiver. If we go to India and visit the colossal statue of Siva, we find under the head-gear of the image a place in which to secrete the lying priest who was to answer questions which the confiding worshiper propounded to the god. A juggler can make the scales of a balance rise or fall at pleasure, as pretended spirit mediums sometimes do to weight-force exerted by spirits, and as is done in the public markets for sport; but yonder in Hindoostan the guilt and innocence and the life and death of the accused are decided in this manner.

Would that we could record that the Roman Catholic Church has kept herself clear of these wicked frauds. But when we read that Pope Simplicius and his former wife (A. D. 497) carried fire coals in their hands, and put them on their clothes without being burned, and when we know that asbestos cloth would guard their hands and a solution of alum would render their clothes incombustible, and that these facts were known at that time, we

---

*Mackay's Memoirs of Popular Delusions, vol. i, p. 188.

are compelled to charge the alleged successor of St. Peter with fraud. When the Hussites were excommunicated, at a given signal tapers in the hands of the priests were suddenly extinguished, and all the people thought the event supernatural, and evidently the priests were willing agents in the deception. And alas, our suspicions receive confirmatiom as we glance over the dark history of the Romish priesthood. At Blois, in France, the blood of a murdered duke came out afresh every year, blood being sprinkled on the spot by the deceptive priests. Pope Sylvester the Second, A. D. 991, gained the reputation of possessing supernatural power by making a speaking head of brass, an acoustic instrument of peculiar construction. A pope professing miraculous power convinced the Emperor Basil that his son was about to come into his arms, by throwing a picture of his son into the air by means of two concave reflectors. As early as the third century magicians produced pretended apparitions of the dead in this manner.

The blood of Saint Januarius, said to have been collected centuries ago, may be seen to-day at Naples. It liquefies and boils when held in the hand. It is a mixture of spermaceti, sulphuric ether, and orchanet. It looks like blood, and may be made to boil by the heat of the hand. This is an old monkish trick, the bones of the saints having been often made to bleed in this way. Peter the Great resolved to put an end to the weeping girl of St. Petersburg, and made the discovery that a reservoir of oil was secreted behind the eyes of the picture, so that when it was heated by the lighted tapers the oil would run out and look like tears. A convincing proof that the blood of Saint Januarius was likewise manipulated by the lying priests of Naples occurred when Naples was attacked by the French. The word went round among the faithful that the blood of the saint would not liquefy as usual, because of the presence of the French. The story reaching the French commander, he sent word to the priests that if the blood of the saint did not liquefy in an hour, his cannon would blow the church down about their heads. The saint relented and his blood liquefied. On the altar of the church at Lisbon was a miraculous egg, which contained letters in relief on its surface. It was given out that these letters were on the egg when it came from the hen. But the miracle disappears and the fraud becomes transparent when we remember that if letters are traced with a pin on an egg covered with a thin layer of wax, and the egg is then placed in vinegar or some other acid, the letters traced will stand out in relief on the eggshell.

We only aim to give those who are ignorant of the art of legerdemain a general idea of the methods by which the senses of the beholders may be deceived. Heathen religions, the papacy, witchcraft, haunted houses, and modern spiritualism have largely been supported by arts of deception. But a separate class of professional jugglers has always existed during historic times, and may be met in most savage and newly discovered tribes. In Norman times the juggler was a "joculator," and was not only a professional trickster, but astrologer, fortune-teller, minstrel, and clown. In the fourteenth century the European juggler began to confine himself to feats of sleight of hand, assisted by machinery, by which he produced astonishing illusions, which often led the ignorant and superstitious masses to regard him as a wizard, assisted by demons.

Chaucer describes the feats performed by jugglers in his day. "Sometimes they will bring in the similitude of a grim lion, or make flowers spring up as in a meadow; sometimes they cause a vine to flourish, bearing white and red grapes, or show a castle built with stone, and when they please they cause the whole to disappear." James the First was sure that the jugglers of his day were aided by the devil. It is well known that the jugglers of India, China, and Japan are wonderfully expert, and they so far excel the average American "medium," that writers on spiritualism often maintain that they are aided by departed human spirits. The rope untying feats of the Davenport Brothers have been found among North American Indians, together with the familiar trick of breathing fire.*

One indispensable prerequisite for a successful juggler is to be a good talker, for the voice can call the attention of the observer from some apparently indifferent, but really essential, movements of the operator or his accomplice. While the audience is convulsed with laughter or deeply interested in a

---
* Taylor's Primitive Culture, vol. i, page 154.

story, the operator is not subject to very close scrutiny. He must be capable of swift movements, for motion is swifter than sight. The spiritualist juggler has a rare opportunity for prosecuting his work. Usually his audiences are eager to be deceived. They will allow him time till the small hours of the night if he demands it, to get the "conditions" right, and get himself *en rapport* with the spirits. He can relate thrilling stories of ghosts and haunted houses, and discourse learnedly on odylic or psychic force. He can plead pausible excuses for failures in his experiments, because it is not a test of his power only, but of the willingness of the spirits to operate, and of the "positive" or "negative" or skeptical condition of the circle.

Light is also a powerful agent to disturb the psychic conditions of the air, and hence the lamps may be turned low or totally extinguished. Skeptics and inquisitive persons may be held by the hands by stout and muscular accomplices, because odylic force flows through circles, and spirits must act in harmony with law. His own private character is not inquired into, because evil spirits are the readiest to communicate, or crude spirits of the lower circles, and they prefer a medium whose moral character is congenial to their own. If he is caught in the act of fraud, spiritist papers will say it was a freak of a mischievous spirit or the medium became tired waiting for the spirits to operate, and, therefore, added a trick of his own to make the *séance* interesting. If a human hand is seen manipulating the machinery, it is believed to be the hand of the spirit, which when fully materialized can not be distinguished from the hand of an ordinary mortal.

With such a sentiment manufactured by the spiritualist press and platform the jugglers of this century have had the dawn of their millennium, and for more than a score of years have filled the land with their pretended marvels. The medium usually, and always for his most successful experiments, must have his own apartments, and must be subject to his own self-imposed conditions. In 1702 A. D., the priest in Guatemala, when allowed no more liberty than this in his experiments, would seem to transform himself into a lion or tiger. Brewster,* the great naturalist, describes how, under these circumstances, pygmies, giants, terrific heads with moving awful eyes and jaws which open and close, may be made to advance towards the audience, the apparently living beings transforming themselves into skeletons, which soon vanish into transparent air. A simple experiment, which may be tried by any one, is to make the room dark, and then cut a hole in the window-shutter, when men and other objects without will be seen on the wall.

Richardson, a notable juggler, who lived in the latter part of the seventh century, appeared to chew melted glass and burning coals. We know not what were the methods used by him, but a modern juggler would not hesitate to repeat the experiment under certain self-imposed conditions. The mouth

---

* Brewster's Natural Magic, page 86.

could be protected by plates of metal, or cold substances could be so painted as to look like live coals at a little distance from the beholders, or by sleight of hand the live coal might be made to appear to enter the mouth when it was really deposited elsewhere, but with such rapidity of movement that the eyes of the beholder could not detect the cheat. That motion is swifter than sight is a law which is ever valuable to the juggler. The fusible metal of Darcet is a compound of mercury, tin, and bismuth, and has the appearance of lead. A spoon made of this compound will melt in warm water, and when melted it may be poured on the tongue or held in the hand without inconvenience. By using this metal jugglers have often made people believe that they were holding melted lead in their hands. It is also a well-known fact in science that melted iron can be held a moment in the hand, and that the hand may be thrust into a mass of melted metal if the hand has been previously moistened. The moisture of the hand is instantly changed to vapor, and the vapor serves as a safe envelope to the hand for a little time, vapor being a very poor conductor of heat. Sometimes, when the juggler or medium seems to thrust his arm into boiling water a fluid which boils at low temperature has been substituted for water. The feet may be prepared to walk on burning coals by frequently rubbing their soles with sulphuric acid, alternating with oil. When treated for a time in this way the soles of the feet become like leather. This experiment of necessity is performed only on rare occasions, and was used chiefly in the ancient ordeals which tested the guilt or innocence of the accused.

We read that Professor Begruss, promised the duke of Brunswick, that during the dinner hour his coat would turn red, and to the amazement of the prince, while he was beholding, the magician's coat turned red without visible cause. In heathen temples the veil concealing sacred objects was often made to change color from a white to a blood red hue, and the people beholding thought it a miracle. There are various ways by which this feat may be accomplished. Pour lime water on beet roots, and cloth soaked in the solution and suddenly dried will turn red after a few hours' contact with the air.

Our modern scientists could become marvelous jugglers if they were disposed to turn their knowledge to such base uses. They can make tears of glass which may be struck with a hammer without being broken, but which will crumble to powder if a thread at one end be broken; and pear-shaped bottles in which marbles may be rolled without breaking the bottles, but the magic bottles would fly to pieces were a grain of flint no larger than a canary seed to be dropped into them. They freeze water into ice in contact with red hot crucibles, and if James the First believed the jugglers of his day were in league with the devil he would certainly charge our modern scientists with sorcery, and burn them alive. Ancient, like modern, diviners made use of jugglery. Cicero relates that in his day they could not pass each other on the streets without putting their tongues in their cheeks.

Jugglers flourish best when, on account of the prevailing ignorance and superstition of the people, they can veil their arts in mystery and assume allegiance with the supernatural. It is for this reason that jugglery in India is better developed than in the United States. The methods of the juggler shall be more fully discussed when we come to speak more particularly of modern spiritualism.

Chapter X.

ORDEALS.

ACCORDING to Tacitus,* some Roman oracles gave responses by means of lots, on which were engraved certain significant words and signs. The modern Hindoos are accustomed to decide disputes by casting lots in front of a temple, believing that the gods are thus compelled to interfere to see that justice is done. The lot has been used in all ages and in all countries. Sometimes the persons using it have employed it as a convenient method of settling questions which would otherwise involve disagreeable disputes, without being influenced by any superstitious motives, but more frequently in primitive ages and nations it has been looked upon as being governed by some supernatural power. The freaks of chance are ever mysterious.

At this point we confront a region of thought which has been dark even to philosophers, and we need not be astonished to find it an object of superstitious regard among the uncultured. The islanders of the Malay archipelago, the people of Kamtchatka, and the Hindoos when near the sacred Ganges, will not save a man who by accident falls into the water and is near drowning, believing that the invisible

---
*Germania, 10.

powers who control seeming accidents are in quest of a human victim, and if the one endangered is saved another victim must soon take his place. The inhabitants of Kamtchatka sometimes attempt to drown the unfortunate man by force, and if he escapes from them they refuse ever afterward to admit him to their homes, or to give him food, regarding him as if he were already dead.

"To haul over the coals" is a reminder of a savage custom among our forefathers, of causing persons to walk on burning coals to attest their guilt or innocence when accused of crime. This popular adage, like many others, serves to remind us of the dark night of ignorance out of which we have emerged. Duels took their origin in the popular belief that deadly weapons would by some magical influence aid the cause of him who was in the right, and destroy him who was in the wrong. In the days of Charlemagne, God was appealed to to preside over such contests, and the issue was regarded as a vindication of the righteousness of the cause of the victor. As a result of this popular belief dueling spread over the country like an epidemic, attacking all classes of society, not excepting the clergy, who were permitted to produce champions to fight in their stead. But after a time the moral sense of the clergy prevailed so far as to cause them gradually to introduce other trials by ordeal which were less objectionable but not less unreasonable—such as casting lots in the presence of the altar, causing the accused to walk blindfolded and bare-foot over a space strewn with red-hot plowshares, holding red-hot iron in the naked hand, plunging the arm into boiling water, and throwing the accused into ponds and rivers to see whether they would sink or swim, as suspected witches were served in subsequent times. When a priest was accused he was required to swallow a piece of bread and cheese without choking, and of course the priests were rarely found guilty. It was but natural that the priests who invented these ordeals should set apart the safest test for themselves.

But after the thirst for blood and indifference to the sacredness of human life had been increased by the Crusades, so that the clergy were no longer able to control them, the ordeal by the duel once more became popular. Under Otho I, all legal questions concerning which the lawyers could not agree were decided by the ordeal of the duel. In the reign of Charles VI, the Parliament of Paris ordered a duel to be fought to decide the guilt or innocence of Sieur Legris. Queen Elizabeth at one time permitted a duel, which was witnessed by the justices and counselors of the court, to decide a difficult question concerning the title to a certain piece of property. Duels were provoked by the slightest causes. The father of Sterne fought a duel about a goose, and Sir Walter Raleigh fought a duel about a tavern bill. Dueling at times became a mania, and the people seemed to be seized with a frenzy for such bloody encounters. Millot, in his history of France, estimates that as many as eight thousand pardons during a period of twenty-eight years were issued to men who had killed other men in duels.

The ordeal of the duel could not be so easily controlled in its issues as those other ordeals which were invented by and under the management of the Roman priests, in the days of Charlemagne. The priest, after satisfying himself of the guilt or innocence of the accused, and having control of the ordeal, could decide the matter in accordance with his desires. Iron could be so painted as to look to be red-hot when it was not heated at all; the plowshares could be so arranged that the accused, stepping at a regular pace, could avoid stepping on them; the hands and feet could be prepared by being rubbed with oils and acids so as to become leathery and uninjured by a brief contact with red-hot metals, and all trace of burning could be made to disappear after the time which would elapse while the accused was under the care of the priest, or the hands and feet could be protected by flesh-colored coverings, and liquids which boil at low temperature could be substituted for water. When the mother of Edward the Confessor vindicated her virtue by walking over a space strewn with red-hot plowshares, as the priests had control of the ordeal, and as they had a motive and the disposition for deception, it is probable in this case as in many others, they used their well known ability in legerdemain on the side of mercy.

Chapter XI.

EPIDEMIC ALARMS.

THE Christian Scriptures clearly teach that the world shall not always endure, but leave us in ignorance of the time when the great catastrophe shall come in which the earth shall be destroyed. It is natural that such a doctrine should have an important influence upon the Christian mind in every generation, and when we remember how susceptible mankind are to epidemic fears we are not surprised to find that no century has passed in which some large bodies of Christian believers have not been seized with a sudden frenzy on account of the supposed nearness of the end of the world.

Before the natural sciences were well developed strange appearances in nature, such as the approach of a comet, a meteoric shower, a pestilence, or even a storm of unwonted violence, would be regarded by many as harbingers of the long-expected catastrophe. Sometimes, when armies were marshaled for war, they would suspend hostilities until the ominous appearances had ceased. An eclipse of the sun was sufficient to convince assembled legislators and worshiping congregations that the day of judgment was at hand. Several times an epidemic alarm, excited by the belief that the end of the world was at hand, has extended over nearly all christendom

In the tenth century it was the current belief that the thousand years which it was supposed were assigned by the Apocalypse as the limit of the earth's existence had then nearly elapsed, and many zealous and excited preachers traveled abroad in France, Italy, and Germany, announcing the near approach of the day of judgment, the opening scenes of which were were to occur at Jerusalem. As the delusion spread business enterprises were neglected, buildings were suffered to decay, and in some fits of public frenzy many costly edifices were pulled down. They would not only cease to build, but they would assist the impending destruction.

During the year 999, one year before that one in which it was expected the world would come to an end, vast multitudes of men, accompanied with their wives and children, having sold their possessions to the unbelieving or the hesitating, started toward Jerusalem, singing hymns, offering penitential prayers, and gazing toward the sky, which they believed was liable to open at any moment to disclose the descending Judge and his twelve legions of angels. During the following year which, as they believed, was certain to witness the final judgment, the number of pilgrims to Jerusalem was greatly increased, and those who had arrived at the sacred place, and were awaiting the day of doom, were filled with ever-increasing excitement. A meteor or a thunder peal would hurl them upon their knees, to weep and pray. Some would be calm in the midst of the general confusion, and with child-like confidence await the approach of the loving son of the blessed virgin; but the majority of them were like crouching slaves, hoping by tears and prayers to avert the avenging lash which they knew they so richly deserved. To them the approaching judgment day was a reality; their faith, though misguided, was perfect, and their feelings were as intense as if they were really listening to the last trumpet blast. But the year 1000 passed by and the earth still stood on its ancient foundations, and the deluded multitudes who had gone to Palestine to meet the Judge of the world, with disappointment and chagrin were compelled to beg their way back to their native lands, and to endure the taunts of their less credulous or less ambitious neighbors, who had resolved to meet the judgment-day around their own hearth-stones.

Again, in 1345 and 1350, a similar epidemic terror occurred when all Europe was visited by the plague, and mourning and alarm filled almost every city, producing that peculiar state of mind engendered by distress, in which the man of crushed heart is incapable of argument, the rush of passion overwhelming the reason. The skeptic can not command his skepticism in time of sorrow, and the man of faith easily imbibes the faith of his counselors. Also distress tends to produce forebodings of coming sorrow. The ravages of the plague engendered a wide-spread conviction that the world was about to come to an end, and nearly all the cities of France, Italy, and Germany contained preachers who fanned the fires of popular enthusiasm.

In the year 1736, an epidemic alarm swept

through London. It was produced by a prophecy of the celebrated Whiston that the world would come to an end on the 13th of October of that year. It was believed that the general conflagration would begin at London, and multitudes of people assembled in adjacent fields to witness the destruction of the city.

In the United States, Millerites and the Second Adventists have repeatedly fixed the time for the ending of the present order of nature, and have assembled in considerable congregations, at different times, to meet the Judge of mankind, who, as they supposed, was about to descend from the clouds of heaven.

In the year 1806, in a village in the vicinity of Leeds, a hen laid eggs on which were inscribed the words, "Christ is coming." The writing on the eggs was looked upon as miraculous, and it was generally believed that the hen had become an unconscious prophet, whose mission it was to warn mankind of the approach of the day of judgment. Some persons went to the place where the hen's nest was, and found her in the very act of laying an egg, upon which was the miraculous writing. The inhabitants of Leeds and of the surrounding country were thrown into an epidemic alarm. Many who had been too thoughtless concerning religious matters, repented and gave themselves up to prayers and tears. But it was soon proved beyond a doubt that the owner of the hen had written upon the eggs with acid, causing the letters to stand out in relief on the surface of the shell, and had afterward forced the egg back into the body of the hen. Those who had been led to repentance by this delusion were soon moving on in their accustomed ways of indifference and folly.

In 1629, while astrologers, fortune-tellers, and other impostors were in high repute, and were constantly uttering their predictions, and at a time when, owing to the poor sanitary arrangements of all large cities, pestilential diseases were of frequent occurrence, some astrologers predicted that Milan was about to be visited by the plague. In the following year the plague broke out, when the would-be prophets ever eager to advertise themselves, reminded the people of their prophecy; or, perhaps, the people themselves remembered the prediction, which under ordinary circumstances would have been forgotten. A comet had appeared, and some of the astrological fraternity affirmed that it was a forerunner of war; others maintained that it was an indication of famine, while others believed that a pestilence was about to occur. There was also an ancient verse which had been preserved by tradition, and which, doubtless, like the prophecies of Mother Shipton, had been so changed as to apply to successive periods, the changes usually being made with reference to decades. This ancient verse just at this time had been made to indicate 1630, as the period when the devil would poison Milan. While the plague was raging in the city, the people awoke one morning to find that all the doors in the the principal streets were marked or daubed with some curious substance, which had been applied by means of a sponge. The earthly mischief-maker who had perpetrated the joke could not be found, and the people, reasoning after the manner of the inquirer at a spiritist *séance*, who assumes that the spirits must do that which can not be traced to mortal agents, concluded that the devil was the perpetrator of the deed, and assigned as a motive which actuated him, the desire "to poison Milan." This last marvel, together with their fear of the plague, drove the people insane. This superstitious terror became more contagious than the plague, and served to increase the latter to redoubled fury. No efforts were made to check the ravages of the plague, for how could they hope to check-mate the devil? Hope gave way, and all sank down under a belief that they would die. The people, as their insanity increased, began to believe that the water of the wells and all grain and fruits, and all objects of touch were poisoned. They dreaded to touch the walls of their houses and the handles to their doors.

At this period it was the common belief that witches and wizards—men and women—could be admitted into terms of intimacy with the devil, and receive certain diabolical powers from him, by pledging to give him their souls after death. A rare chance was thus offered to wicked men to get rid of their enemies, and to enjoy the devilish luxury of revenge. They only had to come forward and testify that they had seen their neighbor going about the streets besmearing doors with the devil's ointment, and the mob would set upon the alleged culprit, or the civil authorities would put him to the rack. Sometimes the poor victim, worn down by torture, would confess his guilt, to hasten his death, and thus escape from pain which he could no longer endure. Such confessions served to confirm the common belief. One old man, eighty years old, wiped off the seat before sitting upon it at church. A cry was raised that he was besmearing the seat with the devil's ointment, whereupon the congregation dragged him out of the church and through the streets till he died. Many suspected persons were executed, and every execution witnessed by the people only increased the violence of their insanity. Scores of persons at last, mistaking the creations of the diseased imagination for realities, related to the credulous people that they had seen the devil riding in his chariot, drawn by four white horses, and that his chariot wheels produced a sound louder than thunder.

Those who were seized with the plague often became insane, and their insanity taking the direction of the popular frenzy, they fancied that they were the ones who were in league with the devil. An incredible number from this cause accused themselves of having distributed the devil's poison. They mistook dreams for realities, and when they dreamed that they were abroad scattering poison, they believed that they were really absent from their sick-beds, and no evidence could be brought to contradict them, for it was thought that the devil's agents often became invisible.

In the month of June, 1523, several astrologers in London united in uttering the prophecy that the water of the Thames would swell to such a height that ten thousand houses in London would be swept away. A few believed at first, but delusion soon became epidemic, until multitudes of people, representing all classes, from the lowest to the highest, fled from London, carrying with them their families and the movable furniture of their dwellings. The prior of Saint Bartholemew's built a fortress at Harrow-on-the-Hill, and stocked it with provisions sufficient to last him and his friends for two months. The fortress was also furnished with boats and expert oarsmen, so that the inmates could escape if the deluge should rise above its summit. A few days before the appointed day on which the river was to swell, the prior and his friends moved into the fortress. He was compelled with sorrow to refuse many wealthy citizens who asked to be admitted into his place of refuge. A large part of the population of London, however, remained in their homes, because it was foretold that the Thames would rise gradually, and they believed they would have ample time to secure their personal safety. Early on the morning of the eventful day the banks of the river were lined with anxious crowds, watching its dangerous waters. The day passed. The Thames ebbed and flowed as it had been accustomed to do from time immemorial, and one more entry was made in the record of human folly.

In 1761 London was shaken by an earthquake, and a month after another shock occurred, producing a dread foreboding lest other shocks still more terrible might follow. While the public mind was in this state of suspense and dread, a visionary by the name of Bell began to prophesy that another earthquake was about to occur, by which the city would be totally destroyed. Mr. Bell announced that as one month had elapsed between the first and second shock, therefore about one month after the second a third would occur of which the first and second were premonitions. He accordingly fixed upon the 5th of April as the day on which the last great convulsion of the earth was to occur, and ran about the streets of London sounding the alarm. Thousands of people were convinced, and taking their families with them fled from the city. As the appointed day drew nigh the excitement increased until all the villages within twenty miles of London were crowded with terror-stricken fugitives, while the poorer classes, who could not pay for accommodations in the crowded villages, encamped in the open fields, while others took refuge in the boats which lay upon the river. Many of those who at first were skeptical caught the contagion of credulity and fear when they saw the multitudes fleeing from the city. The day of doom passed by, and the sun arose upon London standing in all its pride and strength, and the befooled fugitives returned chap-fallen to their former avocations. On further investigation it was found that Bell was insane and the authorities kindly sent him to an asylum.

It is only in very recent times that Christendom has become free from the epidemic alarms created by ignorance and superstition. No longer ago than 1832 the expected appearance of a comet caused great excitement and fear through all Europe, and more especially in Germany, it being the prevailing belief that there was danger that the earth would be destroyed. At the present time, when a comet appears thousands in our own country are filled with dread.

Chapter XII.

THE CRUSADES.

IN the eighth, ninth, and tenth centuries Christian pilgrims from various parts of Europe went in great numbers to Jerusalem, some of them being actuated by a laudable desire to behold the scenes which were associated with the life and death of the world's Redeemer; but the most were prompted by a desire to atone for their sins, because it was the current belief that such a pilgrimage would secure to the pilgrim pardon for all past transgressions. Some of the pilgrims were also actuated by the love of money, for upon their return they were able to sell at extravagant prices bits of wood, as fragments of the true cross, or hair and toe-nails as relics of the apostles, and even wtaer from the Jordan and mold from Mount Calvary. We have spoken of these pretended relics in another chapter.

In course of time, as the number of pilgrims increased, the Moslem governors of Palestine imposed a tax upon them, and thus obtained a very great revenue. At the beginning of the eleventh century an epidemic terror seized upon Christendom, induced by the prevailing belief that the world was about to come to an end. The general alarm was increased by earthquakes, falling stars, and violent hurricanes, until the high-ways leading from Europe to Palestine were filled with terrified pilgrims on their way to Jerusalem, to meet their Judge, who, as they believed, was about to descend in the clouds of heaven. The Turks, by excessive taxation and sometimes by personal abuse, gave great offense to these Christian fanatics, some of whom from time to time returned to Europe to recite the story of their wrongs.

One of these returned pilgrims was Peter the Hermit, who conceived the great idea of driving the Turks out of the Holy Land. He laid his plans before Pope Urban II, who at once gave him every possible encouragement. The pope shortly afterward addressed a vast multitude who stood in front of the cathedral of Clermont, and described to them the boundless wealth of Palestine, the sufferings of pilgrims, and commanded the people to arm themselves and go forth to drive the Turks from the Holy Land, promising full pardon for sin to all who should reach that land. Those who joined the Crusade were liberated from debt, and if they were outlaws they were granted full pardon. Many women burned the sign of the cross on their breasts and upon the tender limbs of their infants, and encouraged their husbands and sons to join the Crusade. Peter the Hermit, with rough clothing, and arms and feet bare, preached the Crusade in many cities with fiery eloquence, and thousands answered his call. Real estate was sold for one quarter of its value, and the proceeds devoted to the purchase of weapons and provisions for the Crusade.

During the year 1096, A. D., the roads were filled with ignorant and armed fanatics, some of whom thought that Jerusalem could be reached in a few days, while others reckoned it to be fifty thousand miles away. As it was believed that all sin would be remitted to the crusaders as soon as they arrived in Palestine, multitudes of them on the way gave themselves up to the extremest practices of drunken debauchery and licentiousness. It is said the number of these crusaders, embracing women and children, was three hundred thousand. As the motives which were used to induce them to join the Crusade were of the worst, this great multitude was mostly composed of the vilest classes of European population.

The horde led by Peter the Hermit, on account of a serious difficulty which had occurred between that city and a band of crusaders led by Walter the Penniless, made an attack on the city of Semlin, in Hungary, and capturing the city, enacted a scene of brutality and licentiousness almost unparalleled. At Nissa the undisciplined crusaders commit such depredations as to bring on another battle, in which they are completely routed and slain by thousands. The army led by Peter had several such encounters as this, in which it generally was beaten with great loss, and soon after crossing the Bosphorus, while their leader was absent in Constantinople, was completely destroyed. The army led by Walter the Penniless engaged the Turks near Isnik, or Nice, and out of twenty-five thousand, twenty-two thousand were slain. The remaining three thousand returned to Europe. About this time another fresh horde of a hundred thousand crusaders set out from Germany, but their depredations in Hungary compelled the inhabitants of that country well-nigh to exterminate them.

Shortly after this other swarms of crusaders started forth from Germany and France, preceded by a goose and a goat, which they believed would aid them in hunting Jews, whom they mutilated and murdered with extremest cruelty. And when there were no more Jews to butcher, they started upon the customary road to Palestine, passing through Hungary. Again the Hungarians are provoked to arm themselves against this horde of robbers and assassins, and slaughter them in such great numbers that the stream of the Danube is said to have been choked up with their dead bodies. This was perhaps the most brutal and licentious army which ever wore the sign of the red cross, and we breathe relief when we learn that it was well-nigh exterminated before it passed beyond the boundaries of Christendom.

When this fit of popular madness passed away a well-planned war of Europe against Asia was conducted by many able leaders, chief among whom were Godfrey, duke of Lorraine, and Raymond, count of Toulouse. When these leaders drew up their forces before Nice, in Bithynia, they found, according to some reliable authorities, that they commanded one hundred thousand horsemen, six hundred thousand footmen, exclusive of women and children. This vast army found great difficulty in procuring food and water in the devastated regions of Phrygia, so that five hundred daily died of hunger and thirst. Shortly afterwards, when laying siege to Antioch, one thousand a day died of disease and starvation; but after a time the gates of Antioch were opened by the treachery of Phirouz, a captain under the command of the Turkish prince, and the crusaders rushing in slaughtered indiscriminately men, women, and children, until the streets of the city ran red with blood. When the crusaders found themselves in possession of Antioch, they saw themselves again confronted by famine and pestilence, so that, in a short time, of the three hundred thousand which had laid siege to the city, only sixty thousand remained alive. Dogs, cats, and rats were sold for exorbitant prices, but even the supply of this sort of food was soon exhausted. But such was the mad enthusiasm of this remnant of the Christian army that they pushed their way onward, encouraged by dreams and omens, until they conquered Jerusalem, and gained possession of the holy sepulcher.

The second, third, fourth, and fifth, and seventh Crusades were each of them less eventful than the first, as it was impossible to create again such a violent epidemic frenzy. The sixth Crusade, although not taking such a firm hold on the popular mind in Europe as the first, was characterized by the extremest frenzy and fanaticism. In the Spring of the year 1213, an army of thirty thousand boys and girls, mostly from the vicious and neglected children of the cities of France and Germany, was raised by two monks, to undertake the journey to Palestine. The preaching of the monks stirred up the children to such a pitch of excitement, that they ran about the streets, crying: "O Lord Jesus, restore thy cross to us." The movement was looked upon with approval by Pope Innocent III, for he said, when informed of the project: "These children are awake while we sleep." Many of these children perished by shipwreck, some were sold into slavery, and the remainder, being landed at a certain port contrary to the instructions given by the leaders of this wicked plot, were induced to return to their homes. It is believed that the two monks who raised this army of children did it with the design of making money by selling them as slaves.

It is not our purpose here to give a history of the Crusades, but simply to present another illustration of the freaks of epidemic frenzy. Europe expended countless millions of money, and the lives of two millions of her inhabitants, simply to satisfy a fanatical desire to gain possession of the holy sepulcher, which contained not the body of the Lord, and which possessed no more value than any other sepulcher; and, whether the sepulcher which they sought was the one in which the Savior lay, was and is, only a matter of conjecture. The crusaders slaughtered even women and children, plundered and burned defenseless cities, and innumerable multitudes of them committed the most horrible deeds of lust, while braving untold privations and dangers, in order to gain possession of a little bit of almost worthless territory, which had once been trodden by the feet of the Lord Jesus. They acted without reason, and under the impulse of an epidemic frenzy.

Chapter XIII.

MONEY-MAKING DELUSIONS.

JOHN LAW, who was born in Edinburgh, in 1671, was a duelist, gambler, and cultured madman, who, after advocating his financial theories in various countries, became the adviser of the duke of Orleans, after the death of Louis XIV. France, having a national debt of three thousand millions of livres, and an income, after the expenses of the government were paid, of three million livres, was on the verge of bankruptcy. A royal edict was published authorizing Law to establish a bank, the notes of which should be received in payment for taxes. The reputation of Law for marvelous financial ability, which his pamphlets advocating his new and startling theories had given him, together with the indorsement which he had received from the government, at once gave him a firm hold upon the public confidence. The baseless currency which he issued was received by the people without question, and became a medium of exchange between capitalists and laborers, so that in a short time every branch of industry was stimulated to activity, and France enjoyed a season of prosperity greater than she had ever before witnessed.

Increasing prosperity in trade served to increase

the credit of Mr. Law. Though he at this time professed to pay coin in exchange for his bank notes, such was the public faith, that the coin was seldom demanded, and when demanded he could always pay at once from the coin placed in his hands by depositors. Branches of his bank were established in many different parts of France, until he handled nearly all of the currency used by the entire country. But as the credit of his banks depended upon the amount of gold and silver which they were supposed to contain, it became necessary to invent some scheme to convince the people that vast quantities of these precious metals were flowing into them. As Mississippi and Louisiana were popularly supposed to contain great quantities of gold and silver, Mr. Law obtained letters patent, giving him the exclusive privilege of trading with those territories. The capital of the company was divided into two hundred thousand shares, valued at five hundred livres each, to be paid for in the old national notes issued before the establishment of Mr. Law's bank. Mr. Law also gained from the government the exclusive control of the sale of tobacco, and the exclusive right of refining and coining gold and silver. After a while his banks were wholly adopted by the government, and became the Royal Bank of France, which immediately issued fictitious notes to the amount of one thousand millions of livres.

In 1719, Mr. Law's Mississippi Company received the exclusive right of trading with the East Indies, China, and the South Seas; and he promised one hundred and twenty per cent profit annually to all who would purchase shares, at the same time issuing fifty thousand new shares. The people by this time had become frenzied with excitement, and three hundred thousand applications were made for the fifty thousand new shares, Mr. Law's house being surrounded by the excited multitudes from morning till night. The Duke of Orleans saw his opportunity for paying off the national debt, and issued three hundred thousand new shares, at five thousand livres each, which were all taken by the excited throngs. As the epidemic spread, it reached lawyers, statesmen, scholars, and philosophers, their better reason giving way before the blind impulse communicated by the excited multitudes.

The highest officers of state were sometimes kept waiting from morning till night to get an interview with Mr. Law, the throng about him being so great. In the midst of the excitement, Madame de Boucha, while Mr. Law was at dinner, gave the alarm of fire, to call him forth to accept her money for shares of India stock. The price of shares sometimes rose and fell ten or twenty per cent in a few hours, affording a rare opportunity for speculation. Large fortunes were made and lost in a day. The love of gambling bore down before it almost all public and private virtue. Money flowed into France from other countries, being brought by travelers and speculators from foreign countries, who were attracted by curiosity and the love of gain; all houses were crowded, and kitchens and stables were occupied by lodgers.

In the midst of this tide of apparent prosperity, Mr. Law was the object of popular veneration. When he rode abroad in his carriage, so great was the crowd which gathered about him, that an escort of soldiers had to be provided to clear the streets before him. His wealth became so vast that he became possessed of nearly all the valuable lands between the Oise and the Somme. As the tide of prosperity had risen to its greatest height, and was now at a standstill, an additional issue of bank notes was made, to the extent of five hundred millions of livres, and all persons were forbidden to buy jewelry, plate, and precious stones, and to have in their possession more than five hundred livres of coin. The execution of this law stirred up popular resentment and disgust, and awakened a suspicion among the people that Mr. Law was not as sagacious as they had believed him to be. People at once began to question the stories concerning the vast mines of gold which were said to exist in Mississippi and Louisiana. To restore the public faith, the government, by force of authority, sent six thousand of the most worthless of the population of Paris to New Orleans, to work in the gold mines; but this expedient failed to quell the rising distrust. The panic became so great that the doors of the Royal Bank were besieged by an excited throng, as large as ever assembled to buy Mississippi stock, but with far different feelings. At one time, fifteen persons were crushed to death against the doors of the bank, by the press of the excited throng. As Mr. Law's life was endangered, he left the country, and his valuable estates were confiscated by the government. He died in obscurity and poverty, at Venice, in 1729.

While the people of France were being agitated by the wild financial schemes of John Law, a similar delusion began to affect the public mind in England. In the year 1711, Mr. Harley, earl of Oxford, originated the South Sea Company, to which was granted, by act of Parliament, the monopoly of the trade with the South Seas. At this time it was believed that Mexico and Peru and the eastern coast of South America contained inexhaustible mines of gold and silver, and it was believed that the natives of those countries would give in gold and silver fabulous prices for English manufactures. Although, on account of political complications with Spain, the South Sea Company held but little commerce with the South American ports, yet the stock of the company was much sought after by capitalists, and money flowed into their treasury. In 1720 the company proposed to redeem and sink the national debt, which amounted to more than thirty millions of pounds, provided five per cent could be secured to them by the government for a certain number of years. The proposal was accepted by the government. The price of stock in the South Sea Company rapidly increased in value, and a rich harvest was afforded the stock jobbers, who invented the most extravagant rumors for the accomplishment of their purpose. It was asserted that Spain was ready to enter into a treaty by which England would be granted free trade with all the Spanish ports of the

Western World. It was commonly believed that silver would become as plentiful in England as iron, and gold would flow into England in indescribable abundance. It was promised that a hundred pounds invested in the company's stock would bring back one hundred pounds per annum to the stockholder. Exchange Alley, in London, was crowded with stock jobbers. It seemed as if the whole nation was seized with a frenzy for speculation. Here and there, along the streets, might be seen an emissary of the South Sea Company addressing a wondering crowd on the wonderful wealth of the countries bordering upon the South American seas. As a result of these efforts, the company was enabled to sell three and a half millions of additional stock, a part of it at a premium of four hundred per cent.

The great wealth which was being gained by the managers of the South Sea Company inspired other shrewd, but evil, men to start other companies, having similar foundations, and inflated with similar pretensions. When these companies were started, the value of their stocks would fluctuate with the fluctuations of public confidence, affording a rare opportunity for speculation. The few knowing ones would invest their money in the new enterprise, prompted not by their faith in the promises made by the projectors, but by their knowledge of the facility with which the multitude could be duped by plausible pretensions. They bought stock from any new company which arose, knowing that they could sell again at an advanced price, while the less intelligent crowd, not knowing their motive, regarded their purchases as an evidence of the real value of the stocks. One company was started, with a capital of a million pounds, to build wheels for perpetual motion; another was "A company for carrying on an undertaking of great advantage, but nobody to know what it is." The projector required a capital of half a million pounds. Each subscriber depositing ten pounds would be entitled to one hundred pounds per annum from the profits of the company. The projector opened his office at nine o'clock in the morning, and by three o'clock in the afternoon one thousand shares had been subscribed for. That evening he left London with his gain, and was never heard from afterward. Permits to subscribe, at some future time, to a new sail-cloth manufactory sold for sixty guineas in the stock exchange.

The following are samples of the companies represented in the stock exchange during this great epidemic of pecuniary speculation and fraud: A company for supplying London with sea-coal, capital three millions; for effectually settling the island of Blanco and Sal Tarlagus; for furnishing funerals in any part of Great Britain; for a grand dispensary, capital three millions; for improving the art of making soap; for insuring and increasing children's fortunes; for importing walnut trees from Virginia, capital two millions; for improving malt liquors, capital four millions; for insuring to all masters and mistresses the losses they may sustain by servants, capital three millions; for extracting silver from lead. Meanwhile the South Sea Company continued to grow in popular favor until their stock arose to one thousand per cent. In one month thereafter it fell to seven hundred, producing general consternation throughout the country. But in one month more, it fell to one hundred and thirty-five. By this time the whole nation was in despair, and public meetings were held in every town of England praying the government to deal out vengeance upon the managers of the South Sea Company. Parliament appointed committees of investigation, who discovered the frauds of the company involving in guilt many persons of high rank and authority in the British Government, some of whom were sent to the Tower and incarcerated for their crimes. Excepting small sums which some of the culprits were permitted to retain to enable them to begin life again, the ill-gotten gains of the company were confiscated and applied towards repairing the wrongs they had done, but the nation which had been so suddenly admitted to "the fool's paradise of imaginary wealth," and so suddenly ejected, came forth with impaired virtue and enfeebled energy.

When the tulipomania was raging in Europe among the wealthy who vied with each other in the possession of rare specimens of the plant, sometimes paying half their fortunes for a single root, the Dutch were affected by an epidemic frenzy to engage in the tulip trade, which extended to the lowest dregs of society, and caused the ordinary industries of the country to be neglected. The mania was sudden and necessarily of short duration, for in a short time the tulip market was so fully supplied that prices rapidly depreciated. But the deluded speculators were so blinded by the rising excitement that they thought that the demand for tulips would last forever, and that the wealthy from every foreign country would send to Holland to purchase the precious vegetable at fabulous prices. Visions of easily gained wealth floated before the minds of the whole population. As every one wished to purchase tulips in order to grow them, the demand was so far in excess of the supply that the most extravagant prices were paid for them. During the second year of the mania, 1635, a fortune of one hundred thousand florins was frequently paid for forty roots. One variety called the Ever Grand, weighing less than two hundred grains, sold for five thousand five hundred florins. One man possessed a tulip of a species called the Viceroy, which he traded for the following articles: Two lasts of wheat, four lasts of rye, four fat oxen, eight fat swine, twelve fat sheep, two hogsheads of wine, four tons of beer, two tons of butter, one thousand pounds of cheese, a complete bed, one suit of clothes, and a silver cup. Tulip exchanges were established in various cities where tulip jobbers speculated in the fluctuations of the tulip market. A spirit of speculation seized almost the whole population, and nobles and chimney-sweeps alike invested their fortunes in tulips. Real estate was sold at a great discount for cash, to enable the owner to invest his money in the precious roots. The mania extended to other countries, which poured their money into Holland to receive tulips in exchange. But after a few months, the more clear headed began to see that the demand for tulips would soon be met by the ever-increasing supply, and sold their stocks, afterward refusing to buy. A panic began, which soon became epidemic, and those who had invested their fortunes in tulips suddenly awoke to find themselves bankrupt. The nation which had been reveling in imaginary wealth suddenly began to send up a wail of distress.

Chapter XIV.

ALCHEMY.

THE pretended science of alchemy held sway over the minds of men in the most enlightened portions of the globe for more than a thousand years. We find the belief in the transmutation of metals current in Constantinople in the fourth century, many books at that time having been written upon the subject. The alchemists believed that all metals were composed of two elementary substances, one being metallic earth and the other sulphur. The pure union of these two elements constituted gold. The other metals contained these two elements, mixed with various foreign substances, and it was the aim of the alchemist to find a substance which would dissolve these foreign substances, leaving only the two elements of gold to remain. This universal solvent which they sought was called the philosopher's stone. When found, it would transmute all the baser metals to gold, and bestow upon its discoverer untold wealth.

The first great alchemist who gave the delusion greater currency than it had ever had before, was Geber, who lived in the year 730 A. D. His real discoveries caused him to be looked upon with superstitious regard by the people. From him we have the first mention of corrosive sublimate, the red oxide of mercury, nitric acid, and the nitrate of silver.

In the beginning of the tenth century, Alfarabi traveled from country to country in pursuit of the philosopher's stone. He was entertained in the royal courts of the lands he visited, and offers of great wealth were often made him to remain to bless some particular monarch with his presence and possible discoveries; but he steadfastly refused the tempting proffers, believing that far greater things were in store for him.

In 980 A. D., Avicenna was born, whose reputation as a man of learning in the known and the occult sciences was so great that Sultan Magdal Douleth made him grand vizier of his realm. Other lesser lights arose in these centuries, and many in humble stations wore out their lives and wasted their substance in the pursuit of great wealth or physical immortality by means of alchemy.

Thomas Aquinas, who died A. D. 1274, was one of the four great theologians of the Roman Church, the most learned man of his age, and has been looked upon with great respect by Christians of all creeds; but he lived in a day when the belief in magic was deeply rooted in the minds of the people. He was an alchemist, and while he did not discover the philosopher's stone nor the elixir of life, yet it was believed that he could work wonders. It is related of him that he "lodged in a street at Cologne, where he was much annoyed by the incessant clatter made by the horses' hoofs, as they were led through it daily to exercise, by their grooms. He had entreated the latter to select some other spot, where they might not disturb a philosopher; but the grooms turned a deaf ear to all his solicitations. In this emergency, he had recourse to the aid of magic. He constructed a small horse of bronze, upon which he inscribed certain cabalistic characters, and buried it at midnight in the midst of the highway. The next morning, a troop of grooms came riding along, as usual; but the horses, as they arrived at the spot where the magic horse was buried, reared and plunged violently — their nostrils distended with terror, their manes grew erect, and the perspiration ran down their sides in streams. In vain the riders applied the spur; in vain they coaxed or threatened; the animals would not pass the spot. On the following day their success was no better. They were at length compelled to seek another spot for their exercise, and Thomas Aquinas was left in peace."*

Alchemy was accepted with unquestioning faith by all, from the humblest peasant to the king on the throne and to the head of the Roman Church. Pope John XXII was an alchemist; Charles VI was an alchemist, and wrote a book on the subject. King Henry VI granted a patent to certain persons to find out the philosopher's stone and transmute enough of the baser metals into gold to enable him to pay his debts. Some of the German kings, when in straitened financial circumstances, seized the most renowned alchemists and thrust them into prison,

---
*Mackay's Memoirs of Popular Delusions, vol. i, p. 100.

furnishing them with all the chemical materials they asked for, with the intention of keeping them in close confinement until they should discover the philosopher's stone. It was also the prevailing belief, even among the alchemists themselves, that the discovery which baffled them had been often made by others. If a man gained prodigious wealth, popular belief ascribed it to his possession of the philosopher's stone, and his stoutest denial would only confirm the prevailing opinion concerning him, for, as they thought, it would be to his interest to keep secret an art by which the gold he manufactured would become worthless by its very abundance. It was for this reason, that the Parliament of 1404 A. D. declared that any Englishman caught in the act of transmuting the baser metals into gold and silver should be accounted guilty of felony.

Nor was this belief confined to those whose vocations did not lead them to a thorough study of the natural sciences. Roger Bacon firmly believed in the philosopher's stone, and spent much of his time in trying to discover it. He was one of the most learned men of the thirteenth century. He invented the magic-lantern. The burning-glass, the telescope, and gunpowder will carry onward his fame forever. He also wielded a facile pen, and wrote books on alchemy, and the adaptability of the natural elements for producing the philosopher's stone. The poor alchemist—while hunger was gnawing at his vitals, and his children were crying for bread—would bend over his seething cauldron of acids and alkalies and metals, expecting that every next moment he would produce the yellow metal which would bestow upon him and his loved family boundless wealth and all that wealth bestows. His laboratory was kept closely guarded on those occasions when he thought success was nigh, lest another should snatch the secret from him when his wan hand should be ready to grasp it.

In the history of alchemy we find many painful illustrations of the credulity of the human mind, when the thing to be believed is in harmony with man's natural desires. Thomas Aquinas, to whom we have referred, spent much of his time not only in pursuit of the philosopher's stone, but also of the water of life. It was believed that he, in conjunction with his tutor, had found at last some of the essential ingredients of the long-sought elixir, and by means of it, under the proper conjunction of the planets, they animated a brazen statue. They proceeded with their work so far that the animated statue performed the office of a domestic servant; they even endowed it with the faculty of speech, but, through some defect in the elixir, it chattered perpetually, and would not be quieted. They tried in vain to mend it, until one day Thomas was in the midst of a very profound mathematical problem, when he could endure the noise no longer; so, flying into a passion, he siezed a ponderous hammer, and broke the statue in pieces. It was sometimes even thought that these wonderful men had power over nature, so that they could change the seasons, cause flowers to spring up from the ground instantaneously, and command the clouds and storms.

ALCHEMY.

As the philosophers believed and taught that it was possible to find a compound which would confer great longevity or physical immortality, and were often at work in their laboratories trying to produce it, the belief would very naturally arise, ever and anon, that the discovery had actually been made. Some wag, or malicious deceiver, would often pretend to give a recipe for making the much-coveted compound. The following is a recipe given by Arnold de Villeneuve, as published in a work entitled "The History of the Persons who have Lived Several Centuries, and then Grown Young Again," by Longeville Harcourt:

"The person intending so to prolong his life must rub himself well, two or three time a week, with the juice or marrow of cassia (*moelle de la casse*). Every night, upon going to bed, he must put upon his heart a plaster, composed of a certain quantity of Oriental saffron, red rose-leaves, sandalwood, aloes and amber, liquefied in oil of roses and the best white wax. In the morning he must take it off, and inclose it carefully in a leaden box till the next night, when it must be again applied. If he be of a sanguine temperament, he shall take sixteen chickens—if phlegmatic, twenty-five; if melancholy, thirty—which he shall put into a yard where the air and the water are pure; upon these he is to feed, eating one a day, but previously the chickens are to be fattened by a peculiar method, which will impregnate their flesh with the qualities that are to produce longevity in the eater: being deprived of all other nourishment till they are almost dying of hunger, they are to be fed upon broth made of serpents and vinegar, which broth is to be thickened with wheat and bran."*

This item was first brought to light near the year 1500, by one Poirier, who professed to find it in the MS. of the philosopher to whom it is attributed. By taking this regimen, it was believed that youth could be renewed every seven years for a thousand years.

Pietro D'Apone, born A. D. 1250, it was alleged, possessed a powder which would cause gold when paid out by him to come back again to his purse without visible aid. Bolts and bars could not restrain it. Sometimes it would become invisible in the hands of him that received it. For this and similar crimes he was tortured by the Romish Inquisition. He probably played some tricks of legerdemain at times by which he started a reputation which at last became undesirable.

Very often the tricks of the juggler were employed to establish a reputation for the alchemist. By mixing in the presence of witnesses some compound in which gold was secretly placed or held invisible in solution, and then by a process simple enough to the operator, but profoundly mysterious to the bystanders, bringing it forth, the alchemist could suddenly leap forth to a position of prominence and veneration in the villages which he might visit, and by means of his new position perpetrated other frauds, by means of which he gained his livelihood. Many a poor dupe was induced to pay out

---
* Mackay's Memoirs of Popular Delusions, vol. i, p. 103.

the hard earnings of years for some worthless recipe for forming a compound to produce longevity, or for turning the common metals into gold. When the unfortunate dupe discovered the fraud he attributed it to the incapacity and dishonesty of his deceiver, and still retained the prevailing belief that the philosopher's stone and the water of life were really attainable by man.

Nicholas Flamel was born in France in the fourteenth century. He practiced alchemy and became very wealthy, which was falsely attributed to the secret arts of his profession. Charles VI sent a messenger to him to find whether he really had the philosopher's stone, but Flamel would make no reply. His mysterious silence deepened the popular conviction concerning him, and served to extend his reputation. He died in 1415. His brother alchemists, in after years, denied his death and affirmed that he would live yet many centuries, having discovered the water of life. This absurd story was believed by many.

In the sixteenth and seventeenth centuries alchemy took upon itself a new phase in Europe. It was pretended that it would bring man into closer relations with God, banish disease and sorrow from the world; that it would render the spirit world visible to man, and its occupants would be the companions and instructors of our race. This religious phase of alchemy was probably excited by the general influence of the religious reformation of Luther and his coadjutors, which then convulsed the world. The alchemist, in order to gain a hearing was compelled to speak of higher themes than silver and gold, or even physical immortality.

Cornelius Agrippa was an alchemist of wonderful renown. He was born at Cologne in 1486. He made the most extravagant pretensions, which were quite generally believed by his contemporaries. The alchemists of Paris wrote for him to come and live among them, to teach them how to proceed in their calling. He was really a man of learning, as is attested by Erasmus and Melancthon. But they speak from their knowledge of his reputation rather than from their personal observations of the man. He boasted of his marvelous attainments, and exercised sufficient caution not to expose his ignorance. He was made secretary to Emperor Maximilian. We then find him physician to the mother of Francis I. Soon afterward he was invited by Henry VIII and Margaret of Austria to reside in their dominions. Many strange tales are related concerning him, which reveal the boldness of his pretensions and the strange credulity of that day.*

"One day Agrippa left his house at Louvain, and intending to be absent for some time, gave the key of his study to his wife, with strict orders that no one should enter it during his absence. The lady herself, strange as it may appear, had no curiosity to pry into her husband's secrets, and never once thought of entering the forbidden room; but a young student, who had been accommodated with an attic in the philosopher's house, burned with a

---

*Mackay's Memoirs of Popular Delusions. Volume I, page 140.

ALCHEMY.

fierce desire to examine the study, hoping, perchance, that he might purloin some book or implement which would instruct him in the art of transmuting metals. The youth, being handsome, eloquent, and, above all, highly complimentary to the charms of the lady, she was persuaded, without much difficulty, to lend him the key, but gave him strict orders not to remove any thing. The student promised implicit obedience, and entered Agrippa's study. The first object that caught his attention was a large *grimoire*, or book of spells, which lay open on the philosopher's desk. He sat himself down immediately and began to read. At the first word he uttered he fancied he heard a knock at the door. He listened, but all was silent. Thinking that his imagination had deceived him, he read on, when immediately a louder knock was heard, which so terrified him that he started to his feet. He tried to say 'come in,' but his tongue refused its office, and he could not articulate a sound. He fixed his eyes upon the door, which, slowly opening, disclosed a stranger of majestic form, but scowling features, who demanded sternly why he was summoned? 'I did not summon you," said the trembling student. 'You did!' said the stranger, advancing angrily; 'and the demons are not to be invoked in vain.' The student could make no reply; and the demon, enraged that one of the uninitiated should have summoned him out of mere presumption, seized him by the throat and strangled him. When Agrippa returned, a few days afterwards, he found his house beset with devils. Some of them were sitting on the chimney-pots, kicking up their legs in the air; while others were playing at leap-frog at the very edge of the parapet. His study was so filled with them, that he found it difficult to make his way to his desk. When, at last, he had elbowed his way through them, he found his book open, and the student lying dead upon the floor. He saw immediately how the mischief had been done, and, dismissing all the inferior imps, asked the principal demon how he could have been so rash as to kill the young man. The demon replied, that he had been needlessly invoked by an insulting youth, and could do no less than kill him for his presumption. Agrippa reprimanded him severely, and ordered him immediately to reanimate the dead body, and walk about with it in the market-place for the whole of the afternoon. The demon did so; the student revived, and putting his arm through that of his unearthly murderer, walked very lovingly with him in sight of all the people. At sunset the body fell down again cold and lifeless as before, and was carried by the crowd to the hospital, it being the general opinion that he had expired in a fit of apoplexy. His conductor immediately disappeared. When the body was examined marks of strangulation were found on the neck, and prints of the long claws of the demon on various parts of it. These appearances, together with a story, which soon obtained currency, that a companion of the young man had vanished in a cloud of flame and smoke opened people's eyes to the truth. The magistrate of Douvain instituted inquiries, and the re-

ALCHEMY.

sult was that Agrippa was obliged to quit the town."

In Germany at one time, Agrippa exhibited to Lord Surrey, in a glass, the image of his mistress. Paulus Jovius, in his book, entitled "Eulogia Doctorum Virorum," soberly relates that the devil, in the shape of a black dog, followed Agrippa whenever he walked out. He also summoned David and Solomon from the tomb to please Emperor Charles the Fifth. He was a bad man and a willful deceiver. The two victims who disappeared, as the magistrates believed, were murdered by him. The image of the lover was doubtless a painting exhibited in dim light by means of a mirror. The devil in the shape of a black dog, of course, was a dog. As to the methods of exhibiting David and Solomon, we refer the reader to the methods resorted to by spiritualist mediums. It is evident that the emperor could not identify the features of those ancient worthies.

Paracelsus was born near Zurich, in Switzerland, A. D. 1493. His name became one of the most famous in the age in which he lived. He traveled into foreign countries, to visit the mines and laboratories of the philosophers, to find the secret principle of transmutation. After a time he returned to his native Zurich, having found, as he professed, a way to manufacture the water of life. He wrote books upon alchemy and medicine, which at once attracted the attention of Europe. The mystery of his words and the obscurity of his ideas lent a charm to his writings, which made them objects of profound study to all who were interested in the mysteries of his art. In 1526, he was chosen professor of physics and philosophy in the University of Basle, where his lectures were attended by excited crowds. He publicly burnt the writings of the standard authors who had preceded, declaring to the crowd of spectators that there was more knowledge contained in his shoe-strings than in the writings of the venerable quacks who had been the guides of the people hitherto. But the badness of his private life, and his pretense that he was aided by a legion of spirits, which he kept imprisoned in the hilt of his sword; and by a legion of demons, with which he threatened those who affronted him, erelong turned the people against him.

But after his death a sect sprang up called by his name, and spread rapidly in France and Germany. They taught that the magical power of medicines was explained in the Bible, particularly in the Apocalypse. They taught that life was an emanation from the stars, that the moon governs the brain, the sun the heart, the planet Jupiter the liver, Saturn the gall, Mercury the lungs, Mars the bile, and Venus the loins. They taught that a spirit, or demon, dwelt in the stomach, practicing alchemy, in the transmutation of food into the substance of the body. They taught that gold which had been manufactured by the transmutation of the baser metals could cure all disease and produce great longevity; and, perhaps, physical immortality, by being applied under certain conjunctions of the planets.

George Bauer, was born A. D. 1494, and for his able work on the water of life obtained the patronage of the celebrated Maurice duke of Saxony. He was a long time superintendent of the silver mines of Chemnitz, where he searched continually for the philosopher's stone. He taught that fire-damp and explosions in the mines from inflammable gases, were spirit phenomena, being produced by mischievous spirits, which inhabit the bowels of the earth. He left behind him a reputation for being one of the most learned men of his age.

Doctor Dee, born A. D. 1527, was one of the foremost scholars in the days of Queen Elizabeth. He had previously received a pension of one hundred crowns from the court of Edward VI, after which he spent much of his time in London, practicing as an astrologer, telling lucky and unlucky days, and casting nativities by aid of the stars. The search for the philosopher's stone, however, occupied the most of his attention. He was charged with attempting to take the life of Queen Mary by his enchantments, but was acquitted. He was consulted by Queen Elizabeth as to the most lucky day for her coronation. Queen Elizabeth visited him at his own home, and when he was sick she sent her own physician to attend him. He was in constant search for the philosopher's stone, believing that by its aid he could not only transmute all metals into gold and cure all bodily diseases, but be able to converse with spirits and learn all the mysteries of the universe. After a time his imagination became diseased, so that, by intently gazing into a crystal, he thought he saw spirits and conversed with them. In order to succeed in his vision, it was necessary that his whole soul be so absorbed as to be unaware of any thing taking place around it. But, unfortunately, when the angelic visitants had fled, and he had come out of his trance, he could not remember the communications he had received. For this reason he applied to a brother alchemist to act as his secretary, and write down at once the communications he should rehearse while the angel stood before him. Edward Kelly became his assistant, but he was not so much of a dupe as his master. Kelly had lost both of his ears as a penalty for forgery (which fact he usually concealed by wearing a skull-cap), and would write what he chose, as coming from the lips of his entranced employer. Kelly soon, however, began to see wonderful visions of his own. These spirit communications were published, and extensively circulated in Europe. Soon Doctor Dee professed that he had discovered the water of life, and that he would never die. People came in crowds to look upon the wonderful man, and to receive such favors as he would deign to bestow upon them. Being in straitened circumstances at this time, and needing money to carry on his experiments, Queen Elizabeth gave him a donation from her private purse.

By means of a "spirit materialization *séance*," such as we shall fully explain in these pages, Doctor Dee and Kelly so far deceived Count Laski, a

Polander of enormous wealth, whom they met at the court of Queen Elizabeth, that he placed his estates at their disposal, to enable them to manufacture the philosopher's stone. They assured the count, by means of pretended prophecies and spirit communications, that he should be made possessor of boundless wealth, and live for many centuries, during which time he would become king of Poland. They lived upon the bounty of the prince until they had made him well-nigh bankrupt. Next we find them making an obedient dupe of Stephen, king of Poland, who placed a large sum of money at their disposal. Soon afterwards we find them commanding for a time the credulity and the estates of Count Rosenberg, in Bohemia. Kelly soon after this received a communication that he and Doctor Dee should have their wives in common. After a time Doctor Dee consented, but the arrangement led to the final separation of the two men.

Dr. Dee then turned his attention to his former friend and patron, Queen Elizabeth. He sent her a piece of silver and a warming pan, telling her that he had manufactured the silver in the warming pan. He sent her a plate of brass containing a hole of the size of the silver, thus proving that the piece of brass which had been cut from the plate had been transmuted into silver. Queen Elizabeth was so far convinced that she invited the doctor to return to England. He set out for that country attended by a train of coaches and attendants becoming a prince. His life became less eventful after this. He was appointed chancellor of St. Paul's Cathedral, and afterward warden of Manchester College. He died in 1608, in the eighty-first year of his age.

We can only make a brief mention of the many great alchemists who flourished in later times. A Scotchman, named Seton, gained so great notoriety that he was seized by the duke of Saxony, and confined in a dungeon until he should manufacture gold enough to pay a million of money for his ransom. Seton, previous to his confinement, had transmuted the baser metals into gold in the presence of an assemblage of learned men. He used sleight of hand in introducing real gold into his compounds so dextrously that his credulous witnesses could not detect the cheat. From this time onward his fame, which proved so uncomfortable, was established. While in prison he was tortured to compel him to reveal his secret art, but in vain. He escaped from prison, but was so injured by his confinement that he died soon afterward. Sendivogius married the widow of Seton, and transmuted quicksilver into gold in the presence of the Emperor Rudolph II, and so far concealed the fraud that the emperor caused a tablet to be affixed to the wall of the room in which the experiment was performed, commemorating the event. The emperor also conferred upon the cunning trickster a gold medal and an invitation to become one of the members of his court. This dupe and deceiver published several works on alchemy, and died near the middle of the seventeenth century. We know that he could deceive the eyes of his witnesses as to the appearance of gold, for he sometimes passed counterfeit gold coin for real money.

The Rosicrucians were a secret brotherhood of alchemists, which flourished in the seventeenth century in almost all parts of Europe. They threw all the learned men of Paris into commotion. Books were published and placards were exhibited announcing the mysteries and powers of the brotherhood, whose dwelling-place no one knew, and whose members no one had seen. The books were read by every body, and public faith was soon established in the preternatural power of the invisible brotherhood. It was believed that the Rosicrucians could ride on the air, penetrate through bolts and bars, speak all languages, reveal the past, and predict the future. It was believed that they would appear at hotels as real and visible guests, and then melt away into the air without settling their bills. Maidens found them in their beds with them at night, but they became invisible as soon as the alarm was raised. It was believed that some people had found gold in their houses, borne there by the invisible brotherhood. The police of Paris searched in vain to find the whereabouts of the Rosicrucians. The monks affirmed that they were followers of Luther, and that for this reason the devil gave them such wonderful power. The invisible fraternity published books and posted placards to repel these attacks, and further announce their mission. They denied all intercourse with the devil, but said they were aided by sylphs of the air, naiads of the water, gnomes from the bowels of the earth, and salamanders, which dwell in fire, all of which were the friends of man, visiting him in dreams, and guarding him by night and by day. After a time the Rosicrucians became visible, and were occasionally caught enticing pearls and precious stones from other people's pockets into their own, and passing lumps of gilded brass for gold made by the philosopher's stone. After a few of them had been hanged, the sect died out in France.

Dr. Fludd about this time wrote a work in London in defense of the Rosicrucians. His work was of so much importance that it called forth a reply from Kepler. Dr. Fludd affirmed the existence of the philosopher's stone, the water of life, and two principles of all things, the northern and the southern virtues, and that demons presided over each particular disease, and he prescribed the method for their expulsion.

About the middle of the seventeenth century John Heydon, "servant of God and secretary of Nature," also an attorney at Westminster Hall, wrote a book in defense of the Rosicrucians. He affirmed that members of this order could see and hear all things, converse with spirits, and transform themselves into all manner of shapes, control the forces of nature, and transmute all metals into gold. He taught that eating and drinking were unnecessary to man, and quotes the works of a certain traveler to prove that a certain race of men living at the source of the Ganges have no mouths but lived only by the breath of their nostrils. Those of them who

ALCHEMY.

became exhausted fed on the aroma of flowers, while those who had enormous appetites put animal food on the skin and took a little of it by absorbtion. Thus all men might fast for centuries and avoid all diseases which are introduced into the system by food.

Joseph Francis Borri was a physician at Rome, being employed in the pope's household. The wickedness of his private life became notorious. He spent much of his time with debauchees and loose women. He was often arrested by the police for engaging in street quarrels, being drunk and disorderly. But suddenly his aspect was changed. He assumed a solemn and sanctimonious air, and professed to have had some supernatural revelations. He had conversed with spirits, who were aiding him in the discovery of the philosopher's stone. As his followers became numerous he planned a revolt against the civil authorities, which, being discovered, compelled him to flee from the country. We next find him in Amsterdam, living in princely style upon the fortunes of his wealthy dupes, who were aiding him in his experiments for the philosopher's stone. But soon his friends deserted him, and he was reduced to poverty. He then borrowed two hundred thousand florins of a merchant named De Meer to prosecute his experiments in his search for the water of life. He also borrowed six diamonds, on pretense that he could improve their beauty, and with his booty fled to seek the protection of Frederick III, king of Denmark, in whom he found a willing patron. The king furnished him with means for making his experiments, expecting every month to be made possessor of boundless wealth. He continued six years in the court of Frederick, until the death of that monarch in A. D. 1670. Being left without a royal protector he soon found his way to the prisons of Rome, where he died, A. D. 1695.

We then find an alchemist named Helvetius changing metals into gold in the presence of the Prince of Orange. Louis XIII also had in his court an alchemist who professed to have discovered the water of life, and the king believed that he would enjoy his crown a hundred years. Glauber, who invented the salts which now bear his name, was a professional alchemist. In 1726 we find one Aluys transmuting lead into gold in the presence of Duke de Richelieu, in such a manner as to thoroughly convince that intelligent nobleman. But the base impostor was afterward proved to be guilty of coining counterfeit money. Count de St. Germain was a most successful adventurer who flourished in the court of Louis XV. He professed that he had lived on the earth two thousand years, and that he could bestow like longevity upon others. He professed to converse with sylphs and salamanders, and that he could draw diamonds from the earth and pearls from the sea by his wonderful arts.

Louis XV believed the pretensions of St. Germain, and spent much of his time in private consultation with him. All Paris resounded with stories of this wonderful man, and it was after a while believed by many that he was born soon after the deluge, and that he would never die. He was a man of a wide range of information and a fluent talker, and would converse concerning the great personages of the past ages as if he had been intimate in their society. He made a great amount of money for a brief period by selling the water of life to those who aimed to attain physical immortality. The mysterious count had a servant to aid him in his deceptions and to corroborate his stories, who professed to have been in his service five hundred years.

Joseph Balsamo was born at Palermo in the middle of the eighteenth century. In early life he was guilty of forgery and robbery. It was generally believed that he had sold his soul to the devil, and had received in return the power of doing many marvelous things. By the aid of confederates dressed to look like devils, and armed with pitchforks, he robbed a silversmith of sixty ounces of gold, for which he found it necessary to flee into Arabia. Some years afterward he returned to Rome under the assumed name of Count de Cagliostro, and advertised himself as the restorer of the Rosicrucian philosophy. He professed to be able to render himself invisible, to change the metals into gold, and to manufacture the water of life. He made money rapidly by the sale of the latter article, traveling abroad to various cities for the purpose. In Strasburg multitudes flocked to him from the surrounding country to purchase the wonderful liquid. At Bordeaux, in France, the crowd was so great that a military guard had to be stationed before his door to keep order in the eager and excited throng. He also professed to call up the spirits to converse with men. Military officers came to him to talk with the spirits of Alexander and Cæsar, and friends came in great numbers to commune with some congenial occupant of the land of shades.

We have given a brief review of the history of alchemy, which might with interest and profit be expanded into volumes. We have, however, in this cursory glance, beheld enough to cause us to turn away with a sad heart from this additional disclosure of the never ceasing influence of superstition and the black art upon the hopes and fears of a large portion of the human race.

CHAPTER XV.

THE WITCH MANIA.

AN epidemic terror of the supposed power of witches and wizards seized upon Europe, and continued for two centuries and a half. No man felt himself safe from the evil designs of those who might at any moment become his enemy and invoke the malignant powers of the unseen world to do him harm. {When men were smitten with disease, or the storms laid waste their crops or blew down their dwellings, and when they suffered from any unusual calamity they at once attributed their misfortune to the preternatural powers exerted by some person whose insanity or repulsiveness of appearance caused her to be popularly regarded as a witch.} All Europe ran mad upon the subject, and trials of witches and wizards monopolized the attention of the courts of law, so that other classes of criminals were well-nigh forgotten.

In many German cities witches were executed at an average rate of two per day. It was believed that the witch, or wizard, in order to possess his occult power, must renounce his baptism and sell his soul to the devil for time and eternity. It was the popular notion that the devil was ever busy on the earth, not only leading men into sin by injecting into the soul evil thoughts and desires, but perpetually seeking to do men harm in their persons and estates. If a person tripped and fell while walking it was thought that the devil had placed his long, invisible tail in the way before him; if a storm arose or an earthquake occurred, the devil was drunk and out upon a spree, seeking to terrify Christians by disturbing the elements. He appeared among men in many visible forms, sometimes as a drunken loafer at a tavern, paying for his drinks in false coin; sometimes as a drake by the wayside terrifying the belated traveler by a quack which would cause the soul to shudder. He was, withal, a great lover of fun, and was never so happy as when playing off some pranks by which to terrify the upright.

The learned authors who wrote upon this all-absorbing theme, during these two and a half centuries, describe the chieftain of hell with great minuteness, and with equal particularity portray the qualities and functions of the imps which assist him in his work. Besides the devil's chief subordinates, there were millions of inferior demons which swarmed upon the earth's surface. They were male and female, and propagated their species with alarming rapidity. When tossed together in great numbers, they excited whirlwinds. Still-born children, persons killed in duels, women who died in childbed, and wicked men, became demons when they passed into the invisible world. The demons were so numerous that men inhaled them at every breath. They inhabited every part of the human frame, and gave origin to all pains and disorders which plague the human body. They were present in frightful or lustful dreams. They were often transformed into shapes of bewitching loveliness. If Satan appeared in the human form he was always out of proportion, one limb was too short, he was overgrown or dwarfish. His tail was always curled up and concealed beneath his clothing, and by that appendage he could always be detected, if a rigorous examination were made. He sometimes took the form of a tree or some object in nature. Sometimes he looked like a monk, and again he was known to take the shape of a coach-wheel. The demons, concealing their tails, sometimes courted and married young women, and had children by them. Such children were always lean, and cried perpetually.

Sometimes the demon would be as diminutive as an insect. St. Gregory, of Nice, speaks of a nun who forgot to make the sign of the cross before she began to eat her supper, and, in consequence of her sinful neglect, she swallowed a demon who was concealed in the lettuce leaves.

On certain set days Satan and all his imps, together with the witches and wizards, met together in council. These days were called the witches' sabbaths. In Italy and Spain the devil, in the form of a goat, transported the witches through the air to the place of meeting. In England and France the witches rode on broomsticks, always going out through the key-hole and returning through the chimney. Lest the absence of the witch should be noticed by the rest of the family, a demon was delegated to assume her shape and lie in her bed, feigning sickness, until her return. At the place of rendezvous the devil, in the shape of a goat with one face in front and one behind, sat upon his throne. All the witches and wizards were first required to kiss the face which was in the rear, after which their chieftain examined them one by one to see if his secret mark was on them. After this the whole company engaged in a furious dance. Initiates who were there for the first time were required to kiss the devil, swear to give him their soul, and spit upon the Bible. During the sabbath there was a general assembly, in which each related the evil deeds done since the last meeting. Those who could not relate a satisfactory experience were flogged until unable to stand. Thousands of toads sprung out of the earth and danced on hind legs while the devil played on some instrument of music. The toads demanded of the witches flesh of unbaptized babes for food, as a reward for their part in the entertainment. When the devil stamped with his foot the toads vanished. Then followed a banquet of most disgusting articles of food, and after the repast a mock service in imitation of Christian baptism was performed.

Sometimes the devil would require the witches to dance naked before him, each having a cat tied around her neck, and with another cat dangling behind, forming a tail. These convocations always occurred in the night. Pope Gregory IX declared of a certain people, known by the name of Stedinger, that they were witches and wizards; that the devil appeared to them sometimes as a goose, sometimes as a duck, often as a pale, black-eyed youth, whose embraces filled them with hatred against the Church; that they met on the devil's sabbath, when they all kissed him and danced around him. He then enveloped them with darkness, when they all, male and female, gave themselves up to the most shameless debauchery. In consequence of this papal declaration the whole race was exterminated. Women and children were slain, and the buildings in which they dwelt were burned down.

A similar charge was brought against the Templars by Philip IV, when the most heart-sickening scenes ensued. In the suburbs of Paris fifty-nine Templars were burnt in a slow fire. In other parts of Europe they were imprisoned and tortured, and many of them burnt alive.

Pope Innocent VIII, in the year 1448, issued a bull in which he called upon all the European nations to exterminate the growing evil of witchcraft. He recounts the horrors which were threatening the country from this cause: Men and women of both sexes have intercourse with devils, marriage-beds are blighted, children are still-born, and the crops are blighted in the earth. He appointed inquisitors in every country, to convict and punish witches and wizards. These inquisitors would place the alleged witches on the rack and apply to them the most exquisite torture, during which they would ask them if they had attended the witches' sabbath, whether they could bring down the lightning and raise the whirlwind, and whether they had had sexual intercourse with the devil. Sometimes the poor sufferers would answer the questions in the affirmative, as that seemed to be the answer the inquisitor desired, hoping thereby to save their lives; but such answers only confirmed the public faith in the reality of witchcraft, and increased the popular frenzy. Forty-one women were burnt in one province alone, in Italy. Sprenger, a German inquisitor, burnt, on the average, more than five hundred a year; in two years five hundred were burnt in Geneva; in the district of Como, in Spain, during the year 1524, one thousand persons suffered death for witchcraft. Those wives and husbands who wept while the poor victims were burning in the flames were at once accused of witchcraft, and met a similar fate. In a township in Piedmont every family lost at least one of their number, who was burnt alive by the pope's inquisitors. Husbands sometimes swore that their accused wives were asleep in their arms during the night on which it was charged they were riding away, on a broomstick or on the devil's back, to attend the witches' sabbath; but in vain. The husband was informed that the devil was sleeping beside him, having assumed the form of his wife. In the year 1561, five poor women of Verneuil, in France, were burnt for having transformed themselves into the shape of cats. Sometimes the poor sufferers would be induced, under torture, to give the names of other persons whom they had met at the witches' sabbath, and many persons thus implicated were executed. In 1573, Giles Garnier, in Lyons, was burned alive, for turning himself into a wolf and devouring little children. Fifty witnesses testified against him, and, when tortured on the rack, he confessed that he had done what was charged against him.

While James VI, of Scotland, was returning from Denmark, a storm arose, which well-nigh wrecked his ship. Dr. Fian was accused of being the wizard who caused the disaster. Some witches, who had been tortured, confessed that they had met him at the witches' sabbath, and that he had entered into a league with the devil to do harm to the king.

Dr. Fian was put to torture, to cause him to confess his guilt; iron boots were wedged upon his legs until he fainted because of the intensity of pain; his finger-nails were torn out with pincers; needles were thrust into his eyes, but he was still unmoved. The boots were again put on his legs until the blood and marrow spouted forth in great abundance. It was proved at the trial that Dr. Fian had gone to the witches' sabbath with a fleet of witches sailing in sieves, at the time of the king's disaster; he led the witches to a church of North Berwick; he blew into the key-hole with his breath, and the door flew open; he blew a second time, and the candles were lighted, when they all beheld the devil seated in the pulpit. The devil's body was hard as iron, his nose was like the beak of an eagle, and his eyes were like fire. After the devil preached a sermon, he brought a newly buried corpse from the churchyard, upon which they feasted. As a result of these investigations, Dr. Fian and twenty-five other persons were hanged for witchcraft.

It is estimated that from the time that Queen Mary passed her law against witchcraft to the accession of James to the throne of England, seventeen thousand persons in England and Scotland were executed as witches and wizards. To be accused was generally equivalent to condemnation; not more than one person in a hundred who was accused was proved innocent. Aged persons usually have some part of their bodies which is so far paralyzed as to be insensible to pain. Such persons, when discovered, were proved by that fact to have the devil's mark on them, and were executed; or, if they escaped death, the persecution which they experienced from their neighbors was but little better than death. During the Long Parliament, in England, three thousand witches were executed. It is estimated that forty thousand were executed in the first eighty years of the sixteenth century.

King James, in his book on Demonology, recommends that the person suspected of being a witch be thrown into the water, and affirms that the water will not consent to receive the vile creatures who have renounced the water of the baptism. By this test the accused would have a poor chance for life; for if she sank in water she would probably drown before all suspicion of her character was allayed, and if her clothing or the accidental position of her body on the water caused her to float, she was taken out and executed as a witch. The poor victims were wrapped in a blanket and carefully laid on their backs on the surface of the water, and, in consequence of this precaution, they generally floated on the surface long enough to secure their condemnation.

This method was first put into practice by Matthew Hopkins, the famous witch-finder, who traveled through England in the practice of his profession, in the middle of the seventeenth century. Another test was to require the suspected witch to repeat the Lord's Prayer and the Apostles' Creed; if they in their agitation in the face of death missed a word, it was taken as evidence of guilt. If these methods failed to establish the guilt of the accused, pins were thrust into every part of the body to find some spot insensible to pain, and, when found, it was established that they had the devil's private mark on them. The aged were often convicted by means of this test. It was also believed that witches and wizards could not weep, excepting, on rare occasions, they might shed three tears from the left eye. If the poor victims on the rack tried to exercise fortitude enough to endure their suffering and not give way to any momentary weakness, which would lead them to make any concessions that would convict them of guilt, their fortitude was taken as evidence against them.

The witch-finder was supported at public cost, furnished with a carriage and attendants, and received forty shillings for every person he brought to execution. One method employed by the "witch-finder-general" Hopkins, was to place the suspected witch on a stool in the middle of the room, and keep her there without food for twenty-four hours. A hole was made in the door or window to let in the imps who would come in the form of moths or flies, or some other insect, to suck her blood; for imps come in such disguises, and delight to feed upon the blood of witches. It was for this reason that old witches were so thin and wrinkled. If any fly or other insect came into the room and alighted on the victim, and afterwards made its escape, the accused was accounted guilty, and sentenced to be burned.

In 1664, Sir Matthew Hale, the eminent jurist, condemned two women to the stake. They had caused a neighbor to have fits and vomit forty pins, and a two-penny nail, at one time. These pins were forced into the mouths of the bewitched by devils, in the form of bees. The celebrated Sir Thomas Browne, a man of great literary ability, was one of the witnesses in the trial. He stated that witches often did in this manner convey crooked pins and needles and nails into the stomachs of their victims. In 1716, a woman and her little daughter, nine years of age, were hanged for raising a storm, by pulling off their stockings and making a lather of soap. It was not until 1736 that the statute of James I, against witches and wizards was repealed, and the witch-finders' occupation, in England, was gone. In Scotland, in 1718, an old woman, named Nanny Gilbert, who was lying in bed with a broken leg, was thrown into prison for transforming herself into a cat, in which shape she had prowled about in her neighbor's back yard.

THE WITCHCRAFT MANIA. 183

But the witch mania was most terrible in Germany, France, Spain, Switzerland, and Portugal. Cologne for many years burnt three hundred witches annually; the district of Bamberg, four hundred; Nuremberg, Geneva, Paris, Lyons, Toulouse, two hundred each. They were executed for raising storms, blighting crops, causing virgins to bring forth toads, and married women to be sterile, or to be with child three years, instead of nine months; for turning the faces of their enemies upside down, or twisting them round backward; for inserting in the bodies of their victims bits of wood, hair, nails, glass, cloth, egg-shells, pebbles, knives, and hot cinders. Tramps, who could not give an account of their occupation, were burnt as witches and wizards. In Wurtzburg more than fourteen children were burned. One boy confessed that he would willingly sell himself to the devil for good dinners and cakes, and a pony to ride every day of his life. For this he was hanged and burned. Sometimes the hangman was sent into the prison at night, dressed to resemble the devil, and promised to insure the victim safety and happiness if she would dedicate herself to his service. Exasperated by the prospect of torture and death, and influenced by her superstitions, she often thankfully accepted the proffered aid. The hangman afterwards would appear as witness against her.

On the 12th of August, 1669, the king of Sweden appointed commissioners to investigate the witchcraft alleged to exist in the little village of Mohra. The commissioners met in a church in the presence of three thousand people. They soon found malicious persons and excited enthusiasts, who were ready to come forward as witnesses. Several persons had journeyed through the air to attend the devil's convocation at Blockula, where they saw his Satanic majesty as a little old man, dressed in a gray coat, and red and blue stockings. These witches had carried children with them in their aerial flight, as was proved by the testimony of the children themselves, the parents also asserting that the next morning they could see spots on their children, where the devil had beaten them black and blue. They also described, in words too vulgar to repeat, the horrible debaucheries of the witches, which they witnessed. The minister of the parish had been troubled with head ache. One poor witch, under the influence of torture, confessed that she had beaten his head with an invisible hammer; but, owing to the thickness of the skull, was unable to break it. As a result of the investigation, seventy persons were condemned to death, twenty-three being burned in one bonfire. Fifteen children were executed.

We are more familiar with the witch mania as it developed itself among the colonists of New England. A girl, named Goodwin, who had fits and was partially insane, imagined that an old Irish lady had bewitched her. As the excitement spread, other nervous people had hysteric fits, which they attributed to the evil influence of some neighbor, against whom they had an especial abhorrence. These fits were generally accompanied with the peculiar choking sensation, now well known as a symptom of hysteria. The mental disease became epidemic, particularly among the women. Sometimes they fainted, asserting, when they revived, that they had seen specters of witches and devils. They gave the names of the witches they saw in their visions, two hundred of whom were thrown into prison. The victims of their dreams were persons from all ranks of society. Nineteen persons were executed, one of them being a little child, only five years old. They also tried and executed a dog, for being a wizard.

The last execution for witchcraft, in the civilized world, took place in Wurtzburg, Germany, in the year 1749. A number of hysterical young women in a convent in that place felt a sense of suffocation about the throat, and went into fits. They swore they saw a certain young woman climbing over the walls in the shape of a pig, and sometimes in the form of a cat. On this evidence, the young lady who was accused was burnt alive in the market-place.

The witch mania was kept alive by superstition and deception. In those days many mischievous lads dressed themselves in the form of devils, to frighten their neighbors; and, from motives of policy, concealing the deception, the affrighted victim would tell his neighbors, and his children, and children's children of his wonderful encounter. Tricksters, who deceive for fun or gain, always flourish best in an age of credulity and superstition. In this age, devils and ghosts who affright people at the road-side are usually laid up with broken bones; catalepsy is no longer attributed to the magical power of the witch; and educated dreamers and hypochondriacs no longer believe in the reality of their visions. Now when children dream of flying through the air, they are taught to believe that it is only a dream, and are not encouraged to imagine that some neighboring hag has taken them away to hold a convocation with the devil. There is now a return of reason, which enables judges and juries to remember that victims on the rack of torture may be driven to make any confession which will insure relief from immediate agony, or may be driven to temporary insanity, in which they may utter statements which are valueless as testimony.

A better knowledge of mental diseases has taught us to believe that in a popular frenzy weak and excitable persons, either through fear or desire, may believe themselves to be in league with the devil. It is also now well known that fits of hysteria and freaks of excited fancy, under the influence of a popular delusion, may become epidemic. If a man comes forward and confesses that he has transformed himself into a wolf, in which state he has devoured little children, we pronounce him insane; the lack of flesh and the wrinkles of old age are no longer proofs that the imps are sucking the blood. Modern physicians have discovered that needles are sometimes known to come out of the arms and side, and other parts of the body, when they have not been placed there by the enchantments of the witch or wizard. Such an occurrence, at one time, would excite the witch mania in any community;

some old woman would be sure to be the victim, and, under torture, she would implicate many others.

We have given but a hasty sketch of the history of witchcraft in the leading countries of the Christian world; we have passed by many illustrious names of those who have fallen victims to this Moloch of superstition, on whose altars such a person as Joan of Arc was offered as a burnt sacrifice. When we turn from the civilized to the heathen world, we find the spectacle to be still more appalling. Among many of the African tribes, the delusion of witchcraft has become such an epidemic, at different times, that whole districts have been well-nigh depopulated by it.

The logic of the witch maniacs was the same as that which, in more recent times, has been employed by believers in modern spiritualism — the logic of ignorance. Ancient judges would say, when a woman had an attack of hysteria, or had swallowed a needle which was voided through her side or arm: "What has caused it? We do not know. Therefore, it must be produced by a witch." Hon. Robert Dale Owen looked upon a "Katie King" séance, and said: "What has caused it? I do not know. Therefore, it must be a spirit." The savage South African reasons in the same way. The foolish fallacy in the argument is this: We do not know; therefore, we *do* know.

We, of this age of scientific and religious knowledge, can scarcely realize that this great and cruel delusion has so recently plagued mankind; we are surprised to learn that Mrs. Dyer bewitched the teeth of Queen Elizabeth, and made them ache, and that Dr. Fian was tortured for having wrecked the ships of King James, by the aid of a company of witches sailing on the sea in sieves.

Chapter XVI.

HAUNTED HOUSES.

CLOSELY allied to the witch mania is the belief in the existence of haunted houses, a belief which, like the former, has sometimes become epidemic. The belief in the existence of haunted houses may be attributed to the same causes as those which we have already considered, a superstitious dread of the invisible world, an excited imagination, ignorance of the laws of nature, an irrepressible desire in the minds of a large portion of the human race which impels them to seek every favorable opportunity for enjoying sport at the expense of another, and the evil designs of men who have sought to accomplish their ends by alarming the credulous fears of those who have stood in their way.

In the thirteenth century King Louis, who was called the Saint, became the victim of some cunning tricks played by six sanctimonious monks. They desired to gain possession of the palace of Vauvert, which had been built for a royal residence by King Robert, but which was then standing vacant. All at once the house became haunted. Frightful shrieks proceeded from it by night, and blue, red, and green lights glimmered and vanished at the windows. The clanking of chains was heard. In a short time the surrounding neighborhood was filled with superstitious terror, and, as the terror increased, the apparitions within the empty palace became emboldened by the assurance that no one would dare to investigate them too closely. At last a specter appeared every night at a window which looked out upon one of the principal streets. He was clothed in green garments, and had a long white beard and a serpent's tail, and assuming a threatening mien he shook his fists and terrified all who passed by. The king sent commissioners to investigate the matter. The commissioners were received by six monks of St. Bruno, who lived adjacent to the haunted palace, and who gave assurance that the disturbance would cease if the king would give them the palace to be used for a monastery. The king, awed by the power which the monks possessed over the specters, gave his consent and drew up the deed. The disturbances ceased as soon as the monks took possession of the royal mansion of King Robert, and the green ghost was sent to sleep with Pharaoh and his host under the waves of the Red Sea.

In France, in the sixteenth century, if a tenant could prove that the house he lived in was haunted, he would be sustained by the civil courts in defrauding his landlord out of the rent. But the loss of the money due for the past use of his building was not the only loss the landlord sustained, for the evil reputation of the house might cause it to stand empty for many years. As we would naturally expect, at this time, haunted houses multiplied in France.

THE WITCHCRAFT MANIA. 191

In the year 1649, commissioners were sent from the Long Parliament in London to take possession of the royal palace at Woodstock, and efface all the emblems of royalty which it contained. They entered the royal residence and took up their lodgings in what had been the king's apartments, and tore down every picture and motto which might recall the name of Charles, of the house of Stuart. But soon they found that they were not the only midnight dwellers in the royal abode. Strange noises were heard. A spirit dog growled and gnawed their bedclothes, chairs and tables danced by means of invisible hands, plates and dishes were hurled about the room, logs of wood were mysteriously placed on their beds, bricks fell down the chimney, and demons ran off with their breeches. At one time a shower of stones, bricks, mortar, and broken glass fell about their heads while they were sleeping. Sounds were heard like the footsteps of a great bear, the jaw-bone of a horse was thrown upon the table, the fire was extinguished by water poured down the chimney, candles and lamps were blown out. Some nights the commissioners were so terrified that they spent the whole night in prayer and singing psalms, but at last, their courage giving way, they fled to London to repeat their marvelous stories to the members of Parliament. The matter remained a profound mystery until the restoration of the monarchy, when it became known that one of the commissioners, Giles Sharp, was all the while a royalst at heart, and by the aid of confederates had produced this protracted and wonderful *séance*.

He had spent his early life in Woodstock, and knew every room and trap-door and secret passage of the royal palace.

The demon of Tedworth, as portrayed by Rev. Joseph Glanvil, in his book entitled, "Sadducismus Triumphatus," gained great notoriety in 1661, and and has since been quoted by believers in modern spiritualism to add probability to the genuineness of the manifestations through spirit mediums. The house of Mr. Mompesson was disturbed by knockings on the outside of the doors and walls by night. The sounds seemed, after a time, to travel about the house in a mysterious manner. Sometimes he heard a thumping on the roof; again, the demon would beat the bedsteads of the children with great violence, even playing tunes. A board was seen to move mysteriously in the day-time, in the presence of many witnesses. Chairs moved and objects were hurled about the room one evening when the minister was present to pray with the family, hoping that his prayers would terrify the demon and cause him to depart. A blacksmith came one night to sleep with the footman, but during the night a pair of pincers was continually snapping at the blacksmith's nose, and other mysterious sounds were heard. At one time the room was filled with a noisome odor, and the room seemed hot, though it was Winter and the room was without fire. As the fame of these wonderful proceedings extended, the king sent a committee to investigate them, but the cautious demon would do nothing in their presence. One night seven or eight devils in human form

THE WITCHCRAFT MANIA. 193

entered the house, but were frightened away by firing off a gun. These devils regarded bullets as unhealthful.

We are to remember also, that the house of Mr. Mompesson contained several servants who doubtless possessed a good degree of human nature; that Mr. Mompesson had caused the arrest and imprisonment of a member of a band of gypsies, who were intensely enraged at him on that account; that the disturbance ceased as soon as the gypsy was transported beyond the sea and his associates had no farther hope of his release; that these manifestations began again as soon as the gypsy returned from transportation; that the gypsy professed to be the cause of the disturbance, and that the excited imagination would naturally add to the manifestations which the enraged trickster really produced.

In 1772 Mrs. Golding, an old lady residing alone in London, with her servant, Anne Robinson, was terrified by a commotion among her crockery. Pots and pans were hurled down stairs, hams and loaves of bread would leap about the floor, and cups and saucers fell down the chimney. Chairs and tables moved mysteriously. Some neighbors came in to witness the phenomena, but fled in alarm. The old lady moved into another house, taking her servant with her, but the same manifestations continued. All London was excited over the affair, and the scene of these singular freaks became widely celebrated. The servant girl was after a time dismissed from service, and confessed to Rev. Mr. Brayfield that she was the cause of the disturbance.

She placed the china on the shelves so that they would fall on the slightest jarring motion. She attached horse-hairs to other articles, so that she could jerk them down from their places without being perceived. Black thread would answer the same purpose, being likewise invisible in the lamplight at a little distance. She also had a confederate in her lover.

A farm-house in Baldarroch, Scotland, was haunted in the year 1838, and so great was the excitement it produced that hundreds of people came to witness the wonderful antics of the invisibles. Sticks and pebbles flew about the back yard, hurled by invisible hands; cups, knives, spoons, and other articles would leap about the room and come rattling down the chimney. The lid of a mustard-pot was put into the cupboard by the servant girl in the presence of scores of witnesses, and presently it came down the chimney. The most wonderful stories were told, and the whole country was in a state of alarm, so that nervous people felt strange sensations when they came into the bewitched atmosphere of the place. At last the trick was discovered. Two servant girls were shown to have hurled the articles about, to have loosened the bricks which fell down the chimney, to have placed the dishes in such a position that the slightest jarring would cause them to fall. By means of dark threads, and other method ssuch as they could devise, they had produced some results which seemed really marvelous, while they invented and gave currency to stories which were false, but readily believed by the family and neighbors after the excitement was begun. The girls were convicted by a process of law for their mischief, and as soon as they were sent away to prison the phenomena at the haunted house of Baldarroch ceased. At an earlier day such an occurrence would have caused perhaps a score of suspected witches to be burned alive. In our day it would only prove to some poor, deluded spiritualists the reality of spirit intercourse, and cause them to renounce the ancient revelations of prophets and apostles for the new.

The believers in haunted houses were guided by the common logic of ignorance: "What is it? We do not know. Therefore, it is a demon." Professor Crookes, F. R. S., and Professor Wallace, F. R. S., witness a "Katie King" séance, and say: "What is it? We do not know. Therefore, it is psychic force." The spiritualist reasons in the same way, and concludes that it is a spirit.

Chapter XVII.

ANIMAL MAGNETISM.

CLOSELY allied with modern spiritualism is the delusion believed in and practiced by the animal magnetizers. The doctrine of spirit communication does not follow from it as a logical sequence, but spiritualists seldom follow logical sequences. The dreams and theories of spiritualists, however, contain much of animal magnetism. It is to them the connecting link between mind and matter, and the subtle force by which mind may influence mind. And with the credulity characteristic of that class of visionaries, they assume that if minds in the body may exert upon others this subtle power, minds out of the body can do likewise.

At a time when alchemy began to fall into disrepute, this new delusion, based upon the power of the excited imagination, arose to take its place, and the chief apostles of the new faith were furnished from among the alchemists, whose "occupation was gone." It appeared under the name of mineral, and, subsequently, of animal magnetism, under which name it still survives.

The mineral magnetizers performed their cures and produced their effects by means of the natural magnet, and, sometimes, by certain rare stones, until Mesmer arose, and gave the delusion a new form.* "Kircher, the Jesuit, whose quarrel with the alchemists was the means of exposing many of their impostures, was a firm believer in the efficacy of the magnet. Having been applied to by a patient afflicted with hernia, he directed the man to swallow a small magnet reduced to powder, while he applied at the same time to the external swelling, a poultice made of filings of iron. He expected that by this means the magnet, when it got to the corresponding place inside, would draw in the iron, and with it the tumor; which would thus, he said, be safely and expeditiously reduced. As this new doctrine of magnetism spread, it was found that wounds inflicted with any metallic substance could be cured by the magnet. In process of time, the delusion so increased, that it was deemed sufficient to magnetize a sword, to cure any hurt which that sword might have inflicted." After a while the sword was magnetized with the hand. If the sword was stroked upward with the fingers, the wounded person would be immediately relieved of his sufferings; but, if the sword was stroked downward, he would at once begin to groan with the most excruciating pain.

The notion then arose that a sympathetic alphabet could be traced on the arms of two persons, though thousands of miles apart. A piece of flesh was to be cut from one arm of each of the two persons, and the flesh taken from each was to be caused to grow into the arm of the other. After

---

* Mackay's Memoirs of Popular Delusions, vol. i, page 264.

which, the absent piece of flesh would feel every sensation experienced by the arm from which it had been taken. Thus, if one of the men would trace letters on his naked arm, the arm of the other would feel the sensation, and thus communication could be established between them. Upon the transplanted pieces of flesh letters of the alphabet were to be tattooed, and, whichever letter one of the persons pricked, the sensation of pain would be felt in the corresponding letter on the arm of the other.

Quacks arose in great numbers, professing to cure diseases by the laying on of hands, and by the application of the magnet. Sometimes the impostor was so surrounded by infatuated dupes as to block up the street of the city near his residence. The theory of animal magnetism developed itself naturally from these preceding delusions. In 1774, Mesmer reduced the doctrine of animal magnetism to a system, and promulgated it to the world. He wrote out his theories and sent them to the learned societies, but they uniformly failed to indorse them. At this time his residence was in Vienna.

"Mesmer did not find his residence at Vienna as agreeable as he wished. His pretensions were viewed with contempt or indifference, and the case of Mademoiselle Œsterline brought him less fame than notoriety. He determined to change his sphere of action, and traveled into Swabia and Switzerland. In the latter country he met the celebrated Father Gassner, who, like Valentine Greatraks, amused himself by casting out devils and healing the sick, by merely laying hands upon them. At his approach, delicate girls fell into convulsions, and hypochondriacs fancied themselves cured; his house was daily besieged by the lame, the blind, and the hysteric. Mesmer at once acknowledged the efficacy of his cures, and declared that they were the obvious result of his own newly discovered power of magnetism. A few of the Father's patients were forthwith subjected to the manipulations of Mesmer, and the same symptoms were induced. He then tried his hand upon some paupers in the hospitals of Berne and Zurich, and succeeded—according to his own account, but no other person's—in curing an opthalmia and a gutta serena. With memorials of these achievements, he returned to Vienna, in the hope of silencing his enemies, or at least forcing them to respect his newly acquired reputation, and to examine his system more attentively.

"His second appearance in that capital was not more auspicious than the first. He undertook to cure a Mademoiselle Paradis, who was quite blind as well as subject to convulsions. He magnetized her several times, and then declared that she was cured; at least, if she was not, it was her fault, and not his. An eminent oculist of that day, named Barth, went to visit her, and declared that she was as blind as ever; while her family said she was as much subject to convulsions as before. Mesmer persisted that she was cured."*

In 1784, a royal committee of the Faculty of Medicine, together with a committee from the Acad-

---
* Mackay's Memoirs, vol. 1, p. 277.

emy of Sciences, in Paris, were appointed to investigate the phenomena of mesmerism, and report upon them. Benjamin Franklin was among the number. But, so far as can be learned, Mesmer failed to meet that honorable body, though formally invited to be with them. Other mesmeric operators were present, and a large number of subjects for treatment. One of the members of the joint commission wrote out the following report:

"The sick persons, arranged in great numbers and in several rows around the *baquet*, receive the magnetism by all these means: by the iron rods which convey it to them from the *baquet*; by the cords wound round their bodies; by the connection of the thumb, which conveys to them the magnetism of their neighbors; and by the sounds of a piano-forte, or of an agreeable voice, diffusing the magnetism in the air. The patients were also directly magnetized by means of the finger and wand of the magnetizer, moved slowly before their faces, above or behind their heads, and on the diseased parts, always observing the direction of the holes. The magnetizer acts by fixing his eyes on them; but, above all, they are magnetized by the application of his hands and the pressure of his fingers on the hypochondres and on the regions of the abdomen; an application often continued for a long time—sometimes for several hours.

"Meanwhile the patients, in their different conditions, present a very varied picture: some are calm, tranquil, and experience no effect; others cough, spit, feel slight pains, local or general heat, and have sweats; others are agitated and tormented with convulsions. These convulsions are remarkable in regard to the number affected with them—to their duration and force; as soon as one begins to be convulsed several others are affected. The commissioners have observed some of these convulsions last more than three hours; they are accompanied with expectorations of a muddy viscous water, brought away by violent efforts; sometimes streaks of blood have been observed in this fluid. These convulsions are characterized by the precipitous, involuntary motion of all the limbs, and of the whole body; by the contraction of the throat; by the leaping motions of the hypochondria and the epigastrium; by the dimness and wandering of the eyes; by piercing shrieks, tears, sobbing, and immoderate laughter. They are preceded or followed by a state of languor or reverie, a kind of depression, and sometimes drowsiness. The smallest sudden noise occasions a shuddering; and it was remarked that the change of measure in the airs played on the piano-forte had a great influence on the patients; a quicker motion, a livelier melody, agitated them more, and renewed the vivacity of their convulsions.

"Nothing is more astonishing than the spectacle of these convulsions; one who has not seen them can form no idea of them. The spectator is as much astonished at the profound repose of one portion of the patients as at the agitation of the rest—at the various accidents which are repeated, and at the sympathies which are exhibited."*

---
* Mackay's Memoirs, vol. 1, p. 284.

These performances were not free from scandal. Operators of bad character engaged in the work, to manipulate the infatuated females so as to gratify their evil passions. The operators were allowed the utmost liberty in handling the bodies of their patients, who were mostly females, very few males being found among them. The learned commission, after long and patient investigation, came to the conclusion that the only proof of the existence of animal magnetism was the effects produced upon those who believed themselves magnetized; that passes or other manipulations were not necessary to produce those effects; that all these passes and manipulations produced no effect if performed without the knowledge of the patient; and, therefore, that the manifestations were all produced by the excited imaginations of the patients.

This investigation well-nigh put an end to mesmerism; but some of the evil seeds which Mesmer had sown were scattered abroad, and took root among the fanatics of other countries. Some operators, becoming weary of manipulating their patients one by one, when they became very numerous, magnetized pieces of wood and other substances, from which the patients were required to take the mysterious fluid second-hand. One of the most celebrated of them, M. de Puysegur, magnetized a tree on the village green, from which, by means of ropes, a whole multitude could receive the magnetic current simultaneously. At one time, he led a patient to the magnetized tree, and joined him to it by means of a rope, when the patient exclaimed, with an air of astonishment: "What is it that I see there?" His head sank down, and he fell into a trance.

A Doctor Perkins, of London, again revived the idea that magnetized steel would cure diseases. He cured many persons whose maladies were of such a nature as to be affected by the imagination, and his fame spread rapidly. He took out a patent for his magnetized plates, or "Tractors," and they were eagerly sought for among the people at five guineas each. But Dr. Hygarth, of Bath, manufactured some "Tractors" of wood, and painted them so as to look like steel, and being of the same form as those invented by Dr. Perkins, he supplied the credulous invalids with them, and the same results continued; whereupon Dr. Hygarth published a book entitled "Imagination as a Cause and Cure of Disorders, Exemplified by Fictitious Tractors." The result was, that magnetism was made the subject of so much ridicule that it disappeared from England for a time.

The history of magnetism, or mesmerism, in this country has been largely involved with that of modern spiritualism. As we state elsewhere, Andrew Jackson Davis began his career as a mesmeric and clairvoyant doctor. Among the first persons who mesmerized him was an old gentleman of our acquaintance, J. Stanley Grimes, author of a book entitled "Mysteries of Human Nature." At that time Prof. Grimes was a believer in and a practitioner of the mesmeric passes. He was traveling about the country, lecturing on the subject and performing public experiments. At one time he had a number of persons before him seated in a row on a bench, and holding to a rope with eyes shut and minds empty, with wills submissive and in a credulous state, according to his instructions. But before he had proceeded further, a message was brought to him which he was required to answer. He went aside and wrote a letter, and when he returned, to his astonishment he found the usual proportion of his subjects were in what was called the mesmeric state. Who put them into that state? Not he, for he had made no passes, and had exerted no silent will-power on them. He concluded that they had put themselves into that condition. Afterward he performed the experiment without making passes, and not only not willing that his subjects should go into that condition, but silently willing with all his might that they should not be acted upon at all. But the result was the same as before. He therefore was confirmed in his conclusion that the sensitive subjects were put into the mesmeric state by the power of their own imagination. He found by experiment that his silent will could not control the mesmerized or entranced subject when in that state. His words or manner, or the attendant circumstances, must create the expectancy in the mind of the sensitive subject as to what results would follow, and the somnambulist simply carried on the half-waking dream which was suggested to him. The mesmerized subject simply becomes entranced.

The idea that the mesmerist or clairvoyant can be put into mysterious sympathy with an absent person by touching a lock of his hair or some garment he has worn, is a survival of a superstition which often arises spontaneously in the lowest stages of culture. In Australia the native doctor attaches a string to the diseased part of the patient's body, and sucks the other end of the string, believing that he draws through the string, from the diseased part, some invisible substance which, when extracted, will cure the disease. In Orissa it is believed that the witch puts herself in communication with her victims by means of a thread, through which she sends her invisible power. The sick Ostyak holds in his hand a cord which is attached to an animal, which is slain for his recovery. Perhaps it is thought the vitality of the expiring animal flows through the cord into the body of the sick man. The Buddhist priests, by means of threads, put themselves in connection with a sacred relic. In ancient times the Ephesians joined their walls to the temple of Artemis, seven miles distant to gain the help of that deity in resisting the attack of Crœsus.

As we turn to Baron Reichenbach's book entitled "Dynamics of Magnetism," we find this superstition elevated to the dignity of a science. Baron Reichenbach's experiments have been indorsed by some of the more superstitious Fellows of the Royal Society in England, and have been the texts from which the more intelligent spiritualists of the United States have elaborated their so-called scientific basis of modern spiritualism. He is the founder of the idea of od or odylic force, since named psychic force by Prof. Crookes, F. R. S., and Prof. Wallace, F. R. S. He began his experiments in 1844.

We will first state the conclusions the baron arrived at by his experiments, and then point out the method of his self-deception. He held a magnet before certain sick and sensitive women, who saw luminous appearances about the magnet in the dark. And by various modifications of the experiment he concludes (page 37): "It follows from this that the magnetic flame is either wholly material or has such for its substratum; further, that the magnetic light is something different from it, and the magnetic flame is a compound, in which some kind of materiality is united with the immaterial essence of the light." This magnetic light is the mysterious something which is named odylic force. Dr. Ashburner, the English translator of the book, remarks, in a foot-note attached to this passage, that persons have seen a gray or blue light emanating from his hand, and persons whom he has put into mesmeric sleep have seen blue light issuing in copious streams from his eyes when he has concentrated his thoughts. This light, he believes, issues from the brain of the mesmerizer and enters into the mesmerized, becoming in the brain of the latter a motive power which he obeys. He professes that he had caused this light to issue from his brain and travel seventy-two miles, producing immediate effect. He affirms that he sat in one room and willed the light from his brain into a pint bottle in another room, and then poured the mysterious and invisible contents on the head of a patient, who went into a mesmeric sleep.

Baron Reichenbach, after long experiment discovers that this mysterious force resides in his hand. He then immediately discovers that this force can be conducted from his hand through wires into the "sensitive" or hysterical woman. He next discovers (page 115) that the mysterious force may be conducted through all substances; that there are no non-conductors. He has now arrived at the old notion entertained by the Australian savage, that invisible forces may be conducted through a string. He finally discovers (page 157) that this occult force can travel quite a long distance without a conductor, and effect the sensitive subject.

On page 173 he states that all substances give out odylic force. His magnets, crystals, and his hand have not a monopoly of these mysterious emanations. On page 185 he discovers that this force, like electricity, is positive and negative, and that one side of his body is cold and the other warm to the "sensitive" Miss Reichel, and hence positive and negative. On page 234 he discovers that odylic rays may be felt at a distance of a hundred yards. This odylic force is represented by spiritualists as the vehicle of thought. Dr. Ashburner declares, in a foot-note, that by the aid of odylic light the sensitive subject can read through solid bodies, and the volitions and thoughts of one man can be conveyed into another man a great distance away.

The experiments of Baron Reichenbach afforded a theoretical basis for modern spiritualism, though, as may be easily shown and as we shall show hereafter, the theory of odylic force, if true, would enable embodied human spirits to produce all the alleged phenomena of modern spiritualism without the aid of disembodied spirits. But how was Baron Reichenbach self-deceived? He overlooked the well-known laws of the excited imagination. He performed his experiments upon "sensitive" women. He preferred cataleptic subjects. On page 157 he remarks: "Catalepsy itself is, therefore, a condition which exalts, in a disproportionate degree, the sensitiveness of the patient to certain unknown qualities of matter; and matter possesses some hidden quality, by means of which it affects the cataleptic peculiarly in an exalted degree, even at a distance, in a manner analogous to that in which it affects patients in the awakened condition, free from the catalepsy by actual contact." It is well known that cataleptic subjects are often subject to hallucinations of the senses, and are very liable to have a diseased imagination.

Miss Reichel, with whom he made most of his experiments, and patients like her, whom he declared to be of extraordinary value for such investigations, was twenty-nine years old. When seven years old she fell from the second-story window to the ground, and, in consequence, had always been subject to nervous attacks, which were often violently spasmodic. She was a subject of somnambulism, talking and walking in her sleep. The other "sensitives" were also subject to fits. With these girls the baron performed his experiments. He wanted to discover some occult forces about a horseshoe magnet which were invisible to ordinary eyes. He held the magnet before the girls when their fits had just passed away, and they were in the highest possible state of nervous excitement. They saw what their fancy, governed by the words dropped by the baron, caused them to expect that they would see—flames issuing from the magnet. When other substances were substituted they still saw what they expected to see—the mysterious flame, as before. Then the baron desired to know whether this force would affect the nerves of these peculiarly nervous girls. He put the magnet in contact with their hands, and they clutched it convulsively and felt sensations. The expectancy of receiving sensations in the hands and arms from the objects presented was created in the mind of each girl, and when asked if she did not feel the same sensations when the magnet was joined to her hand by a wire, she answered in the affirmative. And in this manner the baron proceeded, step by step, evolving his theory, and unwittingly manufacturing his proofs as he proceeded, by creating certain definite expectations in the already diseased imaginations of the girls upon whom he was performing his experiments.

We have seen entranced people controlled by an operator whose words, by creating a certain state of expectancy in his subjects, would cause them to see and hear in their somnambulistic visions whatsoever he desired. He asked them if they saw a river, and they at once beheld it. He asked them if they saw spirit mosquitoes, and they saw them and soon were bitten by them. If the baron had asked Miss Reichel if she saw snakes, and his manner and bearing had led her to believe that she should see them, she would have beheld them. Upham's "Mental Philosophy" contains an account of a soldier who was in the habit of walking in his sleep, and whom his companions would cause to dream and do whatsoever they desired. The dream of the semiconscious somnambule may be controlled either by creating in his mind, before going into that state, an expectancy of what the vision is to be, or by words and acts of the operator while the experiment is going on, the operator thus intentionally or unintentionally determining the result.

CHAPTER XVIII.

MORMONISM.

DOCTOR M'INTYRE, who practiced medicine in the neighborhood in which Joseph Smith resided with his parents, states that Joseph's father was a loafer, and that his house was "a perfect harem."* Joseph and his father belonged to a company of money-diggers, pretending to find where money had been hidden by looking into a hat in which a white stone had been deposited. Joseph used to get drunk, and after a debauch, being badly bruised by one named Stafford, for stealing sugar, he sent for Doctor M'Intyre, telling him that he had been pounded by the devil. After he became a Mormon apostle, his character was not improved. In Kirtland, Ohio, he engaged in a fraudulent banking scheme, for which, and other offenses, he was tarred and feathered by the inhabitants of the village. In Nauvoo he led a mob against a brother Mormon who opposed polygamy, which resulted in his death.

At the time when he professed to discover the book of Mormon, a belief was prevalent that the American Indians were the descendants of the ten lost tribes of Israel, and this prevalent belief was

---

* Human Nature, by J. S. Grimes, page 360.

the chief cause of his subsequent success; for the superstitious would not think it to be unreasonable that divine revelations should have been continued to this lost and wandering portion of His chosen people; and they would further conclude, that if such revelations had been given, it would be probable that divine Providence would not permit them to be finally lost. Accordingly, Joseph Smith professed to receive a special revelation, informing of the place where the golden plates containing this ancient inspiration, together with a pair of spectacles by which the mysterious writing on them might be read, were deposited in the earth. He kept the plates carefully concealed from profane eyes, only three chosen witnesses being permitted to behold them. Several years afterwards, however, these witnesses, Oliver Cowdery, David Whitmer, and Martin Harris, withdrew their testimony, and exposed the fraud. Smith's neighbors also testified that he had made contradictory statements concerning the golden plates.

It was fully established after the "Book of Mormon" was published, that its real author was Solomon Spaulding, who was graduated at Dartmouth College in 1785, and, after preaching three or four years, engaged in secular business till he died, in 1816. In 1810–12 he wrote a romance, in which he described the peopling of America by the ten lost tribes of Israel. In 1813 it was announced in the newspapers that the book was about to be published, and that it would contain a translation of the "Book of Mormon." Mr. Spaulding's widow, on May 18, 1839, published a statement in the *Boston Journal*,* asserting that she placed the manuscript, written by her husband, in a printing office in Pittsburg, and that Sidney Rigdon, who was connected with the office, copied the manuscript, and frequently spoke of possessing the copy. Mrs. Spaulding asserted that the printed Mormon bible was the work which had been written by her deceased husband; and she had ample opportunity for knowing their identity, as her husband was accustomed to entertain his friends by reading from his manuscript. After Sidney Rigdon gained possession of a copy of Mr. Spaulding's manuscript he left the printing office and began to preach and lecture, uttering the doctrines which were afterwards published in the Mormon bible. He became associated with Joseph Smith in 1829, after which time the Mormon bible was published to the world.

Mr. Harris, one of the three witnesses, showed a copy of a portion of the characters alleged to be on the golden plates, to Professor Anthon, of New York, who found them to be a mixture of crosses and flourishes with Greek, Hebrew, and Roman, just such as an ignorant and cunning person would produce with a book before him, containing various alphabets.

Rigdon and Smith then began to preach, using the "Mormon bible," instead of the Christian Scriptures. Converts were made, so that within one year after Smith and Rigdon united their fortunes, a Mormon Church was established in Manchester, New

---

* The American Cyclopædia.

York. Guided, as he professed, by divine revelations, Smith led his followers the following year to Kirtland, Ohio, where he claimed he would establish the New Jerusalem. At this place many converts were made, and their number was increased by many accessions from abroad, the cause of Mormonism receiving strong re-enforcement in the persons of Brigham Young, Orson Hyde, and Heber C. Kimball. From this place the first Mormon missionaries were sent to Europe. But Smith and Rigdon, in 1838, to avoid arrests for frauds in business transactions, fled in the night and escaped to Missouri.

The Mormons were charged by the Gentile inhabitants with murder, theft, and other crimes, and were driven by mobs from place to place, many Mormons and Gentiles being killed in the contests, until they arrived at a place in Missouri called Far West, where they were joined by Smith and Rigdon. Soon afterwards Thomas B. Marsh and Orson Hyde quarreled with Smith, and made oath before a justice of the peace in Ray County, Missouri, that the Mormons had organized a company of Danites, who aimed to conquer the world by bloodshed. At this time, also, several Mormon leaders apostatized, and accused Smith of gross crimes. Soon afterwards the Mormons were again involved in conflict with the Gentile population, and the State militia was called out to quell the disturbance. The Mormons surrendered and promised to leave the State. Smith was arrested and charged with murder, treason, and felony, and sent to prison.

MORMONISM.

The Mormons then established themselves on a large tract of land, in Hancock County, Illinois, which was presented to them by Doctor Isaac Galland, and were soon joined by Smith, who had broken out of jail. He soon received a "revelation," directing him to build a city to be called Nauvoo, and by dividing the land into lots and selling it to his followers at high prices, he gained possession of a large private fortune. The Mormons built a temple and a home for the "prophet," and soon the city grew, until it contained several thousand inhabitants. A military organization was formed, with Smith as lieutenant-general.

Smith having persuaded several women to cohabit with him, to quell the jealousy of his wife, received, July 12, 1843, a pretended revelation authorizing him to practice polygamy. The establishment of polygamy was opposed by the virtuous men and women of the community, and a paper was established in Nauvoo to lead the opposition. Smith, heading a mob, demolished the printing office, and the editor and publisher fleeing to the county seat obtained warrants for the arrest of Smith and seventeen others. The constable who came to make the arrests was driven from Nauvoo, and the county authorities called out the militia to enforce the law. The Mormons armed themselves and prepared for war, but finally, through the intercession of the governor of the State, Smith and his associates were persuaded to submit to arrest and trial. While the prisoners were in jail at the county-seat a mob of outraged citizens fired through the windows of the jail and killed Hyrum Smith. Joseph, attempting to escape through a window, was shot dead.

Rigdon, who was the real author of Mormonism, naturally aspired to be the successor of Joseph Smith, and being offended at the elevation of Brigham Young to that office, he was delivered over to the devil to be tormented "a thousand years." At last the Mormons were driven out of Nauvoo at the point of the bayonet. In 1848 the Mormons, under the leadership of Brigham Young, began to found Salt Lake City, in Utah. Salt Lake City in 1875 contained a population of about twenty thousand, of whom about two-thirds were Mormons. The city contains a Mormon temple estimated to cost ten million dollars when completed; also a Mormon tabernacle, capable of seating fifteen thousand persons. Polygamy has become an established feature of Mormonism. The order of the Danites would still carry on their bloody work were it not for their fear of the authority of the civil government.

Among their superstitions is a belief that Mormon leaders become gods in the spirit world, ever rising higher in authority and power. They also teach that women escape condemnation in the future life by having been "sealed" to a Mormon husband in this world. It is not our purpose to present a full history of the crimes and superstitions of Mormonism, but to bring it forth as one of the many epidemic delusions which have plagued mankind.

Chapter XIX.

THE ORIGIN OF MODERN SPIRITUALISM.

THE movement known as modern spiritualism began not far from the celebrated Mormon Hill, where Joseph Smith professed to find the golden plates containing a history of the ten lost tribes of Israel. The wonderful success of this impostor emboldened the Fox girls and their coadjutors to try a similar experiment upon the credulity of the public.

Before the Fox girls began their exhibitions, the essential idea of modern spiritualism had become a subject of public discussion, by means of the alleged spirit communications through the mediumship of Andrew Jackson Davis. He had been put into the so-called mesmeric state by Professor J. S. Grimes, in Poughkeepsie, New York, and his powers being thus disclosed he was afterward subjected to the manifestations of a tailor named Levington. After going several times into a trance under Mr. Levington's directions, Davis fancied that he could see through the back of his head. As the excitement grew, Levington saw a way to earn money more easily than by plying his needle, and began giving medical prescriptions through the young clairvoyant, who had become subject to his control. As the reputation of the spirit doctor grew, his overseer took him abroad to prey upon the credulous of other cities. Soon after this we find Davis under the control of one Dr. Lyons.

Professor J. Stanley Grimes, who had spent some years in the study of the phenomena of mesmerism, had made the discovery that when he put persons into the "mesmeric" state he could convey ideas and facts to them which they could be made to repeat without knowing the source from whence they had obtained them. The experiment had been publicly performed by Professor Grimes in the cities where the manipulators of Davis resided. While lecturing in Poughkeepsie Professor Grimes took one Potter with him into a private room in a hotel, and after causing him to become entranced, said to him: "I am the spirit of Spurzheim, and will teach you to lecture on the anatomy of the brain." He then repeated to him a number of times some learned words and statements concerning the anatomy of the brain, and brought him back to full consciousness. That evening Professor Grimes again "mesmerized" Mr. Potter in the presence of the audience and said to him: "Now you are a wise man; the spirit of Spurzheim will speak through you." And immediately the uneducated man began to repeat the learned words and statements concerning the anatomy of the brain, which he had previously heard, much to the astonishment of his acquaintances in the audience. This experiment had been publicly performed and explained both at Poughkeepsie and Bridgeport where the manipulators of Davis resided.* Dr. Lyons, therefore, knew how to convey medical knowledge to Davis in such a manner that Davis would think he received it from the spirits, and could cause the uneducated young man to astonish his neighbors by his learned utterances when entranced. Mr. Potter, who had been thus operated upon by Professor Grimes, declared that he had received his knowledge of the anatomy of the brain from the spirit of Spurzheim. And Davis was thus subjected to the manipulations of Dr. Lyons, who mesmerized him twice a day, for several months, before the pretended revelations began.

Davis's acquaintance with Dr. Lyons came about as follows: While Levington and Davis were traveling in Connecticut, at Bridgeport they formed the acquaintance of S. B. Brittain, who afterward became editor of the *Spiritual Telegraph*, a vile free-love sheet. Living with Brittain there was an "irregular" doctor named Lyons. At this time "Doctor" Davis was aided by some medical knowledge, as Lyons became one of the firm, sharing the profits of the business. Levington was magnetizer, Davis the magnetized, and Lyons the apothecary. But soon Lyons turned magnetizer too, and poor Levington went home chap-fallen, uttering bitter complaints against Lyons and Brittain. When Davis became subject to Lyons he was then told of his great mission as one inspired. Lyons boasted that he would prepare a book from Davis's lips which

---

*Mysteries of Human Nature, by J. S. Grimes, Professor of Medical Jurisprudence in Castleton Medical College, page 357.

would take the place of the Bible, and that fifty thousand dollars would be immediately realized from its sale. The copyright of the book was secured to Lyons and Fishbough. But Davis's trance utterances were ungrammatical and full of blunders. He was then young, and not the extensive reader he has since become. So Mr. Fishbough, who also had become a party to the deception, was employed to rewrite these revelations. But Davis was induced to assign all pecuniary profits from the book to Fishbough and Lyons. When Davis rehearsed his lessons in the presence of a few chosen witnesses, Lyons repeated them to be sure they were correct, and Fishbough wrote them down and revised them for the press.

What is called the mesmeric state is really the trance state. The will of the operator does not control the subject, but his voice and previous conversation can give direction to the half-waking dream of the somnambulist. Davis, though perhaps at first a dupe, was not always free from the charge of deliberate fraud. Professor Grimes related in our hearing, in a lecture, the following incident: Davis was lecturing in Cleveland, Ohio, and in the midst of it he gave an extract from an unfinished manuscript of Professor Mahan, in New York City, professing to read the writing from that distance by his clairvoyant powers, and assuring the audience that soon the manuscript would be published, and requesting the audience to remember and identify the extract he had just given. A gentleman arose in the audience, and taking a paper from his pocket, read the extract aloud. It was already in print, and the conviction forced itself upon the audience that Davis had seen and memorized the passage. Thus the idea of spirit communications was in the air.

Soon an idea struck some mischievous young girls in Hydesville, New York. Mrs. Fox was the mother of three daughters. One was married to a Mr. Fish and lived in Rochester. Two were living at home unmarried. They caused an excitement by producing raps and attributing them to spirits. One of the unmarried sisters, having now become quite notorious, came to live with her married sister in Rochester, who soon was also initiated into the secret art. These girls began their tricks in sport, but soon found them a source of revenue and fame. The relatives of the Fox girls were most ready to denounce their frauds. Mrs. Culver, after having duplicated and explained in public the tricks of the Fox girls, made the following affidavit:

"I am, by marriage, a connection of the Fox girls; their brother married my husband's sister. The girls have been a great deal at my house, and for about two years I was a very sincere believer in the rappings; but some things I saw when I was visiting the girls at Rochester made me suspect that they were deceiving. I resolved to satisfy myself in some way; and some time afterward I made a proposition to Catherine to assist her in producing the manifestations.

"I had a cousin visiting me from Michigan, who was going to consult the spirits, and I told

Catherine that, if they intended to go to Detroit, it would be a great thing for them to convince him; I also told her that if I could do any thing to help her, I would do it cheerfully—that I would probably be able to answer all the questions he would ask, and I would do it, if she would show me how to make the raps. She said that, as Margaretta was absent, she wanted somebody to help her, and that, if I would become a medium, she would explain it all to me. She said that, when my cousin consulted the spirits, I must sit next to her, and touch her arm when the right letter was called. I did so, and was able to answer nearly all the questions correctly. After I had helped her in this way a few times, she revealed to me the secret. The raps are produced with the toes. All the toes are used. After nearly a week's practice, with Catherine showing me how, I could produce them perfectly, myself. At first it was very hard work to do it. Catherine told me to warm my feet, or put them in warm water, and it would then be easier work to rap; she said that she sometimes had to warm her feet three or four times in the course of an evening. I found, that heating my feet did enable me to rap a great deal easier. I have sometimes produced a hundred and fifty raps in succession. I can rap with all the toes on both feet—it is most difficult to rap with the great toe.

"Catherine told me how to manage to answer the questions. She said it was generally easy enough to answer right, if the one who asked the questions called the alphabet. She said the reason why they asked people to write down several names on paper, and then point to them till the spirit rapped at the right one, was to give them a chance to watch the countenance and motions of the person; and that, in that way, they could nearly always guess right. She also explained how they held down and moved tables. [Mrs. Culver gave us some illustrations of the tricks.] She told me that all I should have to do to make the raps heard on the table, would be, to put my foot on the bottom of the table when I rapped, and then, when I wished to make the raps sound distinct on the wall, I must make them louder and direct my own eyes earnestly to the spot where I wished them to be heard. She said if I could put my foot against the bottom of the door, the raps would be heard on the top of the door. Catherine told me that when the committee held their ankles, in Rochester, the Dutch servant girl rapped with her knuckles, under the floor, from the cellar. The girl was instructed to rap whenever she heard their voices calling the spirits. Catherine also showed me how they made the sounds of sawing and planing boards. [The whole trick was explained to us.] When I was at Rochester, last January, Margaretta told me that, when people insisted on seeing her feet and toes, she could produce a few raps with her knee and ankle.

"Elizabeth Fish (Mrs. Fish's daughter), who now lives with her father, was the first one who produced these raps. She accidentally discovered the way to make them, by playing with her toes against the foot-board, while in bed. Catherine told me, that the reason why Elizabeth went away West to live with her father was because she was too conscientious to become a medium. The whole secret was revealed to me, with the understanding that I should practice as a medium when the girls were away. Catherine said that, whenever I practiced, I had better have my little girl at the table with me, and make folks believe that she was the medium, for she said that they would not suspect so young a child of any tricks. After I had obtained the whole secret, I plainly told Catherine that my only object was to find out how the tricks were done, and that I should never go any further in this imposition. She was very much frightened, and said she believed that I meant to tell of it, and expose them; and if I did, she would swear it was a lie. She was so nervous and excited that I had to sleep with her that night. When she was instructing me how to be a medium, she told me how frightened they used to get in New York, for fear somebody would detect them; and gave me the whole history of all the tricks they played upon the people there. She said that once Margaretta spoke aloud, and the whole party believed it was a spirit.

"Mrs. Norman Culver."

"We hereby certify, that Mrs. Culver is one of the most reputable and intelligent ladies in the town of Arcadia. We were present when she made the disclosures contained in the above paper; we had heard the same from her before, and we cheerfully bear testimony, that there can not be the slightest doubt of the truth of the whole statement.

"C. G. Pomeroy, M. D.
"Rev. D. S. Chase."

The Fox girls soon traveled among the larger cities, exhibiting their powers and attracting large crowds, and making a great deal of money. They exhibited in New York City, but were soon caught in their deceptions and exposed.*

Mr. C. C. Burr also soon traveled abroad, lecturing and duplicating in public the feats of the Fox girls, and explaining how they were performed. Mr. Burr prepared himself for his work by forming the personal acquaintance of the leading mediums. He declared them not only tricksters, but otherwise immoral as a class.

Professor Lee, of Buffalo, exposed the tricks of the Fox girls, at about this time. This exposé was so thorough and damaging that the Fox girls refused to submit to like examinations ever afterward. Professor Page, at Washington, caught them in the midst of their deception, at that place, and so reported to the public. Exposers multiplied more rapidly than mediums, and soon the rapping mediums were out of date.

---

* Grimes's Mysteries of Human Nature, p. 374.

Chapter XX.

MEDIUMS EXPOSED.

THE "manifestations" since the day of the Fox girls have been changed, to meet the exigencies of the times; but exposures have ever kept pace with the progress of mediumship. We give below some of the exposures, the most of which occurred within a period of two years. These may be taken as specimens of what could have been gathered from any equal period in the history of modern spiritualism. Many of these exposures were reported in the *Religio-Philosophical Journal*, one of the chief organs of modern spiritualism. The paper is published in Chicago, and is the rival of the *Banner of Light*, published in Boston. At the time when these extracts were taken from it, the paper was opposing nearly every phase of physical mediumship, and advocating a close adhesion to mental phenomena. It was for this reason that the exposures of mediums published in the newspapers of the country found their way into its columns.

In 1876, Mrs. Anna Stewart was one of the leading mediums of the West. Her performances were wonderful in the extreme; no ropes could be so tied as to prevent her, or some invisible power, performing wonders within the charmed circle; scarfs and neckties of persons near her were snatched away and afterward returned to their owners; spirits would appear and vanish; the body of the medium became dematerialized, and all trace of it lost for a time in the imponderable elements; the fragrance of flowers was distilled from the atmosphere; and spirits also spoke to their friends in whispers. She was performing her wonders in her rooms in Terre Haute, Ind., and winning converts, and astonishing every body, until—February 6, 1876—Dr. Higgins, filling his hand with lamp-black, shook hands with her familiar spirit, when, on examination, the lampblack was found on the hand of Mrs. Stewart. This exposure was published in the *Religio-Philosophical Journal*, of March, 24, 1877, in the Chicago *Times* and many other papers. The Terre Haute *Gazette*, of January 25, 1876, contained the names of ten spiritualists who denounced the medium and acknowledged the thoroughness of the exposure.

Mrs. Hardy, of Boston, is said to have made $30,000 by her wonderful mediumistic powers. The *Religio-Philosophical Journal*, March 11, 1876, remarks, concerning the statements given below:

"Such test conditions as these are well calculated to confound skeptics." The Boston *Herald* says:

"Mrs. Hardy—being much beset alike by incredulous materialists and doubting spiritualists, to give a molding séance, under 'test conditions'—appeared at Paine Hall, enveloped in a sack, and sat upon the platform, before a large number of spectators, with a view to producing the mold of a spirit hand under circumstances which would preclude the editors of the *Investigator* and the *Spiritual Scientist* from alleging that she 'did it with her feet.' In about twenty minutes from the time the screen was drawn around the table under which stood the pail of water and paraffine, the invisible chemists signified to the medium that their work was completed, and when the table was removed there lay, by the side of the vessel, a perfect waxen mold of a human hand. The sack, enveloping the medium to the neck, was carefully examined by a committee before and after the sitting, and found to be intact, and the infidel member of the committee publicly confessed his inability to suggest any possible human mode of accomplishing the result achieved.

"The séance was introduced by Mr. John Hardy, the husband of the medium, by a well-written and compact history of the origin and growth of the materializing phenomena attending the mediumship of Mrs. Hardy, and cogently claiming for them — whether spiritual or otherwise — the earnest attention of scientific chemists.

"Mr. Seaver and another gentleman in the hall wanted Mrs. Hardy to also inclose the paraffine and water in a bag or screen; but, for reasons best known to the medium and those conversant with the subtle conditions of mediumship, this was declined, although an experimental séance — under the direction of Dr. Gardner, that morning, at the house of the medium — where the water and paraffine were locked within an inclosure of wood and wire, resulted, as usual, in the production of a mold, which was found floating in the water. It is due to the medium to say that this double test, or the interposition of the wire screen, largely added to the draft upon her vitality; but it fully assured Dr. Gardner, if the assurance were needed, that the production of the mold was the unmistakable result of supersensual forces, and gave him confidence to assert in Paine Hall last evening that this was the beginning of a series of experiments which would astonish the world. He even promised Mr. Seaver the pleasure of soon witnessing a spirit in full form standing upon the platform of his materialistic temple. Mr. Seaver said that was just what he wanted to see. *Nous verrons.*"

But even this cunning trickster and her confederate could not carry on their work forever undetected. The *Religio-Philosophical Journal*, of April 15, 1876, contains the following statements: "Doctor Hall, in the dim light, saw under the table at which the medium sat, *toes* instead of spirit fingers, and that a lady who sat nearest Mrs. Hardy saw her dress and handkerchief in motion at every presentation of the spirit hand. Two other ladies, Mrs. and Miss Lane, at one time saw the fingers of a paraffine mold protruding from under her dress. One lady, at another time, stealthily looking under the table, saw Mrs. Hardy's foot manipulating a bell, which she professed the spirits were ringing. At one time, when she was causing the spirits to write on a slate, furnishing their own pencil, she was seen to lift her hand to her hair, and then move her hand in the act of writing. One lady, lifting the cover unexpectedly, saw Mrs. Hardy's hand on the slate. Some persons weighed (without the medium's knowledge) the paraffine, used as it was before the *séance*, and as it was afterward, and found the weight to be the same. The molded paraffine had not been taken from it, as the spectators had been made to believe. A lady also discovered, after the performance, that Mrs. Hardy's stockings on the bottom of the foot, about two inches from the toe, were cut across and left open. It was to enable her to make her foot bare when she slipped off her slippers under the table." This article in the *Religio-Philosophical Journal*, was signed by the names of seven persons. The *Religio-Philosophical Journal*, of May 30, 1876, contains an affidavit, sworn before S. G. Hyatt, commissioner of deeds, New York City; to the effect that Mrs. Harvey was seen taking from her satchel a model of a hand, such as she exhibited in her *séances*, and placing it in a pocket under her underskirt. Other affidavits equally damaging occur in the same paper of the same date.

The *Religio-Philosophical Journal*, of March 18, 1876, contains an announcement of the exposure of a hitherto successful medium, named Jacobs, who performed the ring test. After his hands were handcuffed together by a committee, the spirits would place a solid iron ring around his arm. The same paper, of August 19th of the same year, announces that the medium has been sent to the penitentiary for crime.

The *Portland Press*, Aug. 29, 1876, contains an account of the exposure of Mrs. R. J. Hull, which occurred in Portland, Maine. The medium, when exposed, confessed her frauds. A certain Doctor Greene seized the spirit by the hand, and held on to it until he discovered it to be the hand of the medium.

The *Religio-Philosophical Journal*, July 15, 1876, contains wonderful accounts of the mediumship of W. F. Peck. Spirit faces and hands appear at the window of his cabinet, and some enthusiastic persons recognized the faces as those of dead friends. Spirit lights appear. Guitars float in the air and discourse sweet music. Spirits speak through trumpets provided for them, and the editor of the *Religio-Philosophical Journal* himself convinced, congratulates his friends on the western coast for having such a marvelous medium among them. But alas for all human hopes, his paper of the following October 7th, contains the news that the wonderful medium was traveling about the country exposing himself, performing his tests, and then exhibiting to the audience how they were done! The same paper, of September 16, 1876, notes the exposure of a wonderful Kentucky medium, by the name of Church. When his breeches' legs were sewed to the carpet, to secure him to the satisfaction of the audience, spirits would play on instruments of music. A light was struck, and the medium was found minus breeches (having stepped out of them), playing on instruments himself.

In the issue of January 15, 1876, the *Religio-Philosophical Journal*, contains an account of a "splendid medium," named William B. Little, and details his marvelous feats accomplished by the aid of spirits, which were fully equal to any thing done by any modern mediums. But the same paper, of the following September 2d, gives an account of his exposure and imprisonment for obtaining money under false pretense. Some one lifted the curtain, not at the appointed time, and Little was found unloosed from his fastenings, and doing what he professed the spirits were to do. His confederate, A. C. Barnes, a prominent spiritualist, was arrested at the same time. There are sixteen names attached to the article in the *Religio-Philosophical Journal* which described his exposure. We learn from the same paper shortly afterward, that Mr. Little was traveling in the rôle of an exposer of mediums. At the exposure above referred to Mr. Little was caught exhibiting his own face at the cabinet window as the face of a spirit. As is customary, the light was kept dim to aid the imagination.

To show what the excited imagination may do, we insert a letter taken from the *Religio-Philosophical Journal*, of a date previous to the *exposé*.

COPY OF A LETTER FROM E. SWEETING TO JAMES COWLEY.

De Witt, *July* 25, 1876.

Dear Sir,—I received your letter a long time ago, and delayed answering until now. We have had Mr. William B. Little here for a few days, holding *séances*, and bringing back to our view the faces and forms of loved ones that have crossed the dark river of death. I saw some of my friends as plain as I ever saw them in life, and many other persons recognized their friends also. It was a grand sight for mortal eyes to behold, and I think it furnishes a long lost or broken link between this and the future world; at least it strengthens my belief in a future existence, to which we can look forward with hopes of better days to come, where pain and sorrow are unknown. So we will wait with patience for the dawning of the morning when we shall see as we are seen, and know as we are known. I remain yours truly,

E. SWEETING.

The *Religio-Philosophical Journal,* of May 2, 1876, contains nearly two columns which describe the "wonderful manifestations through the mediumship of Mr. C. B. Cutler," taken from the Denver *News.* We insert the article, as it gives the reader a good idea of the feats of a superior American juggler:

"As was noticed by the *News* a day or two since, Charlie Cutler, the medium, is again at home, after an absence of three or four months in the East, during which time he has been giving *séances,* very successfully, through several of the Middle and Southern States. The history of Mr. Cutler is too familiar with Denverites generally to render any reference to it, at this time, necessary. Some time last Winter the *News* gave an extended report of what transpired at one of his *séances,* in which were described some very wonderful and truly astonishing occurrences; but at two or three *séances* held since his return far more wonderful and strange occurrences have taken place, wonders which surpass the comprehension of man, and which, we think, will baffle all the scientific acumen of the present age to explain.

"The purpose of this article will be simply to relate truthfully just what occurred in the presence of reliable witnesses, and leave the reader to analyze the occurrences and judge for themselves of their significance and import.

"The first *séance* was held on last Sunday evening, at the house of Mr. Arthur W. Cheesewright, in West Denver, at which there were present Mr. Cutler's mother and sister, a few invited friends, and a reporter, in all twelve or fourteen persons. The cabinet used upon this occasion was simply an ordinary clothes closet, four feet square and nine feet high, with the shelves removed, and in the top of which was securely fastened a staple and ring. In the upper part of the door was cut an aperture, fifteen by eighteen inches, over which hung loosely a dark cambric curtain, resting on a shelf that was fastened to the door just under the lower edge of the aperture. An ordinary kitchen chair was then placed inside, upon which the medium took his seat, his hands, feet, and arms being very securely and intricately bound thereto. A couple of medium-sized dinner bells, some blank paper, and a pencil were then placed within and the door was closed. A verse or two of a familiar song was then sung, when, in about two or three minutes, a voice, in the coarse, guttural dialect of an Indian, speaking broken English, said, 'Look in.' On opening the door of the closet the medium was found entranced, but out of the ropes, every knot and loop remaining intact, and just as they had been placed upon him. The door was again closed, and in a very few minutes the medium was bound again, but tied in a very different and more complex manner. Immediately after this the following written communication was thrust out through the aperture in the door, addressed to the reporter: 'Examine the medium thoroughly, we are going to give you a good test. Watch it close." The medium was again examined, and found tied just as before. In a very short time the voice above referred to said, 'Look in quick.' On instantly opening the door a scene was presented which might be described as a mock representation of the infliction of the legally prescribed death penalty, which the quadruple murderer, Gallotti, has just escaped. In short, the medium was found *hanging by the neck*, with his head drawn well up to the ring in the top of the closet, and his feet eighteen inches from the floor. The noose and knot around his neck were made precisely the same as those used by officers of the law in executions, and designated as the 'hangman's knot.' The medium was 'cut down,' placed in the chair, and retied very securely, but the door was scarcely closed before hands and arms were displayed at the aperture. Arms were thrust out as far up as the elbow and held stationary for five or six seconds, while simultaneously the bells were rung with a force and accuracy of time rarely witnessed under the manipulations of the most artistic of professional bell-ringers.

At this juncture in the proceedings a written communication was received by the reporter, as follows:

"'Select your own circle—not to exceed twelve in number—and come on next Wednesday evening, and we will give you a test *séance*, and allow you to shoot at the materialized hands and faces.'

"Accordingly, on last Wednesday evening, the 3d instant, a party, consisting of six gentlemen of indisputable integrity and three ladies, assembled at an early hour at the dwelling of Mr. Cheesewright, and at once proceeded with the closest scrutiny to examine the floors, walls, and ceiling of the closet above described. This closet was found to be without any possible means of ingress or egress, except through the door opening into the lighted room, where the party remained throughout the *séance*. Every thing being in readiness, the medium was placed in a strong wooden chair, and his hands tied together by a most complex knot, both ends of the cord being passed downward on each side toward the lower rung of the chair, around which they were carefully and doubly knotted; thence taken to the corresponding rung at the back of the chair, and again securely knotted; thence passed under and around the medium's arms, crossed in a knot upon his chest, and taken over the back of the chair, about which they were again carefully knotted; thence taken to the lower cross brace of the rear legs of the chair, where they terminated in an extremely multiplex knot. In this position the medium was placed inside the closet, and in exactly one minute and thirty seconds, on examination, he was found sitting in a 'trance' outside of and entirely free from the ropes, which, however, were found tied in the identical manner as when they involved the medium. The tying was done by a well-known surgeon of this city, who consumed ten minutes in doing it, and made, as he asserts, regular surgical knots. The door being closed but a moment, the medium was found again securely tied in a very different manner, and so intricately that it took three of the gentlemen present, with good light, seven minutes to untie him. The door being once more closed, in exactly three minutes and forty-five seconds he was found hanging with a 'hangman's loop and knot' about his neck, as described in the foregoing account of the first séance. His hands were securely bound in a most intricate and painfully close knot behind his back. His feet were six or seven inches from the floor, and his legs closely wrapped from the feet to above the knee. In this position he was suspended, with his head three feet from the beam and ring that supported the rope he was hanging by. He was 'cut down,' and the noose and knot can be seen at the *News* office.

"A breech-loading rifle was mounted on a frame at the side of the room occupied by the party, about ten feet from the closet, and carefully ranged so that a ball from it would pass through the vertical center of the aperture, within six inches of its lower edge. Boards were also nailed to the rear wall of the closet to receive the bullets that might be discharged from the rifle, and to prove the range in any given shot. The medium was then carefully examined, and found to have nothing upon his person except his ordinary clothing. He was then tied in the manner before described and placed in the cabinet, the door of which was not yet fastened before hands were thrust through the aperture in plain sight of all. A message was then written by one of these hands, in plain view, as follows: 'Load the rifle and prepare to shoot at the word fire!' The first shot was laughed at by the 'control,' who said: 'You shoot too high; lower your gun, and shoot whenever you see a hand.' Several hands were shown for the purpose, and one was distinctly seen to bear the mark of the bullet after the rifle was discharged. Instructions were then received to fire at faces that might be shown, and to make this test as perfect as possible, the rifle was so ranged that every subsequent shot passed through the aperture within three inches of the lower edge. Altogether eleven shots were fired at as many hands and faces, and at least three or four of these shots were seen by all to penetrate the objects at which they were aimed. They would flutter tremulously for an instant after the shot and then dissolve.

"At the close of the cabinet *séance*, and before the medium was released, he and the cabinet, or closet, were sufficiently examined by all to re-assure the witnesses that he had in no way been aided by mortal confederates or appliances. The boards in the rear of the cabinet are still in the same position, and can be examined by any and all who wish; skilled mechanics, with ax, hammer, or any other tools, are at liberty to detect, if they can, any secret trap, springs, or other means of perpetrating fraud or practicing deception.

"The doors and windows of the room in which the party sat were securely fastened and sealed, and a dark circle was held, the medium being seated between two of the investigators, and forming part of the circle; bright lights rose from floors or descended from ceilings, there being at times half a dozen or more of them moving irregularly overhead and around the circle. Two large dinner-bells, a guitar, and several articles of clothing were carried about overhead, the bells ringing their loudest, and the guitar thrumming in loud and discordant notes as it passed about the ceiling; hands innumerable, and of varied temperature and sizes, touched in ways that suggested the rollicking and familiar, as well as the caress of affection; voices were heard in different parts of the room, one of the party being addressed by three different voices, each giving the full name of deceased friends whom he had known years ago, in the East, and none of whom, he believes, were ever known to any body in Denver outside his own household. A number of others received similar tests of equal significance.

"The most remarkable and incomprehensible of the many occurrences related in connection with Mr. Cutler's mediumship occurred one evening, at the residence of his mother, 282 Curtis Street, in the presence of about fifteen ladies and gentlemen, including a *News* reporter. The house occupied by Mrs. Cutler is an ordinary five-room frame cottage, and faces the north. The front door opens into the parlor, on the left of which is a small room, entered by a door from the parlor; this little room is lighted by one window, its walls and ceiling being well plastered, flooring sound and unbroken, and there is no possible means of egress from it except through the window, fronting on the street, or through the door connecting it with the parlor. The three or four gentlemen in the party were invited to prepare this little room — in which were a bureau, a trunk, and a bed—for use as a cabinet; and, after thoroughly inspecting it and finding it as before described, they secured the window, and, by means of pins and tacks, fastened a heavy bed-comfort over the entire length, so as to render escape through it without detection impossible, as well as to render it perfectly dark.

"The door opening into the room was filled in the upper half by a temporary frame, in which was a small aperture, and below the frame was loosely hung a heavy bed-quilt. Mr. Cutler, the medium, was then placed in a chair, and his hands tied behind him in such a manner as to suggest pain; the ropes being passed through the back of the chair to the lower cross-brace, around which they were wrapped, and double knotted; thence separately taken to the front legs of the chair and wrapped about the medium's legs so as to secure each to its corresponding chair-leg by quadruple knots. Another rope was then passed around the medium's neck and passed through the back of the chair to the lower cross-braces, around each of which it was knotted, with equal care. The medium was then placed in the darkened room, which was, however, again examined with a light, and found intact, as before explained. The circle joined hands in the parlor, which was well lighted, and in less than three minutes from the time the medium was placed in the dark room, a stunning crash was heard in the dining-room, in the south-west corner of the house—between which and the dark room there intervened two solidly plastered walls—where the medium was found, in a trance, lying prostrate on the floor.

"An immediate inspection of the room where he had been placed disclosed not the least change of any thing: the window was secured precisely as it had been, and the ropes which had bound and involved the medium were found with knots and wraps intact, and precisely as they were tied, excepting only that they did not involve a human body."

In the *Religio-Philosophical Journal* of January 26, 1876, we learn that Mr. Cutler is to be regarded as one of the best and most wonderful mediums of the day; but the same paper, on the 4th of the following October, copied the following, from the *Salt Lake* (Utah) *Tribune:*

"Having seen the great harm that other 'mediums,' as well as myself, are doing to the minds of scores of people, I have determined to come before the public and acknowledge that I have been deceiving them. I shall show all who wish to know, just how I have done all these tricks. I will, next

Saturday evening, at Liberal Institute, give an *exposé* of many of the famous tests of so-called 'mediums.' I will also expose the following tests: I will allow a committee of six reliable citizens to tie me as they please, and I will loosen myself before them in less time than any medium can; I will also tie myself, will allow a solid iron ring to be riveted upon my neck, and I will take the ring off without removing the rivets; I will do Mrs. Compton's celebrated stock test; I will remove handcuffs, materialize hands and faces, and have a form walk out of the cabinet, while I am supposed to be securely bound to my chair; I will allow myself to be ironed to the floor of the cabinet, and will free myself without breaking a chain; I will expose materialization through a table, also slate-writing, and several other tests done by 'mediums.' I guarantee to duplicate any trick any 'medium' can do, after witnessing it twice.

"CHARLES B. CUTLER, 'Medium.'"

Mr. Cutler was, it is probable, being too closely watched by skeptical committeemen to proceed further in the *rôle* of a medium; or he was smitten by his conscience, and therefore went about the country exposing and explaining his own performances.

The *Religio-Philosophical Journal*, having committed itself, for the time, to the idea of reproducing in its columns the exposures of all mediums, as they should occur, is called upon to record the misfortune of one of its best friends — Mrs. Parry — whom, one week before, it had characterized as one of the best public speakers in the ranks of modern spiritualism. The issue of January 27, 1876, contains an article taken from the Rockford, Michigan, *Weekly Register*, giving an account of her frauds as a medium. Ten names are signed to the account of her exposure, and the *Journal* editor pronounces her a fraud. She was—as nearly all mediums are—a free-lover.

The *Religio-Philosophical Journal* of January 22, 1876, contains accounts of the wonderful mediumship of H. Mott; but July 1st, of the same year, it gives an account of his exposure, which was so thorough that he voluntarily gave back to the audience the money he had received from them at the door. An enthusiastic believer, however, exhibits to us the wonderful power of the excited imagination by stating, in the *Banner of Light*, December 9, 1876, that in one of Mott's *séances* he saw the spirit-faces of eight of his dead friends, at his cabinet door. The writer of the article was one of the editors of the *Banner of Light*, Mr. Warren Chase.

The *Religio-Philosophical Journal* of April 1, 1876, publishes the exposure of one Raynor, who had been a successful medium, and remarks:

"All the material for bogus mediums to imitate spirit manifestations, can be so concealed about the person that the most rigid search may fail to find it. A common silk neck-tie, tied around the neck under a paper collar, will conceal a gauze-like texture, white silk handkerchief, etc., sufficient to produce your sister, mother, or daughter, as the case may be. The expert, too, can conceal them in the lining of his pants, vest, and coat, with threads so arranged as to deceive the eye, and in a moment's time they can be taken out, and replaced. Those who have never investigated this matter would be astonished at the small space required for the articles necessary to materialize a first-class spirit. Tissue paper also acts an important part in bogus materialization, it being used on the head, and various parts of the body, to complete the dress. It can be concealed in the lining of the vest, coat, or pants, and you may search for it, but will not discover it easily. It is an easy matter to *deceive* three out of five who attend these bogus circles."

In the *Religio-Philosophical Journal* of February 24, 1877, we learn of the exposure of Dr. Monk and William Lawrence. They had been regarded as wonderful mediums. Dr. Monk was tried, condemned by the civil courts for deception, and sentenced to imprisonment. He professed to play the accordeon under the table, without touching it. The *Journal* frankly confesses his fraud. The fraud of one Blanchard, who took the photographs of spirits is acknowledged in the issue of March 31, 1877. In the issue of April 21st, it confesses the exposure of Dr. Hinton. In May, 1876, we see the exposure of Messrs. Petty; also Mrs. Claire. November 4, 1876, the *Journal* records the exposure of "the wonder, Dr. Mathews," who was confronted by a former accomplice, who arose in the audience and explained how his tricks were performed. December 16th, the exposure of C. H. Watkins is published. He was medium or exposer, according to the complexion of the town he visited.

In the *Chicago Tribune* we find the following from Rockford, Illinois, under date of January 30th: "Never, since the spirit of Bill Tompkins informed Artemus Ward that he and John Bunyan was a travelin' with a side-show in connection with the Shakespeare, Johnson & Co.'s circus, and that old Bun stirred up the animals and ground the organ, while he tended door, was there such a spiritualistic meeting as took place in Brown's Hall to-night. It was in this wise: The great Fire Queen of Chicago, Mrs. Suydam, had just got through bathing in the flames while under the influence of spirits, when Dr. J. Phillips, of Belvidere, arose and offered to repeat this wonderful test without the protection of spirits. The presiding officer, E. V. Wilson, of Chicago, challenged him, and Phillips forthwith walked upon the platform and went through the performance as his illustrious predecessor, the Chicago fire queen, had done. Made bold by Dr. Phillips, James Chandler, a Rockford citizen, ventured up and did the same thing. Then followed a jamboree, which might have terminated in a row had not the police made their appearance. One man got up and boldly denounced the whole affair as a humbug. Dr. Dunn, of Rockford, got up and offered ten dollars if the fire queen would hold her thumb in a lamp flame for forty seconds. Others trebled the doctor's offer, and, amid the great confusion, the meeting broke up."

The *Religio-Philosophical Journal*, of April 1,

1877, publishes Mr. Silas Arthur as the "greatest musical medium living," but on May 12th publishes him as laying no claim to mediumship at all, but simply laying claim to jugglery. The same paper, September 23, 1876, discovers a man who is the equal of Dr. Slade, the great slate-writing medium. The pencil would write, moved only by a spirit hand, and under the strictest test conditions; but on the 21st of the following October his reputed wife, in a fit of anger, exposed his *modus operandi*, and he in turn said that he had been living with her in a state of adultery. On February 19th, we meet the notice of the exposure of Mrs. S. A. Lindsley, for whom, as she professed, the spirits brought doves and flowers. From the *Banner of Light*, November 4, 1876, we learn that the exposure of the frauds of Mrs. Thayer, a notorious "flower" medium, was published in the *Boston Sunday Herald*. The *Banner* tries to shield her by saying that genuine mediums do sometimes practice deception. The same paper, February 10, 1877, denounces H. Fay, a prominent medium, as an impostor, and cautioned the public against him. He had been so frequently exposed the *Banner* could no longer hold him up. His deception was once thoroughly exposed in the city in which we are now writing.

Anna Eva Fay has been one of the most successful mediums. She at one time gained considerable notoriety in London. The learned Professor Crookes called her "a wonderful and gifted medium." Yet she, too, has been unable to escape the scrutiny of incredulous committees. The *Religio-Philosophical Journal*, June 10, 1876, contains an account of the exposure of her frauds, and quotes from the *New York Times* a statement that a judge in New York City had convicted her of jugglery and required her to take out a juggler's license. About this time Mr. and Mrs. Holmes gave "Katie King" *séances*, to the astonishment of all who beheld them. The spirit of Katie King came out in full view, and gave marvelous proof of her identity. "Katie King" had already exhibited in England, and members of the Royal Society had been astounded. Their inability to explain the marvel filled spiritualist books and papers everywhere with the names of men who have F. R. S. attached to their names, as new converts to the modern gospel.

Robert Dale Owen, author of "Foot-falls on the Boundaries of Another World," and similar books, was writing his autobiography in the successive numbers of the *Atlantic Monthly*. He had a chapter in the hands of the publishers, in which he detailed his experiences with "Katie King." He declared that after many years of investigation the "Katie King" tests were the most wonderful he had ever seen. But before the article was in print he and Dr. Childs witnessed the exposure of the "Katie King" fraud, and he had to order that the article should be suppressed. The disappointment well-nigh or quite drove him insane. Dr. Childs discovered the fraud, and found that "Katie King" was none other than Mrs. Holmes, the medium.

From the *Religio-Philosophical Journal*, May 13, 1876, we learn of the exposure of the fraud of Mrs. Miller, who had been regarded as equal to Mrs. Holmes in her mediumship. The same paper, April 8th, records the exposure of the celebrated medium, Livingstone, who performed the tricks first invented by the Davenport Brothers; who, when he was exposed, gave back the two hundred dollars he had received from the audience. He was also caught in the act of deception in Cleveland, Ohio, August 13th, by Mr. Van Tassel. From the *Banner of Light*, in its quotation from the *Boston Sunday Herald*, we learn that Mrs. Huntoon and the celebrated Eddy family were frauds, a representative of the *Herald* having spent a week with them to make the investigation. A correspondent of the *New York Sun* also exposed their secret arts. Evans, a spirit photographer, also is denounced, defense being no longer possible.

The *Rochester Evening Express*, of August 18, 1876, contains a graphic description of the exposure of the frauds of Mrs. Soules Compton Markee, who was a very noted medium for a time. The spirit ventured too near to the *Express* reporter, when he seized her, and had a desperate struggle with her to hold her long enough to identify her as Mrs. Markee, who was supposed to be firmly secured in the cabinet. The result of the exposure conducted by the *Express* was that Mrs. Markee was put under arrest. Yet the *Religio-Philosophical Journal*, of January 20, 1866, says of her: "The manifestations in her presence have been more wonderful than those given under the mediumship of Doctor Slade, Monck, or any other medium of ancient or modern times." Colonel Olcott wrote a book on the wonderful phenomena of the invisible world, as exhibited in the *séances* of the Eddys, Holmes, and of Mrs. Compton, afterwards Markee. The book contained sixty engravings, showing how these marvelous scenes appeared to the eye of the observer. The book lives, and dupes who have not read of the exposures of the frauds of these mediums, will believe that they are receiving evidences of spirit communication.

Andrew Jackson Davis, to account for the almost universal exposure of the mediumship frauds, has recently written a book, called the "Diakka." Diakkas are a species of strange creatures which inhabit the regions nearest the earth's surface, and which are inferior to human beings. He thinks that the mediums of the two years during the epidemic of medium exposure, were possessed by Diakkas.

We take the following from the *Religio-Philosophical Journal*, of October 24, 1876.

"Mrs. Bennett was a successful impostor, and was known in Boston as the celebrated 'West End medium.' Fathers recognized at her *séances* the spirits of their children, the widower 'saw and conversed' with his departed wife, the brother held 'sweet' converse with his departed sister; and to have suggested they might be mistaken subjected a person to a keen rebuke. Her *séances* are illustrative of the wonderful credulity of a certain class who attend such exhibitions, and show the necessity of having strict test conditions in order to protect them from imposition. After Mrs. Bennett had been fully exposed, she demanded another trial, and the result was as follows, as furnished by the Boston *Herald*.

"'The "West End medium" closed her career in Boston last night. Notwithstanding the late thorough *exposé* of her pretensions in the *Herald*, she had stoutly insisted upon their genuineness, and had the moral hardihood, something less than two weeks ago, to challenge further investigation by inviting a number of persons to attend a "test *séance*," at the rooms of a sincere and devout adherent of hers, residing at South End. Among the favored few invited to attend was a representative of the *Herald*; but the result was so incomplete and altogether unsatisfactory, that he found it impossible to say any thing in her vindication. She pleaded great physical prostration, but promised, upon her recovery, to give unquestionable proof of her medial powers. More than that, she agreed to return to the deserted house in M'Lean Street, the scene of the discovered trap, and there demonstrate her power as a 'materializer' without the aid of said trap.

"'In accordance with this promise a number of persons were invited to meet, last evening, at 43 M'Lean Street, and at about half-past seven o'clock a dozen or so ladies and gentlemen, nearly all spiritualists, and including a representative of the *Herald*, were assembled in the familiar apartments of Mrs. Bennett's late domicile. Mrs. Bennett and Mr. Bennett were also present, the former occupying her usual seat, and looked quite like the invalid she is in the habit of claiming to be.

"'The hole made in the floor of the "spirit" room at the late *exposé* had been repaired, and the plastering in the room beneath was still intact. The doors and windows of the former room were secured, and the usual singing commenced, the medium, as usual, joining lustily in the vocal performance.

"'After the lapse of a few minutes the familiar voice of "Sunflower," the supposed Indian maiden spirit, was heard behind the curtain. A little later the curtains were parted and her dusky face and form were imperfectly revealed to a few; but after speaking a few words of recognition to a number present she retreated, and obstinately resisted the most persuasive invitations of the medium and others to again show herself.

"'About this time Mrs. Bennett, who complained of a great draft upon the "pit of the stomach," commenced to collapse, physically, begged for a drink of water, and demanded a light to be struck. Her requests were complied with, and all present were convinced that the show was over for the night.

"'Then commenced another investigation of the premises, especially in the vicinity of the furnace register of the "spirit room," near which Mr. and Mrs. Bennett seemed to linger with something of fond attachment. This circumstance, however, rather sharpened the scent of several investigators, one of whom announced his purpose to pull up the flooring in that vicinity. This announcement gave Mrs. Bennett another collapse, in the course of which she found herself upon the bit of flooring in question, begged for another drink of water, and implored a cessation of search until she had recovered her equilibrium. Mr. Bennett was also literally upon the spot, and although he had n't much to say, he was evidently indulging in an active train of thought, and decidedly opposed to further proceedings. But the resolute gentleman with designs upon the floor persisted in his purpose, and Mrs. Bennett, having finally concluded that further resistance was useless, suddenly abandoned her post.

"'Then up came the flooring between the register and the wall, and as it came there was revealed to the crowd of eager observers, a large recess between the floor and furnace, and snugly ensconced, there was something which looked like a bundle of clothing, but which proved to be a woman, prone and shrinking under the indignant glances leveled upon her. She was speedily routed from her hiding place, and stood in the midst of the spectators, whose curious, questioning eyes she baffled for a time by hiding her face with her hands.

"'Quite a tumult ensued, and some professed to fear that the woman would receive physical violence; but there was no purpose to harm her; after she had been frequently questioned she was allowed to depart. She is a good-looking woman of perhaps thirty years, of good address, and of more than ordinary intelligence. Indeed, her manner and conversation were such as to fully account for the extraordinary talent so long manifested by her in her personations of "Sunflower" and other supposed spirits. Her name was elicited, but only after a pledge that it should not be revealed for the present. The accomplished swindler pleaded that she was under heavy bonds in a criminal suit, and that a revelation of her name would prejudice her cause and ruin her forever. She promises, however, soon to make a clean breast of her part in this great fraud, and to reveal a singular and startling drama.

"'During the removal of the floor, Mrs. Bennett quietly stole away, like the Arabs, and Mr. Bennett soon after as quietly disappeared. They will probably not resume business at 43 M'Lean Street.'"

In the same paper, February 10th, 1877, we learn that Mrs. Bennett, the Saturday evening previous, had given in Music Hall, Boston, "an *exposé* of the means by which she deceived the public for so long a time."

"The Davenport Brothers, assisted by Prof. Fay, gave an exhibition of their *spirit*-ualistic performance on Friday evening last. The endeavor to 'raise up spirits from the vasty deep' would have been a complete success in the eyes of the audience had not Mr. Harding, one of the committee, interpolated a point or spot not down in the bills. When the closet, whence had issued the unmelodious sounds of guitar, banjo, and bells, and in which the brothers had been tied, so that the spirits had to come to their relief, was opened, one of the performers was found to be well marked about the hand and wrist with ink—of course it was the spirit of the Fifteenth Amendment which had been called up—and the audience might have been satisfied of it had not Mr. Harding had the audacity to explain it upon more tangible ground. In short, he showed his own hands to be covered with ink, and explained that while the spirit hands were flashing the aperture of the dark closet, he, not having the fear of the devil before his eyes, had seized a hand and left the impress of blackness upon it. As jugglers, the Davenports are a success, but as developers of unseen agencies, they are arrant humbugs, as have been all their predecessors since the days of the Witch of Endor."—*Bay City Journal.*

The above is an account of one of the many exposures of the Davenport Brothers. They became quite notorious for a time in this country and in Europe. "Crowned heads" were sometimes in their audiences, and they made many converts to spiritualism.

The celebrated Dr. Slade, who so long and so successfully gave his slate-writing tests in New York, came to grief when he went to London. Learned and able men investigated him but too closely. Professor Lankester, in an ill-guarded moment, seized the medium, and found him writing with a piece of pencil which he had concealed from sight. "Dr." Slade was arrested as a vagrant.

D. D. Home, whom spiritualists generally quote as the greatest modern medium, according to Moncure D. Conway, "was detected in his imposture of placing sponges dipped in phosphorus on wires at the top of the house, and confessed his imposture." M. D. Conway further says in writing to the Cincinnati *Commercial:* "Anthony Trollope is also said to have some ugly reminiscences of Home, in Florence; and Adolphus Trollope is credited with having kicked that eminent medium down stairs."

Dr. Gordon, in New York, at one time created a great excitement among the credulous. He exhibited pasteboard faces at the opening in the door of his cabinet, and, covering them with phosphorus and attaching to them dresses of some gauze-like fabric, they were received as spirits of the dead. He even had some of these masks modeled to resemble photographs of the faces of certain deceased persons. The excited audience at one time seized the cabinet and medium by force, and discovered the cheat.

The Rochester *Democrat and Chronicle* of September 12, 1876, contains an account of the wonderful career of a medium by the name of Jennings, in that city. He produced raps, and thus deceived his more intimate friends. As his reputation for mediumship grew, he studied more closely the arts of deception, and the credulity and impressible imaginations of his audience. His own face at the cabinet window and in the dim light, by means of handkerchiefs reducing the apparent size of his face, could be changed to a child's face. His coat-tail, held to his chin, would pass for whiskers. He, however, had invisible trap-doors, accomplices, wigs, beards, masks and wires, and all needed implements for his work. He found that half of the questions asked by the audience of the spirit would, as a rule, be answered correctly if answered in the affirmative; so, by a little shrewdness, he often gave the audience wonderful evidence of his inspiration; but when caught at his tricks, at last, he published a full confession in the above-named paper. He states that every medium of his acquaintance was an intentional fraud.

This epidemic of medium exposure which swept over the country after the discovery of the Katie King fraud, left scarcely any medium of note untouched. The newspapers vied with each other in sending out their reporters to make investigations, and often the reporter came away with physical injury for his attempts at investigation.

The Onandaga, N. Y., *Standard* reporter, provided with lamp-black, exploded the long-famous humbug, at Moravia; and many similar enterprises had been successfully conducted previous to this time, but the movement did not become epidemic till the years 1876 and 1877, resulting in a complete demonstration that all mediums who give physical tests of spirit presence are humbugs and merely clever jugglers. A chance to cheat is always one of the necessary "conditions." The exploded medium often becomes a lecturer or editor of a spiritualist paper; sometimes he reforms and returns to more honorable avocations.

W. F. Jamieson and M'Queen were exposed in Kalamazoo, Michigan, by Dr. Robinson, who struck a light while one of the mediums was supposed to be floating in mid-air and playing on a guitar, to indicate his whereabouts. The medium was standing on a chair, turning the guitar about over his head, thereby producing a well-known acoustic effect. The audience, being unable to see, heard the sound as if it was floating about over their heads. The audience rushed on the mediums, and demanded their money; they also discovered the wires and secret machinery which the mediums employed to produce their evidences of spirit phenomena. The court condemned the mediums for fraud, and required them to pay a fine of forty dollars, or go to jail. M'Queen went to jail, and turned exposer, and now lives in Hillsdale, Michigan, and challenges the mediums of the world to produce any phenomena which he can not parallel and explain immediately. W. F. Jamieson paid his fine, and became editor of the *Rostrum*, lecturer and debater, being a fine speaker. We once held a debate with him for twelve days, on the various phases of infidelity and spiritualism, during which we confronted him with these facts, confirmed by a letter from his friend M'Queen, and others.

We pronounce all test mediums frauds. Trance and trickery will account for the whole of modern spiritualism. Entranced mediums sometimes dream and believe the land of their dreams to be a real land. We might speak of the manner in which the various manifestations of mediums are produced, but we would recommend the reader to any good books on legerdemain. As to the moral character of spiritualist lecturers and mediums, we can only speak briefly, and say as a class they are unworthy of confidence. Free-lovism, individual sovereignty, the divinity of all our impulses, that sin is a lesser good, are their prevailing beliefs. Their testimony as to their phenomena is untrustworthy, because of the badness of their moral sentiments.

Chapter XXI.

TRICKS EXPLAINED.

WE have already indicated to some extent the manner in which spiritualist mediums produce their manifestations. Frequently the same result may be produced in a variety of ways. We propose now to give the reader an explanation of the *modus operandi* adopted by mediums generally in producing some of the more successful spirit manifestations.

The "Katie King" performances were the culmination of the spirit manifestations, which began with the Rochester knockings. At first the spirits indicated their presence by raps; but as the raps were soon produced by professional jugglers and exposers as satisfactorily as any ever produced by mediums, other tests were invented and used, until they in turn became so thoroughly understood as to be worthless as proofs of spirit agency. The exposer would follow in the track of the professional medium, and duplicate and explain his manifestations. So perpetually something new and more startling must be devised by the professional medium. At last spirits were "materialized," and clothed with flesh and blood, appearing and vanishing in the dim light of the *séance* room. Sometimes, after the medium had become emboldened by success, he would submit to be handled by persons present. At this point the "Katie King" exposé occurred, followed by an epidemic of exposure all over the land. Now there is a reaction beginning against all phases of physical mediumship, sympathized with, as we have seen, by one of the best established organs of modern spiritualism, the *Religio-Philosophical Journal*.

D. D. Home, the famous medium, in the midst of the medium-exposure epidemic, wrote a book, entitled "The Lights and Shadows of Spiritualism," in which he admits that almost every medium, but himself, is a humbug.

He says, on page 408: "Behind the cabinet curtains stands the concealed form of the pretended medium. In his hand he has a length of some gossamer-like fabric, arranged to simulate a robe, and gathered at the top into something like the shape of a head, or surmounted by a mask. This puppet-like construction he cautiously advances through the opening of the cabinet until it is in view of the sitters. Let any reader attempt the process, and the completeness of the deception will amaze him. With lights down, the sitters at some distance from the cabinet, and expectation wrought to the highest pitch, this unsubstantial doll will have the closest resemblance to a human form. Should any very enthusiastic spiritualists be present, he need not be surprised if two or three at once recognize a relative, and insist the form to be a materialized visitor from another world, in spite of all the evidence to the contrary that can be offered them."

Mr. Home then quotes from the confessions of Jennings, the Rochester medium, whose exposure we have already recorded: "My accomplice used false hair, wigs, beards, etc., and put flour on his hands to give a ghostly appearance. For babyfaces we had a piece of black velveteen, with a small round hole cut out. This, placed over the face, gave the appearance of the tiny features of a babe. . . . I had my accomplice paint me a couple of faces; the one a man's, the other that of a woman. I then proposed to have two apertures in the cabinet, one in each of the doors, which was done. On the night in question I entered the cabinet, and the singing and music commenced. I straightened out a piece of wire, attached one of the faces to it, rolled the mask up, poked it through the screen, and then unrolled it by turning the wire. I also had a piece of thick, dark, worsted cloth, which I used as a beard for myself. . . . So on this night two faces appeared at once, and almost threw the meeting into ecstasies."

On page 388 Mr. Home says: "I doubt if there remain now five materializing mediums who have not been seized in the act of personating a spirit form."

We have already stated that the epidemic of exposure reached all the leading mediums of the United States. Our author quotes a letter from Sergeant Cox, of England, whose name has been extensively quoted favorably in connection with spiritualism. From it we extract the following:

"All the conditions imposed are as if carefully designed to favor fraud if contemplated, and even to tempt to imposture. The curtain is guarded at either end by some friend. The light is so dim that the features can not be distinctly seen. A white veil thrown over the body from head to foot is put on and off in a moment, and gives the necessary aspect of spirituality. A white band around head and chin at once conceals the hair and disguises the face. A considerable interval precedes the appearance—just such as would be necessary for the preparations. A like interval succeeds the retirement of the form before the cabinet is permitted to be opened for inspection. This just enables the ordinary dress to be restored. While the preparation is going on behind the curtain the company are always vehemently exhorted to sing. This would conveniently conceal any sounds of motion in the act of preparation. The spectators are made to promise not to peep behind the curtain, and not to grasp the form. They are solemnly told that if they were to seize the spirit they would kill the medium! This is an obvious contrivance to deter the onlookers from doing any thing that might cause detection. It is not true. Several spirits have been grasped, and no medium has died of it, although in each case the supposed spirit was found to be the medium.

"But I have learned how the trick is done. I have seen the description of it given by a medium to another medium who desired instruction. The letter was in her own handwriting, and the whole style of it showed it to be genuine.

"She informs her friend that she comes to the *séance* prepared with a dress that is easily taken off with a little practice. She says it may be done in two or three minutes. She wears two shifts (probably for warmth). She brings a muslin veil of thin material (she gives its name, which I forget). It is carried *in her drawers!* It can be compressed into a small space, although when spread it covers the whole person. A pocket-handkerchief pinned round the head keeps back the hair. She states that she takes off all her clothes except the two shifts, and is covered by the veil. The gown is spread carefully upon the sofa over the pillows. In this array she comes out. She makes very merry with the spiritualists whom she thus gulls, and her language about them is any thing but complimentary.

"This explains the whole business. The question so often asked before was, Where the robe could be carried? It could not be contained in the bosom or in a sleeve. Nobody seems to have thought of the drawers.

"But it will be asked how we can explain the fact that some persons have been permitted to go behind the curtain when the form was before it, and have asserted that they saw or felt the medium. I am sorry to say the confession to which I have referred states, without reserve, that these persons knew that it was a trick, and lent themselves to it. I am, of course, reluctant to adopt such a formidable conclusion; although the so-called 'confession' was a confidential communication from one medium to another medium who had asked to be instructed how the trick was done. I prefer to adopt the more charitable conclusion that they were imposed upon, and it is easy to find how this was likely to be. The same suspicious precautions against detection were always adopted. The favored visitor was an assured friend, one who, if detecting trickery, would shrink from proclaiming the cheat. Only one was permitted to enter. A light was not allowed. There was nothing but the 'darkness visible' of the lowered gas rays struggling through the curtain. I have noted that no one of them ever was permitted to see the face of the medium. It was always 'wrapped in a shawl.' The hands felt a dress, and imagination did the rest. The revealer of the secret above referred to says, that when she took off her gown to put on the white veil, she spread it upon the sofa or chair with pillows or something under it, and this is what they felt and took for her body!"

Before this time this kind of manifestations had been accepted and published as genuine by Professor Crookes, F. R. S. The female medium, of course, has a splendid opportunity for deception; but the male medium may be none the less successful. A silk necktie tied under the collar, around the neck, may conceal a gauze-like texture sufficient to drape his face and person, and produce in the dim light a mother or sister of the trembling inquirer. In the lining of his clothes many other necessary objects may be so concealed as to escape the vigilance of an ordinary committee. He may

TRICKS EXPLAINED. 265

thus conceal hands and heads of rubber, which he may, when taken from their concealment, inflate with his breath. A small bit of phosphorus concealed anywhere about his person would be sufficient to produce a glow of light from the spirit world. Sometimes the face which appears at the window of the cabinet is modeled to resemble a photograph of a deceased relative of some one in the audience. One such manifestation would be sufficient to produce excitement and establish the reputation of the medium. The photograph may be had from the family photographer or secured by a confederate.

Mr. Home continues:

"Noise, however, is often caused during the process, and if heard might excite suspicion. The audience are, therefore, requested to sing. The worse the voices of those present, the more readily and loudly they comply. 'Yes, we will gather at the river,' makes night hideous, and effectually precludes the possibility of detection. While the rest of the apartment is thus filled with a gush of most excruciating harmony, the cabinet becomes for the nonce a dressing-room. Possibly the medium is a woman. The doleful sounds without may strike on her ears, but the fair being heeds them not. Like Jezebel she is tiring her head. A pocket-handkerchief or a simple strip of muslin, bound around the face alters it so as to render recognition almost impossible in the dim light, which is religiously preserved. Let the reader put this to the test. Pin together the window curtains and step behind them. Pass around the face such a band as I have

23

mentioned, and take care that the hair is concealed by it. A little cosmetic or rouge may be employed to heighten the effect. Now turn up the eyes in approved 'dying-duck' fashion, and expose the face to those outside. The change from its ordinary expression will be startling. Half darkness is, of course, desirable; but impostors, arrayed in the manner described, have been known to expose themselves even to a strong light without detection.

"If the 'spirit-form' displayed be masculine, some hair on the face is, of course, desirable. And whiskers and mustaches may be cunningly concealed. One person confessed to me that he had carried them fastened in the hollow under his arm. So with the other paraphernalia.

"The exceedingly fine India-rubber masks employed when it is desired to exhibit a variety of faces, females may hide in the gathers of their dress, or even *in their hair*. Indeed, should the audience be sufficiently enthusiastic, and countenances only be on the programme, those countenances may be furnished by so simple a means as a few engravings. Though the likeness held up to the cabinet-aperture be that of a Wellington, one excited beholder will recognize in it his much-loved grandmother, and another dispute the claim by pronouncing it the face of her equally venerated aunt. I have witnessed these sad exhibitions, and know, therefore, of what I speak."

These masks, be it remembered, are so constructed that the medium can inflate them and then cause them to vanish.

We allow Mr. Home to speak because it was he that converted Prof. Crookes and a few learned men of England to a belief in psychic force. Mr. Home has been behind the scenes. He is writing in the midst of the epidemic of medium exposure. His motives for further concealment of the frauds of professional mediums are gone, for all but "five," he says, are already exposed. He will not, however, as yet confess himself a deceiver. He says confederates are often hired by the mediums from among the servants of the house where they give their *seances*. Biddy or John is glad to get an extra dollar, and besides, they enjoy the fun. There is something in human nature which renders enjoyable a practical joke when perpetrated at the expense of another, and the traveling medium may count upon finding human nature whithersoever he goes. The servants he may bribe have a motive for concealing their part in the matter. Mr. Home himself, doubtless, has had some wicked delight in his success, and consequent notoriety, in convincing men who bore the title of F. R. S. of the genuineness of his spirit or psychic manifestations.

"Lights and Shadows," page 422, contains an account of the *modus operandi* practiced by certain mediums as exposed and explained by Mr. M——: His arms are tied behind him. His shirt sleeves are sewed together and then sewed to his trousers. The elbows of his sleeves are sewed together and sewed to the back of his vest. "He is then put into a bag, the strings drawn round his neck, and the ends fastened to the chair-back against which he reclines. You can also tie cords round his legs below the knees. While being put into the cabinet, or behind a curtain, he *unbuttons* one of his sleeves with the fingers of the other hand. He then *lowers* the arm as much as possible, and gets the sleeve and sewings *above* the elbow. The hand and arm can then, as you will easily see, be brought to the front, and, through the bag, take a bell or any such article from his lap, and ring it. If a tray be put in his lap, with a jug of water and glasses, he can easily pour the liquor from the jug into the glasses. With a little practice the glass may be worked by the hand up the bag as far as the mouth, and he may drink. He then lets it slide down into his lap. Rings laid in his lap are also worked up the bag by means of the fingers, until his mouth is reached. He then grasps the article between his teeth; passes his finger through the neck of the bag; and, taking the ring from his mouth, puts it on his finger, or in his pocket. Mr. M—— did this repeatedly in from *nine to twelve seconds.* I think you will perceive from this that the feats in question, although they may appear to the uninitiated 'very wonderful,' and 'beyond human power to accomplish,' prove, like many other things, quite simple, when you come to comprehend *how* they are done."

Mediums at one time sat in their cabinets with hands untied, but would clap their hands together perpetually as evidence that spirit hands and not the hands of the medium, were manipulating the guitar and bells, and other objects with which the medium was surrounded. This was regarded as a capital test until it was found that the clapping of one hand on the forehead or other naked parts of the body would produce the same sound as the clapping of the hands, and thus the medium could still keep the sound going and have one hand free to produce the mysterious manifestations. Of course, the tests may be multiplied when the medium is so situated as to be aided by a confederate. Mr. Home, on page 423, presents a letter he had received from a friend:

"I must name how Miss X——'s business agent made an offer to me by letters which I have now in my possession, that for a sum of money the medium would expose the whole affair, as she was not properly supported by the spiritualists; '*complicating* [I suppose he means implicating] at least six big guns, the F. R. S. people. Miss X—— is now every night materializing, and is *immense;* another point I will give, she is in the RING of all the best mediums in London, and gets letters every day that will be big to work upon.' The managerial offer was not accepted by me."

We gather from this Mr. Home's estimate of the F. R. S. people, of whom Prof. Crookes was one. This must include Profs. Crookes and Wallace, for I think, leaving them out, there could not be found six Fellows of the Royal Society who have given countenance to the idea that any of the pretended phenomena produced by mediums are genuine.

Sometimes the medium takes some man from

the audience into the cabinet with him. The man's hand is placed on the medium's head. The medium then grasps the man's arm firmly with both his hands. The firmness of his grasp deadens the sensibilities of the arm, so that while one hand is still grasping it he is insensible to the removal of the other hand. With one hand free the medium rings a bell violently, and instantly returns the free hand to its former position. The lights are turned on and the medium is found with his two hands firmly grasping the man's arm in the same manner as when the test began. The witness is then asked if he was conscious that the medium had removed either of his hands from his arm during the ringing of the bell, and he is compelled to answer in the negative. The audience is puzzled, and the "faithful" are jubilant. This test is sometimes varied, but the principle involved is ever the same.

Sensations tend to become permanent. Let some one place a silver half dollar firmly against your forehead and then secretly remove it, and you still feel the half dollar adhering to your forehead. If asked to shake it off you will probably make the attempt. This is often tried in parlor entertainments, much to the amusement of the young people.

There are a half dozen processes for producing spirit photographs. The plate upon which a negative has been made is often washed and used again. If the washing is not done thoroughly a misty and ghost-like image of the former picture will appear beside or behind the more life-like image of the one who has been sitting for his photograph. By retouching the picture when taken in this manner, the effect may be modified as may be desired. When the victim of this deception has previously been made aware of the above mentioned fact in the photographer's art, he is allowed to wash a plate to his own satisfaction, but another plate is afterward secretly substituted in its place by the spirit photographer. Also the ghostly figure may be thrown upon the plate while it is in the bath. This impression will remain invisible until after the picture has been developed. We append the following description of other methods:

"Another method is to hold up the sensitive plate—either before or after operating—for one or two seconds, before a jet of gaslight, in the dark room, or even before the yellow-paned windows, as though to examine the coating of the plate, holding between it and the window or gaslight an old negative, transparent positive, or magic-lantern transparency. Two or three seconds will suffice for the clearest of impressions, and the looker-on would probably never dream of deception, supposing that the operator was simply examining the plate, 'to see if it was all right.' According to the distance between the two plates, the ghost-figure will be stronger or fainter. We recently witnessed a splendid operation of this kind at the Boston gallery, in which two seconds sufficed for the production of a ghost-figure by gaslight. By a clever device, the sensitive plate may be impressed with the figure of a ghost while in the dark slide, on the way to or from the operating-room, or even while in the camera; indeed, twenty different varieties of deception may be practiced during exposure. A common artifice is to place a microscopic picture within the camera-box, so that, by means of a small magnifying lens, its image may be thrown upon the plate. Spectral effects may also be produced by covering the back of a sensitive plate with pieces of cut paper, and using artifices well known to retouchers. The 'rope' picture described in our account of the ———— photographs, might have been produced by the adroit use of cotton twine before, or in the camera during exposure, or might have been produced by double printing. Extraordinary spectral effects, such as that of a man shaking hands with his own ghost, cutting off his own head, or followed by his own *doppelgänger*, may be produced by 'masking,' a process which it would take too long to describe here. There is scarcely any conceivable absurdity in portraiture which may not be accomplished by the camera; and the peculiarities of the business are so extraordinary, the opportunities for humbug so excellent, and the methods and modifications of methods whereby spirit-photographs may be produced so numerous, that it is hopeless for any person totally ignorant of photography to detect a fellow like ———— in the act of fraud; indeed, it often requires an expert in photography to detect certain classes of deception. Were we not limited by time and space, in this article, we could readily fill forty columns with an account of the many artifices practiced by spirit photographers."

By means of a confederate, the professional spirit

photographer can get possession of photographs of deceased relatives of a leading spiritualist, who would be likely to visit his establishment, and on certain occasions produce for the astonished applicant a ghostly picture which he must recognize as that of one of his deceased relatives. A few such feats as this would be sufficient to keep up the reputation of the spirit photographer. From a photograph a model can be made by some hired sculptor, and a pasteboard mask taken, which shall represent the features of the original.

In some cases, ghosts have been made to appear by means of a magic lantern concealed from sight. Optical instruments can be so arranged as to throw the image of a photograph into the air; but generally the use of drapery and contortions of the countenance of the medium, aided by the imagination of some hysterical persons in the audience, are sufficient to produce to the view, in the dim light, a variety of spirit forms, some of which are to be recognized by some person present as deceased relatives.

Maskelyne and Cooke, the celebrated English jugglers, and proprietors of the London Egyptian Hall, affirm that the spirits they produced were often recognized by their flesh-clad friends among the spectators. False whiskers, charcoal, pearline, rouge, gauze-like drapery, and contortions of the face are sufficient to transform the medium into a multitude of spirit forms. The hand rubbed dry, and harshly grasping the hand of the investigator, is the rough hand of a strong man; the same hand, relaxed and moistened, and warmed by the breath, and laid lightly on the hand of the investigator, is the soft hand of a woman. The voice may undergo many changes; it can produce the soft whispers of a woman, or the hoarse declamations of a man. The darkness of the room and the guard around the cabinet or medium are proportioned to the skepticism of the spectators.

The rope-tying feats, made prominent by the Davenport brothers, have fallen into discredit among spiritualists. Maskelyne and Cooke, Van Vleck, Bishop, Baldwin, and many others repeated their manifestations and explained the process. A hand of certain shape can easily release itself from its fastenings; the larger the wrist, and the more soft and compressible the hand, the better the medium. Sometimes the tying is done by a confederate, and the ropes are so tied that, while they seem tight and the knots secure, they are so arranged that they may be thrown off in a moment; the medium furnishes his own rope, and exhorts the persons tying it to be thorough in their work, and they tie many knots and bind a great amount of rope about the medium, who, meanwhile, swells out his body to its utmost capacity; then, when left alone in his cabinet, he relaxes his breath and muscles, and wriggles about until he finds the weak place in his fastenings, and then directs all his physical force on that point. The more he disentangles himself the easier the process of disentanglement becomes. If the committee begin to bind the medium in such a way as to render it impossible for him to extricate himself, he interposes objections, complains of pain, and

TRICKS EXPLAINED. 275

some friend in the audience joins with him in his protestations, and a scene ensues; the committee refuse to act, and another committee, more agreeable to the medium volunteers; but such occurrences are very rare.

A guitar may be made to sound as if floating over the heads of the audience, in a darkened room—after having announced that the instrument is to be borne through the air by the spirits, and thus preparing the minds of the listeners—by swinging it around, at the same time vibrating the strings with the finger; the faster the finger is made to pass over the strings, the more rapidly the guitar seems to float about the room. When the medium shows his hands at the cabinet window, he usually keeps them in constant and rapid motion, so that they shall not be recognized as the hands of the medium, and that they may seem to be many hands, instead of two; the fingers are pressed together, to represent a small hand, and outspread to represent a large hand.

The rope-tying feats are performed in various ways: usually while the medium's wrists are being tied together he gives them a twist, unperceived by the person tying him, which seems to tighten the rope, and the committeeman, whose attention has for the moment been purposely diverted by the medium, looks upon the blood-red hands of the medium with evident satisfaction, because he has been doing his work so thoroughly. By reversing the twist, the rope slackens, and the medium can slip his hand out. Sometimes the medium is tied by spirits inside the cabinet. Then a knot must be used which looks firm, but which in reality is not; in the middle of the rope, a square knot is loosely tied, the ends of the rope are then tucked through in opposite directions below the knot, forming two loops into which the medium's hands are to be thrust, after the rest of the tying is done. The medium then ties himself to the chair, with the remainder of the rope, as firmly as possible, leaving just slack enough to enable him, when his work is finished, to slip his hands through the two loops he had first prepared; then, by straightening himself up in his chair, and swelling himself out as much as possible, the loops tighten down on his wrists, which seem to be joined by a genuine hard knot. Thus the "spirits" have tied him; the committee-men confess they could not have tied him better.

Flour is then put into the medium's hands to make it doubly sure that he shall not use them in manipulating the bells and instruments in the cabinet. But the moisture of the hands makes the flour compact, so that it can be all put into one hand without scattering. The little flour that adheres to the empty hand can be wiped off in the pocket, or on the white shirt of the medium. The medium having slackened the ropes, enlarges one of the loops into which he had inserted his hands, has one hand free in a moment, and rings the bells, thrums the guitar, and makes all the racket possible. In an instant he inserts his hand into the loop, and by a jerk of his body tightens the rope, and he calls for the opening of the cabinet door, when lo! there he is bound as securely as when the audience saw him a few minutes before.

Different knots are invented by the "spirits," but all of them are made somewhat after this manner. But it is more difficult for the medium to untie himself when tied by spirits in the flesh, in the form of committee-men; yet the average committee know so little about knots and rope tying that the medium is safe in counting on their lack of skill. By twisting the rope between the wrists while the knot is being made, or by making the whole body as tense as possible while the process of tying is going on, and by furnishing the committee a long rope, so that there shall be as many knots as possible tied about the limbs of the medium, he may by great exertion in a moment draw the rope tighter about one limb and slacken it on another, and thus extricate himself. When this species of spirit manifestation was in vogue, Van Vleck and others traveled about the country, permitting themselves to be thus tied, and extricating themselves in full view of the audience. They did on the open platform what the mediums did behind the cabinet doors.

The raps may be produced in various ways: by a loose joint in the hand (the hand that pens these lines is so constructed by nature as to be able to produce raps in that way) or other parts of the body; by a rattan concealed in the dress of a female medium, which touches the floor when she is in a sitting posture; by a confederate under the floor; by the shoe of the medium tapping against the table leg; by deftly rubbing the finger-nail against the varnished surface of the table; by a knocker inserted in a hollow boot heel, so constructed as to strike the floor when compressed from above by the heel of the foot. By carefully modulating the sounds they may appear to come from a longer or a shorter distance. Sound may be conducted by a board in the floor so as to seem to come from a point at a distance from the place where it actually originates.

Sealed letters may be answered by opening them and reading the contents. The letters can be steamed open, and then resealed and reglazed so as to look as they did before. If sealing wax has been used, the paper under the wax can be split and then fastened together with gum arabic. The letter may be slit open at the end with a razor, and then stuck together and rubbed as soon as the gum is dry, so as to remove all evidence that it had been opened. Sometimes the medium by practice is able to read a name which is being written, by observing the motions of the end of the pen above the hand of the writer. He has also learned to distinguish in this manner the words which are being written to express relationship, as father, sister, uncle, etc. He requires the investigator to write on paper the Christian name and relationship of the departed human spirit with whom he desires to communicate, while the medium is standing at a respectful distance at the other side of the room. Certain performances are then engaged in by the medium as a blind, after which he sits down and writes a letter giving good advice, and signed by Uncle John, or the person whose name had been previously written by the inquirer.

Sometimes the applicant is required to write many names on separate slips of paper, and then roll them up into separate balls. The medium touches them one by one, he being apparently in a trance. During the process he "palms" one of the pellets, brings it below the table, opens it and reads it at a glance, and then, after some further maneuvering, to make the spirits propitious and blind the applicant, he writes out a communication signed by one of the names which had been written. Sometimes the medium furnishes the investigator with a hard lead pencil and several sheets of thin white paper upon which to write a question and the address of the spirit of some deceased friend, after which he is to take the sheet and burn it in the stove or tear it to fragments. The medium then takes the remaining sheets to another room, and carefully inspecting the indentations made on the sheet which was under the one upon which the investigator had written, he reads it and writes out an answer. Other mediums of this class furnish one sheet of thin paper, and request the applicant to write a question and the name of the spirit on the end of it, and then fold the other part of the paper over it. The medium then pretends to go into a trance. He lays his hand on the paper, turns his side toward the inquirer, shuts the one eye which is visible, leaves the other open, rubs his finger over the question, so that he can see through the thin paper, and reads the words under it. Or, if that is not sufficient, he slightly raises the fold which admits the light. From where the observer is sitting the paper seems perfectly opaque.

To render the manifestation more convincing, the medium may retire a moment before answering the communication. He then returns entranced. He unbuttons his shirt sleeve and makes bare his arm and rubs its surface with his hand, when lo! there is the name of the deceased friend coming out on the surface of the skin in blood-red letters. While out of sight of the inquirer he had scratched the name on his arm with some dull-pointed instrument. Bearing on hard while writing, the pressure forces the blood from the capillary vessels over which the instrument passes. The effect is not visible for a time, but can be brought out in a moment by rubbing the skin with the hand. The blood returns in unusual quantities to the capillary vessels from which it had been forced, and becomes visible through the cuticle. The effect may be heightened by pricking in dots with a pin along the lines traced by the blunt instrument. This, at one time, was regarded as the supreme test of spirit agency. There was the double mystery, How did the medium get possession of the name? and how were the blood-red letters made to come out without visible cause before the very eyes of the beholder?

Pianos are played upon by spirits in various ways. Sometimes the medium extricates himself from his fastenings and plays on the keys himself. It is often done by a confederate. Occasionally the instrument in the *seance* room is not touched at all, but an instrument in an adjoining room is played while some stick of solid wood or some opening in the wall conveys the sound from that room to the place where the audience is assembled. It is also difficult to locate a sound when the cause of it is not apparent. Pianos are lifted by machinery under the floor. Tables are tipped by pushing against them while the hand is on the table with the "pisciform bone," which projects from the hand near the wrist, while the opposite legs of the table are furnished with little spikes, which keep them from sliding, or by means of iron hooks attached to the wrist and concealed in the coat sleeve.

A medium can read names and the time by the watch in the dark by covering his head and the name or watch with a blanket, and holding in his hand near the objects to be seen a bottle of phosphorated oil, for thus he can see while not a glimmer of light is visible to any one else. Stout wire spikes, sharpened at the point, coming up through the carpeted floor leave no trace when they are withdrawn, and are often used in table tipping.

The slate-writing tests are performed in various ways. Slade, the great slate-writing medium, when "grabbed" by Professor Lankester, of London, was writing on the slate with the hand by which he was holding it under the table, as was proved in the judicial investigation which followed the exposure. If the investigator is not close in his observations the slate may rest on the medium's knee, while he writes on it with the hand which is under the table. The pencil may be a small piece of slate secured under the finger nail or concealed for use between the fingers. A common and convenient method is to attach the pencil to a rubber cord concealed in the coat sleeve. After the pencil is used it will fly back into the sleeve out of sight. If the investigator is more observant the slate must be held close against the bottom of the table supported by the little finger and the one next to it, while the other fingers are engaged in writing. When the medium is in his own apartments he furnishes his own slate, and then the experiments are more brilliant. The inquirer is seated at the table, while the medium picks up his slate, goes to the water pitcher and pours water upon the sponge to wash the slate, so that no trace of any former writing may be left upon it. One side of the slate he rubs thoroughly. The other he wets all over, but omits to rub a certain portion on which he had written a bit of news gleaned by means of a confederate, concerning the inquirer or his friends, or perhaps a short communication from the spirits on some general topic. He then advances, slate in hand, towards the table. He shows one side of the slate to the investigator with great care, turns the other side so that it slants, forming an angle of about forty-five degrees to the eye of the observer, who sees only a plain black surface. The writing being still wet is invisible when not held squarely before the eye. He then puts a round bit of pencil on the table and lays the slate down over it, taking care that the side which is free from writing shall be uppermost. The medium then places his hand on the slate to guard it from being snatched away by the inquirer, and that the heat of the hand shall cause the slate to become dry sooner. Meanwhile a bit of slate fastened under the table is rapped upon either by a piece of pencil attached to the medium's knees or held in his disengaged hand. This represents the supposed movements of the pencil under the slate. Soon the slate is turned over and exhibited, containing the communication now distinctly visible, the slate being dry. Sometimes the slate is previously written upon by a preparation which becomes visible when warmed or when wet and dried. More frequently another prepared slate is substituted for the one examined by the investigator by sleight-of-hand, when the attention of the observer is, for a moment, diverted by the medium.

The table may be a juggler's table, or the operator may be aided by a confederate. The *modus operandi* is varied according to the circumstances. That the great apostle of this kind of spirit manifestations was a fraud, and was caught in the very act of deception, was sworn to by Professor Lankester in the English courts. The same medium had been previously exposed by the wily reporters of different New York papers.

Clairvoyant tests are given by mediums sometimes as evidence of spirit agency, and sometimes to exhibit the hidden powers of spirits in the flesh. Of course, just to the degree that we enlarge the hidden powers of the latter we diminish the supposed proof for the former. If the medium's own mind can see afar or read the hidden thoughts of the inquirer, that alone would account for the phenomenon without referring it to the agency of disembodied spirits. But clairvoyance is a humbug. The tests are manufactured in different ways. Sometimes the "sensitive" is placed on the platform in presence of the audience, and blindfolded, but her ears are left open. The lecturer discourses for a time and then proposes to the audience to put in his hand any object, as a knife or pencil, etc., and in a few minutes the "sensitive" will be *en rapport* with the lecturer so as to name the object he holds in his hand. Previous to the exhibition the lecturer and his sensitive subject have made out a probable list of all the objects which persons in an audience would be likely to have with them on such occasions. Then a list of words is made out which shall represent these various objects. It is agreed, for example, that "magnetism" shall represent knife, and "heat" shall represent lead pencil, etc. Some one very cautiously puts a knife in the hand of the lecturer. He pauses, waits for the conditions to get right; talks for a blind to the audience, but soon very carelessly remarks that he fears that there is not enough "magnetism" to-night in the speaker to get the sensitive under good control. He pauses and then talks on, and pauses again. Soon he concludes to try the experiment and asks abruptly, "What have I in my hand?" The "sensitive" answers "Knife." He had communicated that information to the ear of his "sensitive" by using the word magnetism. A cough may mean pocket-comb. The falling inflection may mean pocket-handkerchief, and so on indefinitely.

By sending a secret agent on beforehand, the "sensitive" may give tests in mind reading, and be able to recite events in the past history of prominent persons who would be likely to be present at such an entertainment. By shrewdly guessing the occupations of certain persons present, it then becomes safe to venture certain statements concerning their past experiences, for men in the same vocations usually experience the same things. The "sensitive" may take into her hand a lock of hair cut from the head of one who has been found to be a carpenter, and then being put into mesmeric rapport with him, begin to feel a crushing sensation in the hand or forearm of the right arm (the left arm generally keeps out of danger), followed by shooting pains running indefinitely over the nerves of the right hand and arm, after which the "sensitive" declares that the man to whom the lock of hair belongs has at some time sustained a severe injury in the right hand or arm. In nine cases out of ten the "sensitive" has hit the mark. To those who have never thought of it, it will be surprising to know how much one man's history resembles every other man's history. A shrewd lecturer can surprise an audience by selecting a man from among them, and telling him the general outlines of his past life, and his general traits of character. But to be thrilling in his disclosures he must have a secret agent to go before him to gather up specific facts.

It is sometimes thought to be a wonderful thing that professional mediums can unloose themselves from hand-cuffs. But the mystery disappears when we remember that all hand-cuffs of a certain kind may be unlocked by the same key, and that a key may be secreted in the mouth of the medium. There are also some persons who have small hands and large wrists, which will slip from hand-cuffs and knotted ropes. That Mr. Mansfield, who has been the most successful reader of sealed letters among all the spiritualist mediums of America, opened the letters sent to him, according to Barnum's "History of Humbugs," was proved by the fact that a hair or a grain of sand deposited in the letter disappeared after it had passed through his hands.

It is impossible to describe in this chapter all the many tricks of mediums, for they are ever changing; such a description would occupy this whole volume. But if we were disposed to enter upon such a work we would willingly pledge ourself to explain and perhaps parallel any manifestation of a physical kind which any spirit medium in America can produce. We have faced a hundred mediums with this challenge, without the above "perhaps," and have never yet been brought to the test. Others, like Van Vleck, M'Queen, ex-medium Bishop, Baldwin, and Grimes, have traveled over the country giving this challenge, with like result.

Chapter XXII.

SOME OCCULT LAWS OF MENTAL ACTION.

A DOZEN years ago trance was a region as dark and unexplored as that of chemistry in the days of the old alchemists; and the mediomania developed by modern spiritualism has not been an unmixed curse, because it has compelled scientific thought to concentrate itself upon this hitherto unexplored field. The persons most liable to become entranced are women subject to certain bodily derangements peculiar to their sex;* although men of unhealthy bodies and strong nervous organizations are not infrequently affected by it. As is amply demonstrated by the history of the dancers, flagellants, lycanthropes, mesmerists, and devotees at sacred shrines, the trance is contagious; sometimes sweeping through the crowd like a silent but almost irresistible sympathy, leaving its victims in a dazed and dreamy condition, and sometimes manifesting itself in convulsive and noisy demonstrations.

In such a condition the mind is in a state of abstraction and profoundly concentrated upon the

---

* Pathology and Treatment of Mediomania, by F. R. Marvin, M. D., Professor of Psychological Medicine and Medical Jurisprudence, page 42.

one object of contemplation; and if its thoughts are spoken or written will exhibit a power of fancy and sometimes of logic, of which it is incapable when in a normal state. Orators are eloquent just to the degree of their mental abstraction from all outside thoughts and circumstances while addressing an audience. They must for a time forget where they are, and permit the rush of thought to make them oblivious to every thing else. If a short-hand reporter has taken down the address, the speaker will afterward be astonished to see in it metaphors and sentences which he supposed himself to be incapable of uttering. Great musical composers and philosophers, and inventors in their best moments, are so far abstracted that they sit for hours at their work unconscious of what is taking place around them. We read of one philosopher so absorbed in his meditations that he walked a long distance with one foot on and one foot off the sidewalk, troubled with a half-dreamy notion that by some sudden freak of nature one leg had suddenly become longer than the other. Sir Isaac Newton's servant once brought his dinner to his room, and the busy philosopher being oblivious to his presence, the servant sat down and ate the repast himself, leaving behind him the soiled and empty dishes. When the philosopher awoke from his state of mental abstraction he went to the accustomed place for his meal, but turned away, remarking: "O, I have eaten my dinner."

In such a state the philosopher will be more profound, the musician more musical, and the visionary more bombastic than at ordinary times. Andrew Jackson Davis is a fair sample of the latter class. Writing while entranced, this sentence, impossible to mortals in a normal condition, falls from his pen: "Mysterious rappings proceed from the sub-derangement and hyper-effervescence of small conical glandular bodies, situated heterogeneously in the rotundum of the inferior acephalocyst, which, by coming in unconscious contact with the etherization of the five superior processes of the dorsal vertebræ, also result in tippings by giving rise to spontaneous combustion, with certain abnormal evacuations of multitudinous echinorhincus bicornis, situated in various abdominal orifices. The raps occur from the ebullitions of the former in certain temperamental structures, and the tips from the thoracic cartilaginous ducts, whenever their contents are compressed by cerebral inclinations."[†] This passage is sufficient to throw his uncultured dupes into ecstasies, and cause them to aver that the wonderful seer never had a collegiate training from which such profundity could proceed.

It is in this way that ignorant girls sometimes, speaking while entranced at a spiritualist séance, astonish their friends by displays of unusual power, which they, using the common sophistry of superstition, attribute to inspiration by spirits of the dead. On very rare occasions the memory brings forth, for the entranced lips to utter, forgotten events and truths, presenting a phenomenon well calculated to confound the unlearned,

---

[†] Penetralia, page 188.

and sometimes confounding men of scientific pretensions.

It is reasonable to suppose that in the entranced, in extreme moments, the soul may become active and untrammeled by physical hindrances to the extent which is sometimes experienced by drowning men. De Quincey relates that a friend of his while near drowning, saw his whole past life, with its minute and forgotten events, standing like a panorama before his mind. Doctor Adam Clarke relates that he once had a similar experience. Admiral Beaufort fell into the water, and, while suffocating, his thoughts rushed with astonishing rapidity. He saw at a glance even the forgotten details of his childhood days, and concluded that memory possesses a hidden and almost infinite power, with which we are to awaken hereafter. Upham relates two remarkable cases in which memory gave a hint of its unknown stores, while disease had in some way given it liberty to display them. A child was taken from America to Paris. She grew to womanhood, forgetting every word of English; but when sick with a fever, she began again to speak the forgotten words of that language she had learned in infancy. In a German village an ignorant servant girl, in a delirium produced by fever, began to speak in an unknown tongue. The attending physician recognized it as Hebrew, and wrote down the passages from her lips. The inhabitants of the village, reasoning after the manner of the spiritualists, affirmed that the sick girl was possessed of a learned devil. But the physician resolved to trace out the history of the patient, and, if possible, find a solution of the marvel. He found at last that the girl had been a servant in the house of a learned clergyman, who had been in the habit of pacing to and fro in the hall-way opening into the room where the girl was accustomed to work, and of reading aloud from Hebrew authors. The clergyman was dead, but the physician found his library in the possession of one of his daughters, and there were the Hebrew authors he had been accustomed to read aloud in hearing of the servant girl, and of any one who happened to be in adjoining rooms. Turning through the venerable Hebrew books he found favorite passages marked by the pen or pencil, and on comparing them with the passages written down from the unconscious lips of the sick girl, he found them to be identical, proving that the Hebrew sounds, meaningless to her, had entered the memory of the servant girl, to be retained and uttered years afterwards by her when in the delirium of her sick-bed.

If on rare occasions when collusion and fraud are impossible, a spirit medium (so called), when the eyes are rolled back, the breath convulsive, the pulse low and fitful, the extremities cold, the mind abstracted, and the whole being in an abnormal condition, shall give utterance to facts and truths of which she is utterly ignorant when in a normal state, it only proves to us the hidden power of the memory. Before the phenomenon can be attributed to any other source, it must be shown that the medium had never heard or read the statements she utters. When a mundane and natural cause for a phenomenon may be assigned, we must accept that as the cause and seek no other, else we would be justified in affirming that ghosts produce every effect discovered by our senses. Also, when a known natural law will account for a phenomenon, we must not lay it aside and seek some new and unknown cause, else we destroy all scientific knowledge at one blow. We wish it to be remembered, however, that the extraordinary manifestations of the laws of mind in certain abnormal conditions are not of so frequent occurrence as to constitute the real basis of the great epidemic delusion known as modern spiritualism. A slight elevation of the mental powers of the entranced medium — particularly the imagination — occasional guesses which hit the mark and astonish the unsophisticated, together with deliberate fraud on the part of nearly all traveling and professional mediums, constitute the essential elements, without which modern spiritualism could never have arrested public attention.

But occasionally the entranced medium has exhibited powers which have been of such a character, and which have been so well authenticated, as to present a subject for scientific investigation. One of the most conspicuous and perplexing phenomena developed by modern spiritualism was unconscious volition by those who seemed to be in their normal state. A circle of enthusiastic investigators would surround a table, with their hands laid upon it, and in some expected time and manner, the table would move or tip, all the members of the circle solemnly protesting that it moved without their aid. It would be easy for some deceiver in the circle, by pressing his knees against the table, or by having a hook secured to his wrist and concealed by his sleeve, to cause the table to move; but perhaps all the members of the circle were persons of such moral standing that their assertions could not be discredited. The question arises, Did the members of the circle, or some member alone, move the table unconsciously? or was the movement produced by some unknown spirit or force? By the laws of scientific inquiry, as well as by the principles of common sense, we are bound first to direct our attention to the visible, rather than to the invisible, causes which possibly may have produced the phenomenon. If we find that it was impossible that the visible agents could have produced it, then we are authorized to look toward the invisible.

If we were to adopt any other method of procedure we would land ourselves in interminable absurdities. We would be permitted to refer thefts and murders which occur among us to ghostly criminals, and disband our detective and police force, or set them to work, after the manner of barbarians, ringing bells and hurling fire-brands, to drive off the evil spirits which crowd the air. Let us then turn our attention to the visible persons whose hands lie on the moving table. Could they act unconsciously? Let us first begin with those facts which are more remote from the point in hand and more commonplace. We breathe without any conscious volition of the mind, and we continue to breathe when we are sleeping. The fingers of the skillful pianist act without conscious volition. The business man, starting from home to his office, if profoundly absorbed in meditation, not only walks without being conscious of each particular step, but walks on without turning to the proper street, or walks by his office door without knowing what he is doing; his body moves by unconscious volitions, which are neither recorded by the memory nor noticed by the understanding. If men with their eyes open may do this, may they not in certain extreme moments move a table, and yet be unconscious of it? To say the least of it, when we find such a law governing our mental and physical natures, it is sufficient to warrant us in ignoring all invisible agents as the cause of the table-tipping phenomenon until we have made further investigations. What is the mental state of those in the circle at the genuine table-tipping *séance* which we have supposed to occur? Where the performance was successful, only those of "harmonious" temperaments are there; they had been making a desperate and determined experiment, as they believed, trying to lift the awful veil which shuts out the unseen world; they are filled with awe, wonder, and expectation, which are the exciting causes of the trance or semi-trance. It is past the hour of midnight, and the sitters are solemn and half-dazed; the invisible fluids, as they suppose, pass from left to right around the circle; surely the table must be about to move from left to right; it is a moment of suspense and expectation; each hand is unconsciously pressed toward the right to an increasing degree as expectation and desire increase, till the table moves, and all the company are bewildered and gratified. Each member of the eager and expectant circle exerted a little force, and the aggregate force was sufficient to move the table, just as the crowd of Indiamen pull the ropes attached to the car of Juggernaut, and believe that it moves miraculously. In a genuine case of table-tipping a similar cause is at work, as was fully shown by the investigations of the greatest modern English scientist, Professor Faraday, who constructed an apparatus by which the least pressure on the table by the hands of the medium would be indicated by an index, on the same principle as that governing the scales used by grocers; he attached the apparatus to the table, but fastened the indicator so that it could not move; the medium put his hands on the table and caused it to tip, as he declared, without pressing with his hands. The experiment was repeated, the indicator being free this time; but when the pointer moved on the graduated arc, the medium became conscious of the power he was exerting, and ceased to tip the table.

Sometimes, however, the sitters are wrought up to such a state of expectancy that the excited imagination produces the conviction that the table is moved when in reality it is not. W. B. Carpenter, F. R. S., LL. D., was invited to a *seance* where it was expected that a table would rise up under the hands of the circle and remain unsupported in the air, it being alleged that the phenomenon had occurred the preceding night. Dr. Carpenter sat near by and waited patiently until the expected marvel should occur, but taking the precaution to keep his eyes on the legs of the table at the point where they touched the floor; after a time the members of the circle declared that the table had risen a little way into the air, but Dr. Carpenter still saw the table legs planted solidly on the floor, and asked the members of the circle what evidence they had that the table had lifted itself from the floor, and they replied that they felt it pressing upward against their hands. The excited imagination had transformed the sensation produced by the downward pressure of their hands into a conviction that the table was pressing upward.* Dr. Carpenter avers that he had paid a great deal of attention to this subject during twenty years or more, and has failed to find any genuine phenomena in connection with modern spiritualism and kindred delusions which may not be accounted for by unconscious volition, by the power of the excited imagination under the control of a dominant idea, and by unconscious trains of thought, passing on in the mind, suddenly presenting their results before the eyes of the mind.

That the processes of thought are continually active in the mind, whether we are conscious of them or not, is shown to us in our dreams, when in our half-waking state we become suddenly aware of the operations of the mind. When a man forgets some-

---
*Popular Science Monthly, vol. 2, p. 31.

thing it frequently happens that he may cudgel his brain in vain to find the missing link of memory, and when he is engaged upon something else, and has dismissed the former subject from his mind, the desired idea suddenly flashes upon him, the unconscious trains of thought having at last brought it before him. An inventor, who had studied long upon a desired improvement in the construction of the microscope, was reading a stupid novel when the desired idea suddenly stood before his mind, his unconscious thoughts having solved the problem. Our text-books on "Mental Philosophy" contain examples of mathematicians who have solved difficult problems in their dreams, which they had failed to solve in their waking state.

That there is an important realm of the mind lying below consciousness is evident from the almost inexhaustible store of ideas contained in the memory, very little of which we are conscious of at any one time, and from many other well-known facts which it is needless to rehearse. Our unconscious, more than our conscious, reasonings guide us in some practical affairs of life. Common sense decides almost instantly, the using of data and arriving at conclusions, we know not how, a thousand times over against one conscious and labored process of argumentation. Our mental processes are continually going on like the process of breathing, being only occasionally called to account by the conscious reason and conscious volition. The civil courts of Cincinnati, Ohio, in 1867, furnished a valuable illustration of the idea now before us. We extract an account of it from the *Popular Science Monthly*, Volume I, page 635:

"The recent legal contest over the will of Davis B. Lawler of Cincinnati, involved many interesting medical and psychological questions. He died at the age of eighty-two years, without issue, leaving an estate valued at five hundred thousand dollars. The question arose concerning his mental state at the time when certain codicils were added to his will, which gave the bulk of his property to the German relatives of his deceased wife.

"In October, 1867, nearly two years before his death, Mr. Lawler had a severe fall and concussion of the brain, which was followed by loss of memory of written language, and the codicils in question were made about a month after the accident. His physician, who saw him first six months after the fall, says that he ascertained definitely, on his first visit, that Mr. Lawler could see printed characters, but that they conveyed no ideas to his mind. The large head-lines of a newspaper, the Cincinnati *Gazette*, he could not read though he saw them perfectly. He could write his name, and yet could not tell whether what he had written was or was not his name. He could write directions about his business, but could not read the writing, though it was plain enough to others. The sight of written or printed characters failed to be converted into ideas, while his power to make them seemed to imply the possession of such ideas. But such writing as he did was shown to have been done automatically."

Concerning this remarkable case, which has

OCCULT LAWS OF MENTAL ACTION. 299

been providentially furnished to throw light upon some mysterious laws of mental action, the editor remarks:

"It is well known that many acts, at first performed with great labor, by endless repetition come to be performed without will and even without consciousness. Piano playing, dressing, winding a watch, are acts of this nature, and signing one's name may be classed with them. Herbert Spencer says: 'The actions we call rational are, by long-continued repetition, rendered automatic and instinctive.' He further says: 'In short, many, if not most of our daily actions (actions, every step of which was originally preceded by a consciousness of consequences, and was therefore rational), have, by perpetual repetition, been rendered more or less automatic. The requisite impressions being made on us, the appropriate movements follow without memory, reason, or volition coming into play. Maudsley holds that, 'when an idea or mental state has been completely organized, it is revived without consciousness, and takes its part automatically in our mental operations, just as an habitual movement does in our bodily activity.' And again: 'As it is with memory, so it is with volition, which is a physiological function of the supreme centers, and which, like memory, becomes more unconscious and automatic the more completely it is organized by repeated practice.'"

We do not accept the idea advanced by Professor Youmans, that the part of the mind unrevealed by consciousness is incapable of volition, and is an automaton, but we believe that volition proper, wherein man's freedom consists, lies below consciousness, in that vaster and unexplored realm of the soul unknown to our philosophers. In the case of Mr. Lawler we find that he traced letters with his pen, forming words without being able to read them when written, and hence without being conscious of those muscular and mental acts by which the letters were formed.

This law governing the human organism, and which is so conspicuously manifest in certain abnormal conditions of the brain must display itself to a greater or less extent under those abnormal conditions of mind and body which are so essential to the trance medium. It is exhibited in the familiar experiment of holding a bell by the end of the handle until it strikes the hour of the day. The nervous operator's wish unconsciously controls his muscles, to move the bell gradually until it strikes the hour which he has in his mind. The operator, with the witch-hazel or divining-rod, fixes in his mind a locality where he fancies an oil belt or an ore bed may be located, and when his rod is delicately poised his unconscious volition moves his muscles so as to turn the rod in the desired manner. Mind-reading, or muscle-reading as it is now known to be, has become a parlor pastime. Some one secretes some object in some corner of the room, and then a comrade from another room takes him by the arm and leads him about, hither and thither, and by noting his unconscious efforts to avoid the spot where the object has been placed, is able to

OCCULT LAWS OF MENTAL ACTION. 301

lead him to the very spot where the object has been hidden. If this law of unconscious volition is displayed when the operators are in their normal condition, it would exhibit itself more fully in the entranced or semi-entranced medium. Consciousness is still further stupefied and the muscles are convulsive with nervous tension. The medium has gone into her trance expecting to write a communication upon a certain subject; she is oblivious to all else, and we should expect that in such a state of mental abstraction her mental powers would be more brilliant than usual in the discussion of her theme. We need not be surprised if her memory lets slip some words and facts and sentiments which she has heard from her intellectual superiors and which she could not command in her normal state, and which she shall afterward declare were really unknown to her and which are unknown to those present at the *séance*, but which, on subsequent investigation, they may find to be true; we should expect her to write what she could not remember she had written when her trance had passed away; we should expect, moreover, that innumerable mediums, making experiments all over the land, would sometimes make happy hits, by chance, which, when published in the spiritualist papers, and carefully collected into a volume by a devotee like Robert Dale Owen, would look like a formidable defense of the spiritualists' hypothesis.

Really remarkable phenomena in connection with modern spiritualism have been of very rare occurrence, notwithstanding hundreds of thousands of experiments have been made, in Europe and America, during the past thirty years; and, as we have seen, what have occurred are designed not to disclose to us another world, but to suggest the laws which govern our own. That the entranced medium believes that she hears raps and voices, and sees visions of persons living and dead, occasionally, by chance, hitting the mark, astonishing and confounding the ignorant and credulous, is explained in the chapter on the excited imagination, and elsewhere in this volume.

Chapter XXIII.

THEORIES FOUNDED ON FRAUDULENT PHENOMENA.

AS we glance over the books written by able and intelligent men who have been convinced that the phenomena of modern spiritualism are genuine, and that they prove the existence of some occult force in nature, if they are not produced by spirits, we find that their judgments were influenced either by the performances of mediums who were afterward caught in the act of deception, or by phenomena reproduced under the same conditions and explained by professional jugglers. There is no exception to this rule. Challenges of this kind have been repeatedly published to the world by profesional jugglers. Bishop, Baldwin, and Van Vleck traveled in the United States from the Atlantic to the Pacific coast repeating the challenge and giving their exhibitions. Mediums were ever wary of them. One of them offered a thousand dollars for any mediumistic performance which he could not parallel under the same conditions as those demanded by the medium, and published his challenge in the leading spiritualist paper of the West. His offer was never accepted.

William Crookes, F. R. S., was first confounded by the celebrated Home, whose frauds were detected by Robert Browning, and to whom, as Moncure D. Conway states, he confessed his fraud. Home, by this and other transactions, lost his hold on the public and was denounced as a scoundrel whose honesty could not be relied on. Home's experiments with the accordion, which were regarded by Mr. Crookes as unaccountable by any of the known laws of matter, were afterward performed by Dr. Monk, in England, who after a while was caught in his deception and sent to prison. The medium held the accordion with one hand under the table, while his other hand was on the table in plain sight of the spectators. A basket inclosed the accordion, so that the medium could not reach the accordion with his feet. In this condition during the evening the accordion produced music. The trick has since been often repeated and explained. The medium must have the semblance of a key-board, made of some light material, concealed in his coat sleeve or about his person. This he attaches to the bottom of the accordion which he holds in his hand. Then when unobserved, while the learned professor is "taking down his notes" for the public press, he reverses the accordion, and attaching the false keyboard on the bottom by means of a small hook attached to it, fastens it to the side of the basket; having now the real keyboard in his hand he is able to produce musical sounds. Afterward the accordion floated about in the basket under the table, without the contact of Mr. Home's hand. This subsequent phenomenon was given to avoid immediate examination of the first by keeping Professor

Crookes in suspense, and giving the medium time to reverse the instrument and conceal in his clothing the false key-board which had been on the bottom of the instrument. The accordion was suspended by means of a small hook fastened to a dark thread, which would be invisible in the gas-light. The next test exhibited the weight of the "psychic force" by means of a plank, one end of which was suspended by a pair of scales, while the other end was in the hands of the medium. The medium doubtless performed this trick by means of iron hooks attached to his wrists and concealed by his sleeves. By deftly inserting the hook under the plank and lifting up with his wrists while bearing down with his fingers, he could make the other end of the plank bear more heavily on the scales by which it was suspended. The learned professor meantime was busy taking "notes" for the *Quarterly Journal of Science.*

By means of these concealed hooks the table tippers generally astonished the onlookers. Professor Crookes also flashed the "electric light" on the spirit form of Katie King, much to his satisfaction. But shortly afterward the Katie King business was going on in this country under the same "test conditions," when Dr. Childs, of Philadelphia, flashed another light on the phenomenon, to the profound and sorrowful bewilderment of the venerable Robert Dale Owen. The arrant impostor, Anna Eva Fay, as we have already seen, contributed data to establish the professor's theory of psychic force.

Alfred R. Wallace, F. R. S., based his opinion

on the tricks of Home, spirit photographers, and others whose arts have been duplicated and explained in nearly every city of this country. He rests largely upon Prof. Crookes's experiments.

Epes Sargent, a popular writer of this country, wrote a book entitled, "Proofs Palpable of Immortality," basing his arguments on the phenomena of modern spiritualism. But unfortunately for him, he wrote just before the recent epidemic of medium exposure began. He rests upon Home's exhibitions at the Hazzard House, in Moravia, New York, the exposure of which we have already noted; upon A. S. Haywood, a vile free-lover of Boston, who has been arrested for obscenity; upon Dr. Slade, the slate-writing medium, whose frauds have been exposed and published by the New York *Sun* and other leading papers of that city, and by Professor Lankester of London; upon the Holmeses and Katie King; the Eddy mediums, who have been since exposed, as we have already noted; Mumler, the spirit photographer, whose art is now known to most photographers, and who has since been denounced as a fraud by the leading spiritualists; and others like these. He makes much of the Holmeses and "Katie King," who were then in the midst of their triumphs. He quotes with enthusiasm Robert Dale Owen concerning "Katie King" and the Holmes medium:

"Mr. Owen testifies in the strongest terms to the genuineness of the manifestations. He writes July 1, 1874:

"'All my former experience in spiritualism, favored as I have been, pales before the new manifestations witnessed by me in the course of last month. After the strictest scrutiny, with every facility promptly afforded me by the mediums to detect imposition had it been attempted, I here avow my conviction that the phenomena are genuine; that I have again and again, on more than twenty occasions, seen, heard, touched forms to appearance human and material, and to sense tangible; that these forms have stepped up close to me; that I have held conversations with them, occasionally receiving advice, sometimes having my thoughts read and adverted to; that I have received, written under my very eyes, by a luminous, detached hand, a communication of some length, purporting to come from an eminent English clergyman (the Rev. F. W. Robertson) who died twenty years ago; the style and the signature serving further to attest its genuine character; finally, that I have seen the form which had spoken to me a minute or two before, fade away till it became a dim shadow, to reappear, a few minutes later, in all its brightness.

"'I have seen, during a single sitting of an hour and a half, three separate forms, completely materialized, walk out from the cabinet to within a foot or two of where I sat, have touched all three, have conversed with all three; and this has occurred in the light, *without any one in the cabinet*, both mediums sitting beside me. Again, I have witnessed, on six different occasions, the levitation (that is, floating in the air) of a materialized form.'"

Alas! that Hon. R. D. Owen, who has done

more than any living man towards making modern spiritual phenomena to be held as worthy of investigation by the more intelligent, after his life-long experience, and after all that he had written upon the subject, should write, "All my former experience in spiritualism, favored as I have been, pales before the new manifestations witnessed by me in the course of the last month," and then shortly after be compelled to confess that even that phenomenon was a fraud. We do not wonder the old man went insane.

What must be the feelings of Epes Sargent when he now glances over the eloquent pages of this "Proof Palpable"! On page 112 Mr. Sargent continues:

"Dr. Rane, of Philadelphia, a physician of the highest standing, was present at the *séance* of August 9, 1874. He assured himself by a close examination that there was no inlet or outlet to the cabinet. The two mediums remained outside among the spectators. After some music the curtains of the holes in the partition were raised, and several hands became visible. Soon a whole arm appeared, and, as in salutation, was waved to and fro in a graceful manner. Katie shook hands from the window with those who went up to it. She talked, too, repeatedly; for instance, she answered the question of 'How do you like the present company?' by 'I'll tell you after a while;' and, later, 'I love you all.' At another time she said, 'I feel now as natural as when I was in earth-life.' Her voice was mild and somewhat whispering. Of her issuing from the cabinet in a full materialized form, Dr. Rane says:

"'The door opened and Katie appeared, slowly moving her hands as though saluting or declaiming, and clad in a tasteful white robe, and a mantilla of gauze or lace. Her waist was encircled by a belt, fastened with a gold clasp or buckle. At her throat appeared a gold cross or similar ornament. Afterwards she emerged entirely from the closet, sat down upon a chair next to Mrs. Holmes, rose and receded slowly into the closet again.

"'The question was then put to her whether she could not show us *how* she materialized herself, and was again answered by 'I will try.' After a while the door of the closet opened once more, and we saw, in the right corner of it, a kind of gray mist or cloud, from which, within a short time, Katie's whole figure was developed in a wonderful manner. Her disappearance was similar; it was a gradual fading and dissolving. The white figure *was not illumined by external light, but had a peculiar blueish-white and brilliant splendor, that seemed to come from within.* I do not believe that any mixture of earthly colors would be able to produce the same effect. The gold of the belt-buckle and the necklace appeared more golden than the finest gold.'

"Here was a proof palpable—but of what? Surely of immortal spirit, whether we call it psychic force or independent spirit power. Admitting that there was no delusion—and the reader who has carefully weighed the testimony I have adduced will hardly adopt so insufficient a theory as that of fraud or deception—what can it be *but an intelligence and a will, exercising, through some centripetal and centrifugal use of the invisible constituents of matter, the astonishing power of materializing and dematerializing a human form with its appropriate clothing?"*

On page 120 Mr. Sargent also presents the spirit tests given by Charles H. Foster, a medium whose manifestations were, at the time, quite wonderful, but who has since been brought to grief by the Boston *Daily Globe* and the reporters of the New York papers. Also, on page 229, our author quotes the performance of the medium named Mott, whose exposure we have already noticed. We would also note that the Eddy mediums, upon whom our author places much reliance, afterward exposed themselves, confessing their deceptions.

If we were to dissect Hon. Robert Dale Owen's "Foot-Falls on the Boundaries of Another World," or any other book recounting the evidences of modern spiritualism, it would share the fate of this once very popular work by Epes Sargent. Mr. Owens's most astonishing confirmation of spiritualism, as he confesses, was the "Katie King" *séance*, which he afterward acknowledged to be a fraud. If we turn to the article on Spiritualism in the "American Cyclopædia," we find that the Fox girls, Home, the "Katie King" *séance*, the Eddy brothers, Mott, Mrs. Stewart, Mrs. Markee, are the conspicuous examples of mediumship. That they were frauds has been sufficiently established in the preceding pages.

The well-known Joseph Cook, of Boston, has also recently asserted that, although a large portion of so-called spirit mediums are impostors, yet some of them are able to produce results which can not be accounted for by any known mundane causes, and he hails these manifestations as powerful aids to assist him in his warfare against atheistic materialism. We think that he has no need to resort to such a doubtful method of defense. He indorses as genuine the tests performed by Mr. Home in the presence of Professor Crookes, and which we have already sufficiently explained. He makes much of that bold impostor, "Dr." Slade, who flourished for a time in the city of New York, being one of the chief pioneers in the slate-writing tests. Reporters of the New York daily papers discovered the method of his operations, and published them to the world, so that he found it desirable to seek some new field in which to carry on his operations. Leaving New York, he went to London, and, by vigorous advertising, soon gained sufficient notoriety to attract the attention of some scientific investigators, among whom was Professor Lankester, who caught the medium in the act of writing on the slate with his own hand while, as he professed, the spirits were doing the writing—a fact which Professor Lankester positively asserted in his testimony before the civil courts.

"Dr." Slade was arrested and tried for vagrancy; but, owing to the indefiniteness of the law in its bearings on the case, he was acquitted, but was immediately re-arrested and released on bail. We next find him in Germany—Joseph Cook's earthly paradise, from whence all knowledge is supposed to proceed. Mr. Slade in New York is not worthy Mr. Cook's attention, but Mr. Slade in Germany becomes in his eyes at once a most wonderful personage.

If we were to turn trickster, we would much rather begin our operations in Germany in the presence of some German transcendentalist who has spent half his life dreaming over his mug of beer than in the city of New York in the presence of the matter-of-fact reporters of the daily press. When Mr. Slade has succeeded in astounding and bewildering certain men in Germany, with reputations for strange transcendental notions and possessing difficult German surnames, then Mr. Cook, the disciple, follows his master into this new vagary, and comes forth with his lectures on modern spiritualism. Why did he not indorse Mr. Slade before he left New York? By what transcendental law did Mr. Slade acquire additional psychic force by going into Germany? So far as the experiments performed by Mr. Slade in Germany are reported in Mr. Cook's lectures, we can see a half-dozen ways in which he could have hoodwinked his German converts; but Mr. Cook gives us the result of a private investigation of his own, which we shall examine more minutely:

1. We suggest that Mr. Cook, who had already indorsed the idea that Mr. Slade, by effort of will, and without physical contact, could make a pencil write on a slate, and that a large sea-shell could sink through a solid board without leaving any trace behind, had attained such an abnormal state of cre-

dulity that he was in a condition to be easily deceived by his Boston medium.

2. Mr. Cook admits that mediums, as a class, are immoral, and, as he fails to give the name of his medium or any evidence that he was an exception to his class, we are to conclude that the medium performing the experiments was of bad character. To begin with, we must look upon him with suspicion.

3. Of the nine persons present at the experiments four were spiritualists, who, as a class — as Mr. Cook declares in this same lecture — tend to immorality, and we must look upon them as persons who would be likely to join with the medium in perpetrating a fraud upon the already over-credulous Mr. Cook.

4. The medium had also a powerful motive for deception, because it was certain that through private channels he could convey to the public the indorsement of Mr. Cook. Another medium had recently accumulated $30,000 by similar frauds.

5. Mr. Cook states that care was taken to see that the slates were clean before the spirits or the psychic force began writing on them. We have already explained how the slate may seem to have no writing on it when it contains writing which, after a while, may become visible.

6. The reading of names written on paper and then crushed into the shape of pellets, Mr. Cook thinks may have been a case of mind-reading; but we have already shown how it can be done by fraud.

7. At this stage the "psychic" began to suffer contortions, which would be very useful in diverting attention from the pellets or from the slate, enabling the "psychic" to perform some sleight-of-hand operations necessary to the success of the experiments.

8. He then placed two slates on the table and his open hand on them.

9. The "psychic" then seemed to make a strong effort of will, and expressed doubt about the success of the experiment. This was to quiet the doubting and yet hoping investigators, so that they would be content not to meddle with the slates upon which he or his confederate had written during or before his "contortions."

10. He then exhibited the slates, containing the yet invisible writing, and put a bit of pencil between them. Writing was heard, the sound being produced as we have explained in a preceding chapter.

11. When the slates were opened a bit of pencil was found between them—worn, as if it had been used in writing. A philosopher like Mr. Cook ought to know that the "psychic" could have bitten off the end of a pencil already worn, and that one side of the fragment would thus be worn before it was placed between the slates; or he could have secretly substituted one piece for another. It is very evident that Mr. Cook did not examine the pencil before it was bitten.

12. The writing gave the year of the birth of Mr. Cook's father. Mr. Cook was a public person-

age in Boston, and the medium by a little previous inquiry could have found out this fact.

13. In the next experiment (as, perhaps, in the first) the slates were washed with a wet sponge, and examined after the washing, to see that in the interval they had not been written upon. In the daylight, as we have previously explained, writing may exist on a wet slate when it seems to be clean, and much more might this occur in the gaslight. Why thus wet the slate after Mr. Cook had wiped off the previous writing with his handkerchief? This last precaution was doubtless suggested by the medium, or one of his four probable confederates, to give him an opportunity to write upon the wet slate, or secretly to substitute another slate. Then Mr. Cook gets a bright idea and demands that the wet slates be fastened together with clamps. And to astound the public, Mr. Cook exhibits said brass clamps to his audience. This time the medium exhibits no effort of will, and does not go into contortions. These are not needed as a blind now, because the writing is within the wet slates, and will be revealed as soon as they are dry. When the slates are opened at last, they contain no astounding revelation, but a simple: "God bless you all. I am here. Your loving friend, Fanny Conant." Fanny Conant was a person of whom our philosopher had never heard. She was quite notorious in Boston, but she had never lived in Germany.

14. The *séance* was held in the house of a spiritualist, and four spiritualists were present besides

the medium, with only five investigators, including Mr. and Mrs. Joseph Cook.

15. The five investigators assert that they can not apply any theory of fraud, and that they do not see how the writing was done, unless the pencil was moved without physical contact. Well, suppose Mr. Cook had possessed the humility to confess that there was one phenomenon in the universe for which he could not at present give an explanation, would it not have been more in accordance with the spirit of a true philosopher? We find him falling down into the use of the old, yet ever surviving sophistry of superstition: "If it is not . . . what is it? I do not know; therefore, it is . . ." Or, in other words, I do not know; therefore, I know.

16. But Mr. Cook makes some fatal admissions. He admits that his attention was several times diverted, particularly in the pellet tests. At these times Mr. Cook should have known the medium "palmed" a pellet, and brought it below the table to open and read it. He admits that two or three times the medium and a "friend" of the medium left the room, and conferred together in the hall. This was done in order to perfect arrangements for substituting slates, which were to be concealed under the skirts of their coats. The medium also objected to those test conditions which did not suit him, and at one time parleyed a quarter of an hour during which time by assumed anger, he could call off the attention of the observers, and prepare the forthcoming marvel.

In conclusion, we express our sorrow and surprise that the great and eloquent translator of the latest German thought should not possess as much common shrewdness in dealing with charlatans and impostors as the average newspaper reporter. However, we have seen enough of the world to know that it would be far easier to play a practical joke upon a transcendental philosopher than upon the average boot-black who has knocked against the rugged world of realities.

Chapter XXIV.

SPIRIT AGENCY THE LAST HYPOTHESIS.

EVEN if for the sake of the argument we grant that no spirit mediums have been impostors, and that all our explanations have been inadequate to account for their manifestations, we would not yet be justified by the laws of scientific investigation in assuming that they are produced by disembodied human spirits; but we would be required to join with Professors Crookes and Wallace in their attempts to prove the existence of psychic force. That failing us, we would have to go with Baron Charles Von Reichenbach, into his laboratories, with his magnets, rods, crystals, and hysterical and epileptic females, to determine the existence and properties of odylic force. We are permitted to seek a supermundane cause for any effect which we see around us only after we have exhausted every other hypothesis. And if we should be driven to this last hypothesis, the immoral tendency of spiritualism, the universal corruption of its literature, the dissolute character of the majority of its active advocates, would compel us to believe that the devil himself is the cause to which the phenomena of spiritualism are to be attributed. But the physical theories propounded by the unanimous consent of leading spiritualists are so extravagant as to account for all their alleged phenomena and tenfold more, even if there were no spirits, angels, or devils.

It is affirmed that in certain states the mind is freed from the body sufficiently to possess senses of its own, and for a time has no use for those in the body. And at such times the clairvoyant not only sees and hears without the aid of the bodily organs, but in such states the various faculties of the mind assume new power—the memory, for example, often beholding all the occurrences which have passed before it since the time of infancy.* It is affirmed that a mesmerized subject sees any object which the magnetizer wills that he shall see;† that persons in the circle, by the mysterious influence of mind upon mind, may compel the medium to reproduce their own thoughts and desires, the same being also true of persons not in the circle. ‡ Hudson Tuttle affirms that magnetism (which, according to his notion, is the medium of influence between mind and mind), travels with greater velocity than light;|| that this mysterious force may be felt not only by contact, but at the distance of the stars, and is positive and negative;§ that animal magnetism can be transferred to all bodies;¶ that persons separated by a great distance may influence each other in their dreams;** that by touching an object we leave on it an *aura*, which, if touched by another person, will cause in his brain the same vibrations

---

*Arcana of Nature, vol. ii, p. 63. †Page 70. ‡Page 89.
||Page 110. ?Page 115. ¶Page 119. **Page 134.

as exist in our own, and thus he may know our mental state;* that in this manner the medium may read the thoughts which were in the mind of another;† that some persons in the magnetic state (and they may go into it without an operator) can read a portion of the contents of a book by putting their hands upon it;‡ that sometimes the mind can hear and see at great distances, sometimes also reading the thoughts of persons when far away.‖ The author accounts for this statement by the hypothesis that the brain excites undulations in ether which are impressed on other brains. He says that a sealed letter can be read by the medium by simply touching it and receiving the *aura* of the writer, and without spirit aid,§ and that this life-ether emanating from the brain of the medium, if directed against a table, will produce raps.¶

The same theories are announced by Ashburner in his notes on Reichenbach's "Dynamics of Magnetism;" see pages 38, 337, 356, 387. Judge Edmonds in his "Spiritual Tracts, No. 7," relates that he identified at a *séance* the spirit of his friend, who reported himself to be dead, but who shortly afterward turned up alive and well, and Andrew Jackson Davis, commenting on the occurrence, assumed that the judge may have obtained the thoughts of his friend while he was "in some distant part of the globe."** Mr. Davis also admits that the magnetic forces in the medium, without spirit agency, may move ponderable bodies and

---

* Page 147. † Page 149. ‡ Page 158. ‖ Page 162. § Page 174. ¶ Page 176. ** Evans's Spiritualism on Trial, page 51.

produce raps.* One author declares: "The clairvoyant sees in your thoughts what you no longer think, but what you have thought; what you no longer see, but what you have seen; what you no longer hear, but what you have heard." †

We thus have a view of the natural philosophy peculiar to modern spiritualism. The natural laws invented by spiritualists to enable the spirits to produce the phenomena of modern spiritualism are freely admitted by them to be universal, and hence they can not avoid applying them to spirits in the flesh. Therefore, the phenomena may be produced, as they allege, equally well by embodied and disembodied human spirits.

Assuming that either one of two causes may be assigned, they make their selection in accordance with their desire, but not with reference to the ordinary principles of common sense. It might be admitted that a troop of frolicsome spirits could demolish a garden of herbs, but if we saw a drove of cattle standing in the inclosure, we would be justified in charging the missing vegetables to the bovine rather than the angelic intruders.

According to the physics of spiritualism, a medium without spirit aid could sit quietly in her chair, and cause the ether to vibrate to a place a thousand miles away, producing raps at will on the table in some séance-room, reading at the same time the secret thoughts of the sitters, answering by means of the tiny rap their spoken and silent interrogatories, revealing to them sights and sounds they

---
* Spirit Intercourse, p. 50–54. Spiritualism on Trial, p. 89.

had long since forgotten. Therefore, in order to prove that a communication at a *séance* comes from a spirit, it would be necessary to put all human beings on earth under oath to swear that they had not sent out ether vibrations from their brains at the time the communication was received. But that would not be sufficient, because it is asserted that if persons in or out of the circle are too positive and the medium too passive, they may, unconsciously, compel her to reproduce their own thoughts and desires. To read a book without spirit help, by simply touching it, would be a small matter. The magnetic waves emanating from the brain, and under the control of the will, it is alleged, may be concentrated upon ponderable bodies, inducing in them certain positive or negative conditions, so as to move them or lift them into the air without physical contact. Distance is no obstacle. Therefore the medium should sit unattended by spirits, and, in her easy-chair, lifting at will a table and sending it through the air across the ocean. Railroads and steamships, doubtless, will soon be remanded to the crude past, in which the superstition of Christianity will lie buried. A slender female has often professed to lift pianos without physical contact. She should be able to exert an equal force upon smaller articles. Therefore, by concentrating her will upon the soles of her shoes, the zœ-ether vibrations emanating from her brain should be sufficient to lift her into mid-air, and carry her to most distant places.

In the light of this new philosophy the man

who pulled at his boot-straps until he lifted himself to the moon, becomes real and commonplace. We turn away from this chapter possessed (if possessed at all) by the spirit of Carlyle impelling us to say: Surely man must be the biggest fool in the universe.

Chapter XXV.

DELUSIONS AND THE EVIL PASSIONS.

EXTREMES meet. Skepticism and superstition frequently unite in the adoption of some theories by which to justify the free indulgence of the evil passions. Mohammed and Brigham Young sought some vision of the excited imagination which should permit them to gratify their lusts, while Diogenes, who practiced the most revolting form of licentiousness in public and in open day, and the French atheists of the period of the revolution, invented some false theory of natural science by which to justify their conduct. An infidel who enjoys his infidelity is invariably immoral.

There are no exceptions to this rule. He is guilty of some open or covert crime against his conscience or human society. If he is a true man at heart he will send up a wail before he extinguishes the lamp kindled in the sepulcher and strikes a blow at the religious sentiment upon which public happiness and morality depend. If by some strange process of thought he has entered upon such a work, and is sincerely seeking the right, he must of necessity enter upon his work with sorrow, and a minor tone of sadness is heard in all his utterances. Infidels of this temper constitute a very small minority of their class. And we are well acquainted with the crimes so frequently connected with excessive superstitions—witches seeking supernatural power in order to torment and destroy their neighbors; witch-finders torturing and burning their victims; the worshipers of Saint Peter's toe-nails, and phials supposed to contain the tears or milk of the Virgin Mary; flaying and burning heretics; human victims bleeding on heathen altars in heathen temples in Corinth and Babylon, and in nearly all the ancient world of more enlightened paganism; fornication and adultery practiced in the name of religion; licentiousness sometimes practiced by early mesmerists, flagellants and dancers, and by crowds of deluded and half-frenzied devotees at shrines and magical fountains; Mormonism, resulting in polygamy; Oneida communities, spiritualism, and superstitious schemes of social reform, resulting in free-love, or, more properly, free lust.

Let us take, for an example, the superstition which is just now passing away—modern spiritualism. It has a philosophy stolen from French and German atheists and pantheists, rechristened with the name Harmonial. Optimism is an essential ingredient. But while dreamy Germans and volatile Frenchmen may hold a theory aloft in the cloud region of speculation, or may discourse glibly concerning it in the parlor, and forget it when out on the street, the deluded and persevering Yankee will not fail to carry it out into practical life. Hence the saddest chapter which we are called upon to write in the composition of this volume is this one, in which we record the corruptions attendant upon modern spiritualism. Andrew Jackson Davis affirms: "Sin, in the common acceptation of the word, does not really exist."* "Again, the innate divineness of the spirit prohibits the possibility of spiritual wickedness or unrighteousness."† Dr. Hare, a leading spiritualist, affirms: "There is no evil that can be avoided. The devil could be nothing else but what Omnipotence would make him."‡

Doctor A. B. Childs, in 1860, published a book, entitled, "Whatever is, is Right," which ran rapidly through five editions, and was regarded as a most valuable contribution to the Harmonial Philosophy of Andrew Jackson Davis. Its publishers present in the back part of the book notices of the press, which show us how thoroughly it was indorsed by the spiritualist papers. It is enthusiastically indorsed by the *Shekinah, Herald of Progress, Banner of Light, Boston Investigator, The Spirit Guardian,* and *The World's Paper.* The book also contains indorsements by the following individuals: Silas Tyrrell, Doctor Paige, L. J. Pardee, P. B. Randolph, H. D. Huston, J. S. Loveland, Horace Laver, Mrs. J. H. Conant, Emma Harding, Lizzie Dalton, A. J. Davis, L. C. Howe, Leo Miller, and other leading spiritualists. But what is the book which the spiritualist press and leading teachers have thus indorsed? "Every desire is religion to the soul that produces the desire." "Whatever the desire may be, whether it be called good or bad, that desire is the natural religion of the soul that

---

* Nature's Divine Revelations, page 147. † Page 413.
‡ Spiritualism Scientifically Demonstrated, page 31.

develops the desire."* "Vice is sand-paper to the earthly covering of the soul." "Vice and virtue too, are beautiful to the eyes of the soul. Both are right and in place."† "The soul can not be injured." "The soul can not go backward."‡ "A lie is a truth intrinsically; it holds a lawful place in creation; it is a necessity." "Every opinion is right."|| Our opinion is that a class of people who believe lying is right, may lie, and we receive their testimony concerning alleged phenomena with caution.

"The degradation of prostitution is a phantom of materialism that belongs to self-righteousness." "Prostitution, so called, is really an *undisguised* condition of life." "The vision that sees a wicked man is sensuous; consequently, must fail to see realities that are unchangeable." "What are called wicked deeds are lawful effects of one soul as much as what we call holy deeds are lawful effects of another soul."¶ When Leo Miller, for example, indorses this doctrine, we are not surprised to find him inducing Mattie Strickland, to the great grief of her parents, to live with him as an affinity, temporary or permanent, as the case may be, without marriage. When moral restraint is taken off, the evil passions go uncontrolled. Davis himself broke up a family to secure his "affinity." The prominent spiritualists that have continued unsullied by these theories in their practical life are very few.

Doctor Childs also published a book, entitled,

---

* Whatever is, is Right, page 5.   † Page 8.   ‡ Page 16.
|| Page 18.   ¶ Page 19.

"Christ and the People," which contains the following statements: "Erelong man will come to see that sin is for his spiritual good." "Holiness lays up treasures on earth." "Sin destroys earthly treasures and causes them to be laid up in heaven."* "There has been no deed in the catalogue of crime that has not been a valuable experience to the inner being of the man who committed it."† This book is also strongly indorsed by the *Banner of Light*, the leading spiritualist paper of the United States and of the world.

At the Rhode Island State Spiritualist Convention, Mr. Wheeler, speaking in the name of spiritualists in general, and his remarks apparently receiving the indorsement of the convention, said, as reported by the *Christian Standard*, Oct. 20, 1866: "As spiritualists we have not acknowledged that there is such a thing as moral obligation." "Drunkenness is just as good as soberness; vice is as good as virtue." J. F. Whitney, who was for a long time editor of a prominent spiritualist periodical, confesses that mediums generally become sensual and immoral.‡ T. S. Harris, a leading spiritualist, makes a similar confession, as does A. J. Davis, the father of modern spiritualism, who attempts to account for it by the supposition that mediums are usually controlled by evil spirits, who inhabit the lower spheres, which are nearest to the earth.

There is a large house kept by a prominent

---

* Christ and the People, pages 32 and 33.   † Page 137.
‡ Spiritualism on Trial, by F. W. Evans, page 355.

official of the spiritualist society to accommodate affinity hunters. Six spiritualist editors, and that is about all of them, are free-lovers. Out of three hundred spiritualist speakers, two hundred and fifty are loose in their morals.* The notorious Victoria Woodhull, whose advocacy of free-lovism became too grossly indecent to be endured by the civil authorities, became president of the United States Association of Spiritualists. D. M. Bennett, a notorious free-lover, and editor of the *Truth Seeker*, is now in the penitentiary for sending obscene literature through the mails. The *Religio-Philosophical Journal* has just now published a letter of his, in which he used his philosophy to break down the virtue of a young girl in his office and induce her to become his concubine, his wife being still alive.

The Crucible is edited by Moses Hull and Mattie Sawyer, who published the fact that they were living together as man and wife, without legal marriage, being joined by a private contract which either party could break at will. W. F. Jamieson once published a spiritualist magazine, called the *Rostrum*, entering upon the work of an editor after he had been caught in the act of fraud in conducting a public *séance*, in Kalamazoo, Michigan. He was condemned by the courts to pay a fine of forty dollars, or go to jail. His companion in distress turned "exposer," and now offers to parallel by legerdemain the manifestations of any medium who will consent to meet him. Mr. M'Queen has joined

---
* G. T. Carpenter's Spiritualism Condemned, page 25.

the Methodist Church, and now resides in Hillsdale, Michigan.

Hull's *Crucible* of May 19, 1877, in an editorial by the editor-in-chief, contains the following statements: "We hold damning facts against . . . nearly all the spiritualist lecturers." The editor had been gathering proof to show that all other spiritualist editors and lecturers were as deep in the mire of free-lovism as himself. He says that S. S. Jones, who had tried to make his paper "respectable," and who was the leader of that wing of spiritualism, was guilty of the crime for which he was shot by the husband of Mrs. Pike, and gives the following proofs: "The verbal and written confession of Mrs. Pike, whom he had seduced; when Jones organized the Religio-Philosophical Publishing Association, he (Moses Hull) was aiding him, and was taken by Jones to a certain 'boarding-house,' where he told us we could, if we chose, take a woman and be perfectly free, and there would be no danger of exposure; Jones himself stopped at that place." Mr. Hull then presents the testimony of four female mediums to show that Jones practiced free-lovism in its grossest form, and gives his own personal knowledge of his having occupied the same bed with a woman who was not his wife. All this Mr. Hull does not condemn, but he does condemn the cowardice of Jones, which made him try to appear "respectable" in the eyes of the misguided public. Hull's *Crucible* of March 24, 1877, says the *Religio-Philosophical Journal* establishment was the headquarters of "thieves and libertines." The same paper, in May, 1877, records three murders committed in the above named house, in a period of three months, and reveals the atrocious crime committed by Mrs. Robinson, one of the paramours of Jones, who had obtained an orphan girl from an asylum to serve as a common drudge and mistress of her son. Blows and abuse, and at one time a pistol shot in her head from the hand of her tormentor, at last had driven her to suicide.

If this, then, is the character of the one spiritualist publishing house which aimed to be thought "respectable," what must be the character of the remainder, which permit public sentiment to interpose no check upon their conduct? It is from such dens of iniquity as these that the stories of spirit phenomena proceed, to pass into the current literature of the day; and surely we must believe that theories built upon such data should be rejected.

E. H. Heywood is also the publisher of a paper in the interests of spiritualism, but his opposition to legal marriage and to all civil laws is so pronounced and bold that only a glance at his vile sheet would satisfy the most doubtful as to his character. All of these publications indorse the idea that sin is a step in human progress, and that "Whatever is, is right." The *Banner of Light* is decidedly opposed to the marriage system, and indeed the only spiritualist paper or periodical existing or defunct which ever upheld legal marriage is, we believe, the *Religio-Philosophical Journal*. We now proceed to give some miscellaneous extracts, to show the moral tendency of modern spiritualism.

In the *Banner of Light*, November 25, 1876, Emma Hardinge Britten admits that spiritualism has succumbed to the "social reformers." April 7, 1877, a spirit reports through the columns of the *Banner* that in almost all cases earthly love changes. It follows, then, that nearly all husbands and wives should separate and seek new affinities. October 28, 1876, what purports to be the spirit of "Jim Fisk," the celebrated millionaire who was shot by Stokes, and was detestable for his licentiousness, communicates to the message department of the *Banner* a denial of human accountability, and affirms that in the spirit world men do not draw back from him and say: "I am glad I am not like him." The convention assembled in Philadelphia to celebrate the twenty-ninth anniversary of spiritualism, resolved that "Society has no right to punish any individual." "We know that what to a man seems evil, to the angel world and God is but undeveloped good." (A Spirit, in the *Banner of Light*, April 21, 1877.)

"Human affections, flowing as they do out of the inmost fountains of love, irresistibly cling to and climb about whatever acts upon them as a natural attraction. They have no innate power of deciding *pro* or *con*—whether they shall or shall not—because they are pure, and superior to all thought and intention. When they are attracted, they go; when repelled, they retire in silence." (Andrew Jackson Davis, in *Banner of Light*, January 6, 1877.)

In the same number we learn that the infamous

Victoria Woodhull has been president of the Universal Association of Spiritualists, and was indorsed in glowing terms by the Michigan State Convention of Spiritualists, who

"*Resolved*, That the only open door out of our difficulties is the entire abrogation of all merely man-made marriage laws, leaving the sexes free to seek harmonious associations under the laws of nature."

Hull's *Crucible* of April 7, 1877, in an editorial, declares "governments a fraud," and that "a government founded on the will of the people is, of a necessity, a failure." And again, "It [spiritualism] knows no high, no low, no good, no evil; but recognizes every thing that exists, true to the conditions that produced it."

The *Crucible* of June 2, 1877, says: "O, strike! Wait no longer. Make a perfect Chicago and Moscow bonfire of steeples, court-houses, taxes," etc.

The same paper on May 12, 1877, contains an article boldly advocating the promiscuous intercourse of the sexes. In the same paper Stephen Pearl Andrews charges that nine-tenths of legal marriages are adultery, the married not being affinities.

The constitution adopted by the State Association of Spiritualists in Massachusetts, in 1868, affirms "the divinity of man and the humanity of God," and that there "is no antagonism between them," and opposes "all institutions which subject one man to the will of the many." "All sin, and all there is of sin, is a necessity." "Fatalism is the alphabet of human existence." "Murder, drunkenness, licentiousness are sequences, behind which there is a cause sufficient to produce the effect."

"So far as man's earthly well-being is concerned, obedience to the Ten Commandments is of importance, but so far as man's spiritual well-being is concerned disobedience to them is of greater importance." "There are greater uses in sin than in holiness." (*Banner of Light*, January 30, 1869.) After quoting the above from A. B. Childs's book, the editor remarks: "It abounds in spiritual wisdom, and we do not wonder that A. J. Davis canonized its author." He also says that the doctrine "has been recognized and accepted by leading spiritualists." "No arbitrary decree can make or unmake a relation at once so intricate and fruitful of either happiness or misery," referring to marriage. "Laws and ceremonies do not make rights for us." (Editorial, *Religio-Philosophical Journal*, January 13, 1869.)

The *Banner of Light*, February 13, 1869, claims that governmental laws with regard to marriage are useless. "Do you mean that it is right for a man to follow the inclinations of his appetite, which lead him to excessive intoxication? We answer that by simply saying, Yes." Virtue and vice "both contain deific elements." "What, then, is vice, but virtue?" "In licentiousness we find the outcropping of the God-element in man." (Editorial in *Religio-Philosophical Journal*, February 20, 1869.) This is the editor who was regarded as the leader of the conservative wing of spiritualism. There is some satisfaction in knowing that the villain was shot.

We again remind the reader that these are the men who manufacture and publish accounts of spirit phenomena, standard *séance*-rooms being under their control in the buildings in which their papers are published. "The time will come when worship will be a thing of the past." (Editorial in *Ohio Spiritualist*, October 24, 1868.) "All civil rule is the result of ignorance and barbarism." (A Spirit, in *Banner of Light*, October 31, 1868.) "There is a marriage which belongs to the soul. The soul utters its own ceremonials, makes its own bonds and breaks them." (*Banner of Light*, February 22, 1869.) "No deed can be evil." (*Present Age*, October 10, 1868.) "We thank thee for all conditions of men, for the drunkard, for the prostitute." (*Banner of Light*, December 3, 1862.) "I can not think that libertinism injures the immortal soul of man." (*Banner of Light*, February 8, 1862.) "O thou prince of darkness and king of light, God and devil, greater and lesser good, perfect and imperfect being! we ask and demand of thee that we may know more of thee." (*Banner of Light*, March 1, 1862.) The same paper of December 21, 1861, contains a prayer addressed by Lizzie Doten to Lucifer.

When a leading spiritualist, John M. Spear, by direction of the spirits had become a father without being married, the *Spiritual Telegraph*, then the leading spiritualist paper of this country, applauded the mother who dared to "rise up in the dignity of her womanhood and declare, in the face of her oppressors and a scowling world, I will be free."

We have already given as many extracts from this vile literature as we can permit to appear in this volume, for we must not scatter abroad the pernicious seeds we seek to destroy. We were, at one time, living in a community in which the literature of modern spiritualism was being introduced, and in order that the people of the place might not receive the doctrine of devils unawares, we, with the help of some generous, orthodox persons, bought all of the leading spiritualist papers and magazines published within the United States and one prominent spiritualist monthly magazine published in Europe; we also purchased two-thirds of the spiritualist books which were mentioned in the largest catalogue of such books to be found in this country; and we found them all to be pervaded, to a greater or less extent, with the sentiments exhibited in the extracts which we have already given.

The philosophy underlying these sentiments is old, and is continually reappearing whenever the mind throws off the restraints of Christianity and is swept along by the current of evil desire. There is first the choice of sin; and afterward the will compels the intellect to seek some apparent philosophy by means of which sin may be excused and defended. The old subterfuge is the new one, namely: Man is but an irresponsible machine, and therefore God or Nature is the cause for every thing, sin included, and therefore sin must be right, and all sinners, even by means of sin, are continually progressing. The next natural inference is almost universally adopted by spiritualists, namely: that sin and the desires called evil should not be interfered with; and, therefore, all civil laws, the marriage law in particular, should be abolished.

Chapter XXVI.

THE BIBLE AND MODERN SPIRITUALISM.

THE account given of the witch of Endor in 1 Samuel xxviii, has often been quoted by spiritualists as favoring their theory of spirit communication, and has been a source of perplexity to many students of the Bible. But we believe that a careful review of the passage will show that it is a very strong proof-text against the claims of spiritualists. When the witch of Endor professed that Samuel appeared to her, she cried out with a loud voice as if in a state of great agitation and alarm. Her alarm was either feigned or real. If feigned, she was an impostor; if real, she was meeting an experience to which she was not accustomed, and which was permitted as a special providence of God. Either horn of the dilemma is fatal to the claims of the spiritualists concerning the mediumship of the witch of Endor. The Bible does not assert that the witch had a familiar spirit, but that Saul's servants made such an assertion. "The woman saw Samuel," and "Samuel said to Saul," are expressions such as we would use in speaking of personations on the stage. Saul did not see Samuel. He was visible, if visible at all, only to the imagination of the witch. We notice, also, that Saul notified her beforehand that he desired to communicate with Samuel, whereupon she professed to see an old man coming up covered with a mantle. This evidence alone was sufficient to cause Saul to "stoop with his face to the ground and bow himself." The witch must have known enough of a man so celebrated as Samuel had been to know that he was an old man when he died, but to avoid a more minute description she finds it convenient to say that he is "covered with his mantle."

It is to be remembered that this *séance* occurred in the night, when the witch could have been aided by confederates. Modern spiritualists will hardly hold that the witch really saw Samuel when they are reminded that she professed to see him coming up from the under world, where we now locate the earth's hot center. But whatever view we may adopt as to the nature of this phenomenon, we must admit that the Bible condemned Saul for consulting the witch of Endor. This was one of the sins for which Saul suffered death. (I Chron. x, 13.)

The Hebrew word "oboth," rendered "familiar spirit," implies a kind of frenzy, and suggests that peculiar hysterical excitement so often witnessed in trance speakers. There are no words in the original Hebrew Scriptures which imply that witches or sorcerers could really call up the dead. The original word for wizard signifies "a knowing one," and whether or not he uses his shrewdness in deceiving or instructing mankind can not be determined from the word, but from its relations in the passages in which it occurs. Surely the word was not used in a good sense, for wizards were to be put to death. The original word rendered "sorcerer," according to Gesenius signified "One who professes to call up the dead."

That such "mediums" and those who consulted them were condemned by the Bible is abundantly shown in the following passages: Micah v, 12; Leviticus xix, 31; xx, 6–27; Deut. xviii, 10–12; Isa. viii, 19, 20; lvii, 3, 9–12; xix, 3; viii, 19; ii, ʽ, Ex. xxii, 18; 2 Chron. xxxiii, 6; 1 Sam. xv, 23; 1 Chron. x, 13; 2 Kings ix, 22; Nahum iii, 4; Joshua xiii, 22; Jer. xxvii, 9; Acts xvi, 16; Gal. v, 19–21; Rev. ix, 21; xxi, 8.

That the false prophets "saw nothing" when they professed to consult the dead is proved by Ezek. xiii, 2–7.

That spirits can not communicate with mankind is proved by 2 Sam. xii, 22, 23; Luke xi, 31; 2 Pet. i, 21; Job x, 20; xvii, 22. The passage in 2 Chron. xxi, 12, has been quoted by spiritualists in favor of writing mediums. We answer that Elijah had been dead seven years, but he wrote the message referred to before he died. The margin adds: "Which was writ before his death." We would refer the reader to any good commentary upon this passage, to confirm our interpretation of it.

But what of the demoniacal possessions which occurred in the days of our Savior? We accept the simple statements of them as given in the New Testament, with no desire to explain them away, regarding them as having been especially permitted at that time so that our Lord could demonstrate his power, not only over the material elements, but also over the unseen world. Without this especial display of his dominion over the evil powers of the unseen world the revelation of his kingship would have been incomplete. With Christ on our side, we may defy all the evil powers of the universe. We can trust him in time and in eternity.

THE END.

www.ingramcontent.com/pod-product-compliance
Lightning Source LLC
Chambersburg PA
CBHW030326240426
43673CB00040B/1291